RELATIONSHIP DISTURBANCES IN EARLY CHILDHOOD

RELATIONSHIP DISTURBANCES IN EARLY CHILDHOOD

A Developmental Approach

EDITED BY

ARNOLD J. SAMEROFF

AND

ROBERT N. EMDE

IN ASSOCIATION WITH

T. F. Anders · D. Reiss · P. H. Leiderman
L. A. Sroufe · A. H. Parmelee · D. N. Stern

BasicBooks
A Division of HarperCollins*Publishers*

Figures 5.1 and 5.2 reprinted by permission of *Family Process*.

Library of Congress Cataloging-in-Publication Data

Relationship disturbances in early childhood: a developmental approach
/edited by Arnold J. Sameroff and Robert N. Emde.
    p.   cm.

  Bibliography: p. 239.
  Includes index.
  ISBN 0–465–06897–9
  1. Child development deviations. 2. Parent and child.
 3. Socialization. I. Sameroff, Arnold J. II. Emde, Robert N.
  [DNLM: 1. Child Development Disorders. 2. Parent-Child Relations.
 3. Socialization—in infancy & childhood. WS 350.6 R382]
RJ506.D47R44 1989
618.92'8—dc19
DNLM/DLC
for Library of Congress   88–47892
                                                     CIP

CONTENTS

v

PART II

DISTURBANCE

PART III

CONTEXT

PREFACE

Developmental thinking has forced a revolution in the study of psychopathology. The stability of the known psychiatric universe has been disrupted by the need to integrate dynamic models of behavior into a world where each individual had been thought to occupy a definable niche. We thought there were normal people and disordered people; if a normal person was relabeled as disordered, we decided that we had not been sophisticated enough to notice the disorder earlier. But the study of development revealed that people do change. They can move from one stage of life to another and show an entirely different set of adaptations and talents. In many cases these changes are for the worse, but in other cases these changes are for the better. The dynamics brought to light by developmental research forced a rethinking not only about the permanence but also about the location of order and disorder. For many the source of pathology can be found in a disordered or disorganized family or social context that has prevented the adaptations found in normal development. This book is a search for the locus of behavioral deviancies in young children.

The contributors to this work originally came together to share views on developmental processes and childhood disorder. A special-project group at the Center for Advanced Study in the Behavioral Sciences met regularly during 1984–1985; Thomas Anders, Robert Emde, Herbert Leiderman, Arthur Parmelee, Arnold Sameroff, and Alan Sroufe were resident fellows, and David Reiss and Daniel Stern were visiting scholars. Members of the group were clinicians and developmental psychologists, and there was a concentration of experience in the area of early human development. Our aim was synthetic—to bring together knowledge from a variety of research contexts in hopes of envisioning new directions. After initial discussions dealing with surveys of literature and with theories of development, we found ourselves focusing on the developing infant–parent relationship and its clinical aspects. We discovered that, in many ways, the individual-based nosology for adult psychopathology could not easily be extended downward to early childhood. We felt that the classification of early disorders might be approached with advantage from a new perspective, namely, that of relationships and their disturbances. Accordingly, we set ourselves the specific goal of articulating a model of early development that could serve as a basis for a future nosology of relationship disorders. We were entering uncharted territory, but the prospects for adventure and discovery were exhilarating. There was no established nosology of adult relationship disorders, nor had one been suggested for infancy. Still, based on our preliminary synthesis of the literature on infancy, we felt we were on the right path. We could see the beginnings of a useful developmental model, and we felt that an associated scheme for clinical classification could soon follow. Certainly an assessment scheme based on a developmental model for relationships and their disturbances would make more sense for this early period in life, when an internal self is just being formed and when, from a practical point of view, clinical intervention is usually directed at the level of the caregiving relationship.

Our goal continued to fuel our enthusiasm during the course of the year, although the evolution of our thinking and our consultation with others led to a shift of emphasis. We concentrated less on trying to solve the particular dilemmas of nosology and concentrated more on formulating a developmental model that would be applicable to a future nosology of relationship problems. Our thinking gave primary emphasis to early developmental processes, but we sought a model that could eventually find application in later life as well. Our collaborative discussions and exchanges of reviews and working papers began to yield an approach which, in some respects, seemed paradoxical. Our developmental model needed to give emphasis to an adaptational, individually oriented perspective for relationships, and yet it also needed to serve as a basis for abstract classification of disorders beyond individuals. In addition to including external features of developing relationships, our model needed to include internal representations within the context of the infant–parent relationship. In other words, meaning needed to be conceptualized, in terms of both its internal individual referents and its social contextual referents. But paradox gives momentum for change, and we entertained the hope that struggling with these issues would lead us to a more dynamic model.

From the outset, we found our group interactions remarkably rewarding. We established a collegial tone of openness about our challenges, and our interchanges became lively and free-ranging. Although our common expertise was concentrated in infancy, our individual professional training, experiences, and theoretical orientations were quite varied. We came to highlight some of our differences while appreciating common values and aspirations for generating a workable model.

A word about the strategy of our group process. Instead of identifying differences in viewpoint and carving out separate approaches to our task, we opted for a consensus approach for our model building. We attempted to work through problems as they arose in order to achieve a common solution. (We might mention that although the chapters in this book are identified with particular names, in most cases authorship was determined by writing assignment and all chapters had contributions from the group as a whole.) A vivid crystallizing moment occurred after about a month of our work, when someone said, "Perhaps there is no psychopathology in the infant; for developmental reasons, disorder can only be in the infant–caregiver relationship." Surprised by the simplicity of this statement, everyone agreed that taking a position based on it would be a challenge to our creativity and would take us in exciting new directions. Our commitment to working on a new model followed.

We soon came to appreciate the balance that was needed between clinical-practical and research-theoretical approaches as we tested new ideas. In crossing boundaries between disciplines, we often encountered gaps in knowledge, hidden assumptions, and new questions.

The consensus strategy brought out some advantages, but it also had disadvantages. One disadvantage was the potential undue influence of social pressure for agreement. To counter this tendency, we periodically acknowledged the value we placed on differences of view. Consensus working also meant a commitment to group work, so to some extent this took time away from individual effort. But the most significant disadvantage we recognized was that group members could develop common implicit assumptions. Unless we were forced to make these assumptions explicit, their logic and empirical bases could not be examined. This made presentation of our viewpoints to others outside the group essential. We therefore especially want to express appreciation for the consultations of a number of individuals who pointed out our blind spots in logic, emphasis, and review of others' work. We acknowledge with thanks the consultation of Calvin Settlage and the Interdisciplinary Forum on Development of the San Francisco Psychoanalytic Institute, which he chaired and which hosted us for a day's presentation and discussion. We also appreciate the consultations of Michael Goldstein and John Strauss, who spent a day with our group in Palo Alto, and Michael Rutter, who also responded to our ideas in Palo Alto. We want to acknowledge the comments of the large group that attended our research forum discussions at the annual meeting of the American Academy of Child Psychiatry, held in San Antonio, Texas, in 1985. In addition, we are grateful for the discussion of our work by Robert Hinde and by Louis Sander at our symposium at the Third World Congress of Infant Psychiatry and Allied Disciplines in Stockholm, Sweden, in 1986.

Turning from intellectual to material issues, we want to acknowledge the institutions that provided the financial and personnel support for our project. First and foremost, we are grateful to the Center for Advanced Study in the Behavioral Sciences in Stanford, California, where Gardner Lindzey and Robert Scott were our gracious and supportive hosts. Next we wish to express thanks to the John D. and Catherine T. MacArthur Foundation and to the Research Scientist Program at the National Institute of Mental Health for providing support for a number of our fellowships. We also wish to thank the Foundations Fund for Research in Psychiatry and Irving Harris, an institution in himself, who helped us with several of our group's miniconferences. Finally, we give a special thanks to Judy Bandieri, without whose nimble fingers at both the computer keyboard and the telephone dial we would never have gotten this manuscript together.

Robert N. Emde
Arnold J. Sameroff

RELATIONSHIP
DISTURBANCES
IN EARLY
CHILDHOOD

Introduction

Understanding Early Relationship Disturbances

Robert N. Emde and Arnold J. Sameroff

Who can resist feeling uplifted by a smiling baby who gazes into our eyes from the security of her mother's arms? Who isn't distressed by a toddler who shrieks and turns away from his mother as she tries to make her way through the supermarket checkout counter? Infancy compels us. Not only are we predisposed to empathy but we are drawn to the infant's obvious need for consistent caregiving and love. Growth and development are rapid. Therefore, when things go well, there is a tangible sense of thriving and accomplishment for caregiver and baby, and this is shared with others who see it. When things go awry, the opposite happens. Distress and frustration, although normal and necessary in the short run, can be unmanageable in the long run. Chronic strain, behavioral problems, withdrawal, and, in extreme instances, interference with development can result.

Most parents are all too familiar with periods of chronic strain, recalcitrant problems in feeding, sleeping, and discipline, and distressing temper tantrums, sadness, and apathy—to mention only a few examples. But, unfortunately, more severe problems in behavior are also widespread, as health care professionals and the general public have begun to appreciate. Problems include, on the one hand, those related to child maltreatment syndromes and, on the other hand, those related to a variety of other syndromes characterized by distress, maladaptive behavior, and developmental interferences. A new field—infant psychiatry—is burgeoning, with its own literature (Call, Galenson, & Tyson, 1983, 1984; Greenspan, 1981; Minde & Minde, 1986), its own journal *(Infant Mental Health Journal)*, and professional organizations (World Association of Infant Psychiatry and Allied Disciplines, International Association of Infant Mental Health, and the National Center for Clinical Infant Programs). Researchers and clinicians attempt to address what they perceive as widespread problems in the first years of life and are optimistic that early help can be successful in relieving distress and preventing later childhood disorder.

Early development is indeed unique, and infancy is subject to its own disorders. Still, though disorders in infancy are widespread and are being treated, unlike disorders in older children and adults, they have defied classification. Current diagnostic classification systems provided by the American Psychiatric Association's (1987) DSMIII-R and the World Health Organization's (1977, 1979) ICD-9 are inadequate. They are not considered useful by clinicians. Why not?

Initially we thought the lack of a nosology for psychiatric problems during infancy could be explained by our general human tendency to deny the existence of problems that are too distressing to consider. Infants, after all, are not supposed to be abused, neglected, or depressed. When they come to us in these states it is such a painful violation of our caregiving tendencies that we overlook the conditions. Indeed, health care professionals for too long did not recognize the existence of child abuse syndromes or see childhood depression. Further consideration, however, led us to reject this train of thought. Infancy problems were not being ignored. Many professionals were involved in the clinical care of infancy problems, and—more to the point—successful interventions were occurring even though the disorders were unlabeled. Instead, the answer seemed to lie in an unexpected domain—that of relationships and their disorders—in which clinical theory and classification had not caught up with clinical practice or developmental knowledge.

We found that infancy clinicians had apparently learned from trial and error that relationships are important, that problems in relationships are central in their work, and that intervening in relationships is what helps. But, in general, clinicians are not taught to think this way; traditional training has it that disorders are diagnosed in individuals and that treatment follows accordingly. No classification of relationships and their disorders exists, let alone a proposal for assessment. Family systems approaches have placed relationships in a central role but have not had much effect on official diagnostic schemes; further, these approaches have not differentiated among families with children at different developmental levels. Clearly, we came upon a gap that needed bridging.

4

Relationships and Health

Developmental research has generated substantial evidence concerning the importance of social relationships. Social relationships that are supportive have been shown to promote health, provide buffers against the onset of known classes of disorder, and prevent the recurrence of major mental disorders. Conversely, social relationships that are nonsupportive or stressful have been implicated in the etiology of disorder. Moreover, relationships seem to have a life of their own. They have normative functions. We could not survive without early caregiving relationships, and later relationships in the midst of family, work, and leisure are also essential. Some might assert that individuals, in the psychological sense, exist only in the context of being with other individuals—through relationships. Our sense of self, of agency, and of coherence are all based on relationships between ourselves and others. We are continually involved in internal dialogues as well as in real interactions with significant others in our lives. At times of uncertainty, we consult with individuals who are important to us and who, in particular contexts, provide reference points for action.

Adaptation throughout the lifespan depends on social relationships. John Bowlby (1980) put the matter succinctly, using his concept of attachment: "Intimate attachments to other human beings are the hub around which a person's life revolves, not only when s/he is an infant or a toddler, but throughout adolescence and the years of maturity as well and on into old age" (p. 442).

The authors of this volume came to realize that although recent research has provided considerable developmental knowledge about relationships (Hinde & Stevenson-Hinde, 1986), this has not been integrated into clinical thinking. Correspondingly, there has been little systematic thinking about the classification of dysfunctional relationships (for a review see Fisher, 1977; Wynne, 1984). This lack is all the more striking since many relationships seem persistently disordered, with mutual misery and maladaptation in the participants. Problems of the most intense kinds of relationships—those in marriage and in parenting—make up a substantial part of clinical consultation as well as social policy concern. Moreover, clinical practice indicates that intervention at the level of the relationship is often what is most helpful for individuals.

The Diagnosis and Classification of Relationship Problems

From the point of view of childhood psychopathology, we could outline the problem of diagnosis as follows. When a child's behavioral adaptation is disturbed, the cause could be located (a) in the child, (b) in the child's relationships with others, or (c) in the aspects of relationships that become internalized as part of the child. Each diagnostic focus has different implications for intervention. The first leads to considerations of change within the child, the second to change within the relationships, and the third to change within the internal representations or working models of the developing relationships. A developmentalist would want any diagnostic scheme to aim for etiological clarity—that is, to indicate what leads to what under what circumstances. It is therefore important to know how the individual and relationship mutually influence each other. For adults, cogent arguments have been made for opposing positions—that disordered individuals cause disordered relationships and that disordered relationships produce disordered individuals.

From a developmental point of view, it would be strategic to find a time when only one system in a causal chain can show disorder; this line of thinking led us to infancy. Infancy can be considered a time of life when only the relationship has psychological meaning, when the individual taken alone has not yet reached the developmental "achievement" of being capable of sustained emotional disorder. Therefore we decided to bring together developmental and clinical thinking about the beginnings of childhood, hoping to generate a model that could be used for a needed classification. Still, the reader may very well ask, Why not go more directly to classification? Why not propose a scheme for the classification of relationship disorders, based on current knowledge? The answer to these questions resides in the meaning of the classification of disorder. Profound issues, we discovered, permeate classification. Clearly, if a classification of relationship disturbances were obvious, others would have formulated it before. And a premature, ill-considered classification scheme could be misleading.

Classification is not without its pitfalls, especially that of referring to individuals instead of disorders. Michael Rutter and Madelyn Gould (1985) are emphatic on this point:

> It is wrong to classify people. . . . It is historically wrong because medical classifications were developed to note diseases and disorders and not types of persons. . . . It is scientifically wrong because it assumes a persistence of psychiatric disorders and a fixity of personality that is completely out of keeping with what

is known about development and about the course of disorders. . . . It is morally offensive because it is treating humans as if they were merely the vehicle of problems. It is no more reasonable to talk about a neurotic child than it is to refer to a measly child. In both cases the label (neurosis or measles) may accurately reflect the current problems of the child, but it does not reflect the qualities of the child himself. (p. 317)

Diagnostic labeling when applied to individuals is especially malicious in infancy and early childhood since it can lead to parent blaming and child blaming. This in turn can foster self-perpetuating expectations and maladaptive patterns of behavior instead of leading to helpful interventions. Why, then, should we classify?

Classification is the ordering of information according to similarities and differences. All classifications involve presuppositions and choices. Presuppositions for any classification are rooted in the culture of its origins; a scientifically based classification, in contrast to an intuitive/artistic one, is distinguished by the degree to which the presented view is coherent and based on an articulated set of verifiable hypotheses and methods (for example, see Heisenberg, 1952; Kagan, 1984). Thus we need to generate a conceptual model for classification that can articulate hypotheses in a way that presuppositions are made explicit. An articulated model that precedes classification might also identify patterns as well as point out areas in which research remains to be done—or even areas in which research is required before classification is attempted.

Rutter and Gould (1985) have pointed out that classification can be regarded as a language for professionals to communicate about the disorders they investigate and treat. In the health care professions, such a common language often reflects a lowest common denominator effect—only widely tested and accepted features of classification are included in a recommended scheme. In contrast, a research-oriented classification scheme might contain hypotheses to be tested rather than propositions that have wide acceptance.

These considerations confronted us with a dilemma. We wished to generate a scheme that would be generally useful to practitioners, especially those working with early childhood disorders. But we realized that the state of our knowledge did not justify our proposing such a classification scheme, let alone presenting it for wide acceptance. Rutter's useful criteria for an adequate classification of child psychiatric disorders include: definitions based on verifiable operations; established reliability with terms used in the same ways by different clinicians; differentiation between disorders with established validity with respect to etiology, symptoms, course, or treatment; and demonstrated everyday clinical usefulness. Rutter also enumerated conceptual criteria for classification, which include logical consistency with a set of principles, as well as clear decision rules; further, most disorders in the scheme should apply at all ages, although some will arise only at particular ages.

In light of these criteria, it was clear that we could not propose an adequate classification of childhood disorders. Instead, we aimed at forming a model that would lead to a classification scheme for early relationship disorders that would be testable and that would prove useful in a multiaxial system of diagnosis. In a multiaxial framework a diagnostician is not limited to a list of categories but instead can supplement clinical psychiatric syndromes with other important features. The American Psychiatric Association's classification of DSMIII (1980) and DSMIII-R (1987) has four axes that supplement a primary axis of "clinical syndromes." The axes are "developmental disorders and personality disorders," "physical disorders and conditions," and ratings of "severity of psychosocial stressers" and of "highest level of adaptive functioning."

Although it is now recommended as a standard for adult psychiatry, this system came into use only recently. In fact, a multiaxial classification for mental disorders was originally proposed for childhood—first in Europe (Rutter, Schaffer, & Shepherd, 1975) and then in the United States (Tarjan & Eisenberg, 1972). Early ideas for multiple axes included assessments of intellectual level and etiological factors in addition to the classified clinical syndromes; later ideas included assessing associated social factors. In a study of practitioners, a World Health Organization–sponsored report concluded that a multiaxial system of classification was easier to apply and corresponded more closely to usual clinical practice than did a single axis system (Rutter, Shaffer, & Shepherd, 1975). Since DSMIII adopted modified versions of these ideas, various practitioners have pointed to the shortcomings of the current multiaxial scheme for infancy. Constructive criticisms have been that a future scheme should include (1) more intensive developmental assessments and (2) specific assessments of social context (for example, see Call, 1983; Kreisler & Cramer, 1983; Greenspan, Nover, & Scheuer, 1987).

This brings us to two related issues. First, current nosological schemes—DSMIII-R and ICD-9—are descriptive. They say little about etiology or development. Therefore, how can we apply them to early childhood, a period for which we are centrally concerned with processes leading from antecedent factors to risk of disorder as well as to disorder? Second, the DSMIII-R system has been designed so that two observers can achieve reliability about designated categories of behavior. But a central principle of a developmental approach to psychopathology is that behaviors, syndromes, and states of adaptation change over time. How do we reconcile developmental changes with the demands of reliability and of prognosis that have been hallmarks of adult-based classification schemes of disorder?

One of the areas of difference between a scheme for the classification of disorder based on development and one, like DSMIII-R, based on individual characteristics is the view of symptoms over time. Symptoms in isolation have little meaning other than as a perturbation in expected behavior, unless they disturb the adaptive functioning of the person in social or work settings. To the extent that disturbances extend over long periods of time they are judged to be disorders. For children many problem behaviors become transformed into altered adaptive capacities for the future. The core of the Freudian perspective was the recognition that the child's relationship experience in regard to developmental issues—for example, the oral, anal, and phallic—facilitated or distorted later features of individual development. Similarly, in our current perspective, the behavioral manifestations of disordered relationships may change over time: for example, feeding disturbances become sleep disturbances, attachment problems become exploration problems. As a consequence, a clear understanding of the normative dynamic transformations in child behavior must be the basis of any scheme for understanding deviations.

Perturbation, Disturbance, and Disorder

A consistent theme in our presentation will be the contrast between perturbations, disturbances, and disorders. The concept of perturbation is implicit in development. Development advances through the meeting of challenges and the overcoming of problems. Rolling over, sitting and standing, getting attention and communicating, and sleeping through the night are all major challenges that each child must struggle with. Frustration, overinvolvement, and negative affect associated with each of these developmental milestones reflect normative perturbations in behavior. For most children these perturbations are soon resolved as competence is reached in the new area. For others, however, a failure to attain a given developmental milestone becomes a disturbance if it interferes with other areas of adaptation and a disorder if it persists far beyond normative bounds.

We will apply these same important considerations to the classification of relationships. Our position will be that relationships cannot be evaluated out of their developmental context. Children frequently present to their parents developmental surprises that require adjustments in thought and action. The burgeoning independence of the one-year-old soon becomes the intentional oppositionalism of the two-year-old and produces in parental relationships expected perturbations that require family adaptation. To the extent that the family is unable to adapt within a reasonable period of time and maintains outmoded patterns of interaction, relationships become disturbed and behavioral difficulties become apparent, usually in vegetative functions such as sleeping and feeding. Disorder results when behavioral problems spill over into other adaptive domains and constrict the normative activities of either child or parent. Examples of these developmental issues in classification and treatment will be more fully discussed in the chapters that follow.

The Adult's View and the Infant's Experience

A core problem in the appreciation of relationships in infancy stems from how adults typically view the infant's experience. To think of a caregiving-relationship experience and its significance is foreign to many. Furthermore, families tend to attribute new beginnings to infancy and to endow the infant with a variety of values. The infant is often seen as a way to overcome social disappointments and fulfill dreams of success. Many idealize infancy as a blissful time. Perhaps it is because the infant cannot speak that many adults make attributions about complex mental functions such as fantasy formation in infancy without having confirmatory evidence. We may tend to see the infant in terms of what we imagine we once possessed and lost, whether it be a special mother or a life with fewer frustrations. We may tend to see the infant as a diminished or opposite version of what we value as ideal in adults, namely, as presymbolic egocentric or as having unmodulated "infantile" sexual impulses.

Although clinicians and theorists are aware of the adult-oriented attributions aroused by infants, they have been reluctant to pursue the young child's relationship experiences as being important in adaptive functioning. Perhaps they have simply been unaware that such experiences are important in the generation of developmental problems; yet, considering the literature on the topic, this explanation seems unlikely.

Bowlby (1973) suggests there may be a powerful but unacknowledged tendency for collusion between professionals and parents. Troubled families may "scapegoat," or see family or relationship problems as residing in a single individual; they may also seek a cause outside the family and therefore beyond their influence. Pediatricians, psychiatrists, and psychologists—most of whom are parents themselves—tend to accept the parental view. They tend not to examine the child's everyday experience within the context of family relationships. Bowlby also points out that emotional communications from the child tend to be reified (that is, "the child has a fear" or a "bad temper") instead of being viewed with their situational referents. Along this same line, causes of behavioral problems are sought elsewhere than in the child's experience—in physical illness, unusual circumstance, or impulses or temperament. Bowlby's suggestion may sound extreme to some, but it is consonant with the historical fact that we long failed to recognize the child's experience in conditions of child abuse, parental seduction, and infantile depression.

The Developmental Approach of This Book

The chapters that follow are intended to provide the reader with as complete an understanding of relationship disorders as current knowledge permits. The book is divided into three parts: "Development," "Disturbance," and "Context." Part I presents the dynamic principles through which early relationships must be understood. Part II explores the distortions to be found in the development of relationships. Part III examines the variation found in the organization of relationships produced by developmental status, family, and cultural context.

In the first chapter in Part I Arnold Sameroff presents a view of development as a regulated system from both internal and external perspectives. Internally, biological development is regulated by the genotype to provide a basis for behavioral organization. Externally, an environtype carries the developmental agenda of society, the family, and the parental figure; this gives shape, direction, and organization to the child's personality. Because developmental regulation is carried out through relationships, they become the primary source of variation in early socio-emotional development.

In chapter 2 Robert Emde goes on to present a view of relationships from the perspective of the child. He reviews the functional aspects of relationships in the many domains of parent–child interaction touching on protection and intimacy. The child and the parent are seen as biologically organized to engage in relationships regulated by affective interchanges. Affect is universal among the human species and fundamentally social, permitting emotions to serve as organizers of experience by providing incentives and coherence. Affective organization is repeatedly transformed through biobehavioral shifts during the first and second years of life as autonomy and individuation increase.

The basis of individuation is supported by the development of the child's representational abilities, as described in chapter 3 by Daniel Stern. He focuses his presentation on three questions: (1) Where does a relational pattern reside, in the individual or in the dyad? (2) What gives relational patterns continuity? and (3) What is a representation of interactive history? He answers that the development of relationship representations is hierarchically organized. The hierarchy goes from specific lived moments to memories and generalized representations of those moments to representations of scenarios to internal working models to narrative models. These representations provide a basis for the internalization *within* the individual of what occurs *between* individuals, so that relationships become a major determinant of individual behavior.

In chapter 4 L. Alan Sroufe examines the role of social relationships in the emergence and organization of the individual self. He presents a conceptualization of the self within an organizational perspective in which it is not the particulars of behavior but their organization across time that is the core of self. The phases of self-organization are based on Sander's (1975) model, which moves from dyadic concerns with physiological regulation to autonomous action and self-constancy.

Once the developmental model for understanding early relationships is described in the first part of the book, we turn to descriptions of how relationships go awry in the second part. Sroufe begins in chapter 5 with definitions of relationships and of their disturbances. He describes relationships in terms of quality, patterning, functions, and goals. Disturbance is characterized symptomatically by complaints of pain and functionally by a set of factors: rigidity, structural and boundary distortions, and limitations on future adaptive behavior. He ends with descriptions of categorical and dimensionalized assessment schemes for separating ordered from disordered relationships.

Thomas Anders follows in chapter 6 with a classification scheme for parent–child relationships during the first years of life. He begins with a description of the principles of psychiatric classification that are not currently met by classification schemes of early disorders. He then describes a multidimensional scheme that classifies relationships in terms of their developmental appropriateness, their interactional regulation, the contributions of the individual characteristics of parent and child, and the extant social supports and stresses. Within this scheme the clinician can separate relationships that are perturbed from those that are disturbed or more seriously disordered.

In chapter 7 Arthur Parmelee describes one of the key contributors to relationship regulation, the physical condition of the child. He argues that in the first years of life concerns with physical growth and health dominate parent–child relationships. Because frequent illnesses—colds and infectious diseases—are a universal characteristic of human infancy, they provide a common source of perturbation in early parent–child relationships. The manner in which parents and professionals negotiate such physical perturbations will contribute to whether relationship disturbances or disorders result.

Part III of the book is an attempt to place early relationships in a broader context of other relationships through the lifespan. P. Herbert Leiderman begins chapter 8 with a description of the changing characteristics of intimate relationships from infancy through childhood to adolescence. He enlarges upon these descriptions by highlighting cross-cultural variations in relationship patterns: the Western mother, for example, may take on all relationship roles with her infant; in other societies there may be one nurturing partner—mother—and other play and teaching partners—siblings or other adults. Leiderman lists and explores relationship types, including caregiving, affiliating, mentoring, and romantic. His conclusion is that children enter into many dyadic relationships, both inside and outside the family, and that relationship disturbances can arise after infancy during many developmental stages.

The context of the family is elaborated by David Reiss in chapter 9. The earlier chapters of this book assume that individual psychological disorders arise only when the child develops the capacity to internalize representations of disordered relationships. Reiss argues that even adult members of families maintain relationships without demonstrated family representations. Some aspects of family relationships are not conscious and are not represented even within individual members! He describes many levels of coordinated practice in families, only some of which are subject to representation. He concludes that any model of relationship disorder will have to take into account both the represented and the practiced aspects of family functioning.

From the perspective of developmental psychopathology this book considers three questions:

1. What adaptational functions do early relationships provide for the child?
2. What are the effects of variations?
3. What is the connection between the quality of early relationships and the quality of later relationships?

To understand the adaptational functions of early relationships we need to understand early development. We will view individual development in emotional and cognitive functioning in light of a child's history of social involvements.

From the clinical perspective, it is essential to identify good relationships and bad relationships and to analyze the determinants of those relationships. How much do the individual characteristics of the child contribute to the quality of the relationship, and how much does the nature of experience with the caregiving environment contribute?

The quality of the child's current relationships may or may not be important for those that follow. The questions to be answered here are whether good early relationships can insulate the child from later distortions and whether bad early relationships can be remedied through later improved social interactions. To answer we need to understand how children represent their relationships. For early experiences to affect later experiences, they must be carried at some level of organization in the child's psyche. Yet some dimensions of family functioning that affect the child may not be represented at all.

How successful our approach will be for studying the significance of early relationships will be judged at the end of this work. After the discussions of the nature of relationships, the nature of their representations, and their significance for current and future competence, we will try to identify where we have succeeded and where we have failed. In the instances in which we have failed, we will be faced with the question of whether our shortcomings derive from limitations in our ability to conceptualize the problem or from limitations in our empirical base. The answer will lead to an agenda for future explorations of early relationships and their pathology.

PART I

DEVELOPMENT

Chapter 1

Principles of Development and Psychopathology

Arnold J. Sameroff

The study of relationships runs counter to dominant movements in behavioral theory and practice, which have long been devoted to understanding the person apart from context (Kessen, 1979). Only in this century have we come to realize that individual behavior is enmeshed in social behavior; thus individual development has been reconceptualized as the adaptive establishment of interpersonal boundaries. The construction of these boundaries, which are formed anew with every adult relationship, begins with the infant's first relationships. The contours of these relationships are based on expectations of interactive behavior: if I do A, then you will do B; and if you do C, then I will do D. Each individual's expectations are based on a lifetime of relationship experiences, beginning in infancy.

Before we can approach these early manifestations of relatedness, we must address some new concepts that provide the lenses through which these relationships will be seen and, we hope, understood. These views are within the domain of a relatively new subfield, developmental psychopathology, which integrates developmental and psychiatric thought. Because we anticipate that most readers of this volume will be better grounded in pathology than in development, the bulk of this chapter will center on the developmental understanding of human behavior. Within this understanding the case will be made that each individual grows within a regulated context. The theme of regulation is the key to understanding development, and the details of human growth are in the interplay of biology and experience. Similarly, the theme of regulation is the key to understanding pathology. Variations in the quality of regulation, in its coherence and purpose, have major consequences for the quality of each individual's adaptation to life.

Developmental Psychopathology as a Field

The emerging field of developmental psychopathology has begun to affect child psychiatry by illuminating new possibilities for understanding the etiology, future course, and treatment of many childhood problems. One of the best redefinitions of psychopathology in developmental terms has been provided by L. Alan Sroufe and Michael Rutter (1984), who saw the discipline as "the study of the origins and course of individual patterns of behavioral adaptation" (p. 18).

> It is the "developmental" component of developmental psychopathology that distinguishes this discipline from abnormal psychology, psychiatry, and even clinical child psychology. At the same time the focus on individual patterns of adaptation and maladaptation distinguishes this field from the larger discipline of developmental psychology. (p. 17)

Rutter and Norman Garmezy (1983) summarized the status of the field in a major review of research in developmental psychopathology. For them development "specifies a concern with the general course of psychosocial development, with changes that take place with developmental progression, with the processes and mechanisms that underlie the developmental transitions, and with the implications that follow their occurrence" (p. 776). They cite Leon Eisenberg's (1977) persuasive argument that developmental issues are essential underpinnings for the psychiatry of both childhood and adulthood.

> The process of development constitutes the crucial link between genetic determinants and environmental variables, between physiogenic and psychogenic causes, and between the residues of prior maturation or earlier experiences and the modulation of behavior by the circumstances of the present. The developmental perspective requires us to take account of continuities and discontinuities between infancy, childhood, and adult life. (Rutter & Garmezy, 1983, p. 776)

Rutter and Garmezy go on to elaborate the difference between developmental psychopathology and other disciplines. They argue that developmental psychologists assume an essential continuity in functioning so that severe symptoms (such as depression) are placed on the same dimension as normal behaviors (such as sadness or unhappiness). In contrast, traditional psychiatry is based on an implicit assumption of discontinuity so that disordered behavior is interpreted as different in kind from normal behavior. Developmental psychopathologists make no prior assumptions about continuity or discontinuity. They are concerned centrally with both the connections and the lack of connections between normality and disorder.

THEORIES OF PSYCHOPATHOLOGY

A new orientation to the etiology of psychopathology is needed because the customary models fail to explain how disorders arise and are maintained. The traditional medical model of disorder is based on the presumption that identifiable somatic entities underlie definable disease syndromes. Within traditional psychiatry the current dominant view of disease is still strongly biomedical, with little role allowed for social and psychological factors in the etiology of mental illness (Engel, 1977), although they may have an important role in the maintenance and perhaps treatment of mental disorder. In this view individuals are seen not as integrated systems of biological, psychological, and social functioning, but rather as divided into a biological and a behavioral self. If the biology changes, either through infection or cure, the behavior changes. Three principles that emerge from this model are frequently applied to the study of psychopathology:

1. The same entity will cause the same disorder in all affected individuals, whether children or adults.
2. The same symptoms at different ages should be caused by the same entity.
3. Specific disorders of children should lead to similar adult disorders.

Diabetes is an example of a disease that approximates this model: (1) All individuals who have the same degree of insulin deficiency will exhibit similar symptoms independent of age. (2) If one has symptoms of increased urination, thirst, and problems of growing or maintaining weight, then the underlying cause is generally diabetes. (3) Almost always if one develops diabetes during childhood, one will continue to have the disorder through adulthood. However, there are many medical disorders that do not fit this model. Chicken pox will have different effects and symptoms depending on the age of the individual; the symptom of fever can be caused by a wide variety of factors; and having a cold in childhood does not lead to having a cold in adulthood.

The failure of this disease model is evident in the fact that none of these three principles can be generalized, especially with respect to the study of psychopathology. First, the same underlying problem can be related to quite different behaviors in children and adults, for example, the genetic deficit thought to underlie schizophrenia. Research on children at high risk for the disorder is focused on the identification of early markers of a process leading to schizophrenia. These markers are not themselves schizophrenia, but given a certain unique set of developmental experiences they can lead to schizophrenia (Watt, Anthony, Wynne, & Rolf, 1984).

Second, the same symptoms may be caused by quite different processes at different ages. The sadness that is a primary characteristic of adult affective disorders is a common reactive condition in childhood. The proportion of unhappy children increases from 10 percent at age ten to 40 percent by age fifteen, when adolescence is taking its toll (Rutter, Tizard, & Whitmore, 1981). For most of these cases there is little evidence that depression in childhood has the same biological causes as depression in adult life.

Finally, for many emotional and behavioral problems in childhood, there is little evidence of continuity into adulthood. Most childhood emotional problems do not persist, and there is little empirical evidence to connect adult neuroses with childhood conditions. Even when continuity of symptoms has been found, the connection to underlying entities is complex. Some children with depression did go on to have a psychiatric problem in adulthood; in these individuals, although depression was generally a component of the later disorder, it was the primary adult diagnosis in only a minority of cases (Rutter & Garmezy, 1983).

THEORIES OF DEVELOPMENT

The developmental approach expands upon traditional models of mental disease by incorporating biological and behavioral functioning into a general systems model of developmental regulation. Within this approach underlying entities do not exist independent of developmental organization. The expression of biological vulnerabilities can occur only in relation to the balance between coping skills and stresses in each individual's life history (Zubin & Spring, 1977). Continuities in competence or incompetence from childhood into adulthood cannot be simply related to continuities in underlying pathology or health. The relations between earlier and later behavior have to be understood in terms of the continuity of ordered or disordered experience across time interacting with an individual's unique biobehavioral characteristics. To the extent that experience becomes more organized, problems in adaptation will diminish. To the extent that experience becomes more chaotic, problems in adaptation will increase. The developmental approach identifies the factors that influence the child's ability to organize experience and, consequently, the child's level of adaptive functioning.

Although there is some consensus on the contents of the field of developmental psychopathology, there is less agreement on a theoretical framework. Sroufe and Rutter (1984) believe that there is no single developmental theory that can encompass the field; but they suggest that there are a number of accepted guiding principles that underlie all major developmental positions. These include concepts of holism, directedness, differentiation of means and ends, and mobility of behavioral functions (Santostefano, 1978). These principles overlap significantly with a developmental model that is based on general systems theory and that includes principles of wholeness and order, adaptive self-stabilization, adaptive self-organization, hierarchical interactions, and dialectical movement (Sameroff, 1983, 1989). Obviously there is a great gap between such principles and the data collected in typical empirical studies of psychiatric disorder. Bridging this gap becomes the scientific agenda for a discipline of developmental psychopathology. The task is to relate a general theory of development to the data of both normality and deviance.

Regulatory Systems in Development

What kind of theory is necessary to integrate our understanding of pathology and development? It must explain how the individual and the context work together to produce patterns of adaptive or maladaptive functioning, and it must relate how such past or present functioning influences the future.

The first principle to emerge in such a general theory of development is that individuals can never be removed from their contexts. Whether the goal is understanding causal connections, predicting outcomes, or intervention, it will not be achieved by removing the individual from the conditions that regulate development. A great deal of attention has been given to the biological regulators of development; the environmental regulators of development now need equal attention.

The development of each individual is conditioned by interactions with a number of regulatory systems acting on different levels of organization. The two most prominent of these are the biological and social regulatory systems. Interactions with the biological system are most prominent in embryogenesis, during which the changing contemporary state of the organism's phenotype triggers the genotype to provide a series of new biochemical experiences. These experiences are regulated by the turning on and off of various gene activities directed toward the production of a viable human child. These processes continue less dramatically after birth, with some exceptions—for example, the initiation of adolescence and possibly senility.

Interactions with the social system dominate most of the period from birth to adulthood. Again the state of the phenotype—that is, the child—triggers regulatory processes, but now in the social environment. Examples of such coded changes are the reactions of the parents to the child's ability to walk and talk and the changes in setting provided when the child reaches preschool or school age. These regulations change the experience of the child in tune with changes in the child's physical and behavioral development.

The result of these regulatory exchanges is the expansion of each individual's ability for biological self-regulation and the development of behavioral self-regulation. Advances in motor development permit children to maintain the thermal regulation and nutrition that initially could be provided only by caregivers: they soon are able to dress themselves and reach into the refrigerator. Through psychological development they are able to self-regulate cognition, on the one hand—with the growth of perceptual constancy and the conceptual organization required for representation—and affect, on the other—with the growth of social referencing and defense mechanisms. Despite this burgeoning independence in thought and deed, each individual is never freed from a relationship to an internal and external context. Should we forget this connectedness, it takes only a bout of illness or a social transgression to remind us of our constraints.

THE ENVIRONTYPE

Just as there is a biological organization, the genotype, that regulates the physical outcome of each individual, there is a social organization that regulates the way human beings fit into their society. This organization operates through family and cultural socialization patterns and has been postulated to compose an *environtype* (Sameroff, 1985; Sameroff & Fiese, 1989) analogous to the biological genotype.

Developmental adaptation is the consequence of the transactions among the phenotype, genotype, and environtype. In figure 1-1 can be seen the bidirectional relations that comprise these transactions across developmental

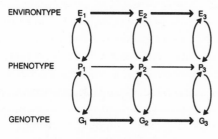

FIGURE 1-1

Transactions among environtype, phenotype, and genotype in development. (Subscripts represent successive points in time. See pp. 26–27.)

time. The upward arrows from genotype to phenotype represent the action of genes on the child's biological characteristics. The downward arrows are the characteristics of the child that trigger gene activity. The downward arrows from the environtype to the phenotype represent the experience provided by the child's physical and social context. The upward arrows are the behavioral characteristics of the child that trigger specific sets of experiences. Initially, the arrows across time for the phenotype are much thinner than those of the environtype and genotype, representing the relative lack of self-regulation in the infant. However, with growth the line thickens as the child becomes increasingly able to take control of his or her own behavior and development.

During human growth, there is a shifting balance between the probabilistic triggering of these transactions and more purposeful manipulations. The purposeful behavior of the genotype is never a factor in an individual's life but may be evident across evolutionary time (Wilson, 1975). The purposeful behavior of the phenotype emerges as the infant increases in motor, emotional, and cognitive capacities. These burgeoning powers permit manipulation of both external and internal experience. Eventually external choices can be made in the parts of the environtype to be engaged, and internal choices can be made for arousing and dampening biological activity, even to the level of the genes (McClintock, 1987). The purposeful behavior of the environtype varies as well, from biologically based reactions of caregivers to the appearance and behavior of the infant to encoded legal systems that prescribe society's response to individual behavior.

Urie Bronfenbrenner (1977, 1986) has provided the most detailed descriptions of environmental organizations that affect developmental processes within categories of microsystems, mesosystems, exosystems, and macrosystems. The *microsystem* is the immediate setting of a child in an environment with particular features, activities, and roles—for example, the home or the

23

school. The *mesosystem* comprises the relationships between the major settings at a particular point in an individual's development, as between the home and the school. The *exosystem* is an extension of the mesosystem that includes settings that the child may not be a part of but that affect the settings in which the child does participate—for example, the world of work and neighborhoods. Finally, the *macrosystem* includes the overarching institutional patterns of the culture, including the economic, social, and political systems of which the microsystems, mesosystems, and exosystems are concrete expressions. Bronfenbrenner's ecological model has been fruitfully applied in the analysis of a number of clinical issues, including the effects of child abuse (Belsky, 1980) and divorce (Kurdek, 1981).

For our present purposes we will restrict the discussion to levels of environmental factors contained within the culture and the family. Developmental regulations at each of these levels are carried within codes, the cultural code and the family code. These regulations are encoded to direct cognitive and socio-emotional development so that the child ultimately will be able to fill a role defined by society.

Although the environtype can be conceptualized independently of the child, changes in the abilities of the developing child are major triggers for regulatory changes and in most likelihood were major contributors to the evolution of a *developmental agenda* that is each culture's timetable for developmental milestones. The cultural code is influenced by a variety of characteristics of society, including the customs, beliefs, and patterns of support and control.

Most behavioral research on the effects of the environment have focused on analyses of dyadic interaction patterns in which each partner's activities are labeled. Only recently have these relationships themselves become empirical issues of inquiry. Ross Parke and Barbara Tinsley (1987), in an extensive review of family interaction research, have identified an important new trend: father–child interaction is being added to the study of mother–child interaction, and both types are being combined into studies of triadic interactions and behavioral patterns of entire families. Behavioral research is slowly overcoming the technological difficulties embodied in analyses of multiple interacting individuals. Another growing empirical base comes from the study of beliefs rather than behavior (Goodnow, 1988; Sigel, 1985; Sameroff & Feil, 1985). Investigators have become increasingly articulate at defining the dimensions of parental belief systems, with the goal of describing the effects of these belief systems on parental behavior and, ultimately, on the behavior of the child. For the present, however, these research domains have only promised future contributions to successful intervention efforts.

THE CULTURAL CODE

The cultural code is the complex of characteristics that organize a society's child-rearing system, which in turn incorporates elements of socialization and education. These processes are embedded in sets of social controls and social supports based on beliefs that differ in the amount of community consensus, ranging from mores and norms to fads and fashions. It would be beyond the scope of this chapter to elucidate the full range of cultural regulatory processes that are potentially relevant to an understanding of developmental psychopathology. Instead, a few points will be highlighted to sketch the dimensions of the cultural code.

Although the common biological characteristics of the human species have produced similar developmental agendas in most cultures, differences in many major features often ignore the biological status of the individual. In most cultures formal education begins between the ages of six and eight (Rogoff, 1981), when most children have the cognitive ability to learn from such structured experiences. But informal education can begin at different ages depending on the culture's attributions to the child. The Digo and Kikuyu are two East African cultures that have different beliefs about infant capacities (deVries & Sameroff, 1984): the Digo believe that infants can learn within a few months after birth and begin socialization at that time; the Kikuyu believe that serious education is not possible before the second year of life. Such examples demonstrate the variability of human developmental contexts and the openness of the regulatory system to modification.

One of the major contemporary risk conditions toward which many programs are being directed is adolescent pregnancy. Although for certain young mothers the pregnancy is the outcome of individual factors, for a large proportion it is the result of a cultural code that defines maturity, family relationships, and socialization patterns with adolescent motherhood as a normative ingredient. To focus on the problem as one that resides wholly in the individual would be a gross mistake.

THE FAMILY CODE

Just as cultural codes regulate the fit between individuals and the social system, family codes regulate individuals within the family system. Family codes allow a group of individuals to form a collective unit in relation to society as a whole. As the cultural code regulates development so that an individual may fill a role in society, family codes regulate development to produce members that fulfill a role within the family and participate in the shared system.

Families have rituals that prescribe roles, stories that transmit orientations to each family member as well as to the rest of the world, shared myths that influence individual interactions, and paradigms that change individual behavior in the presence of other family members. These represented and practiced ingredients of the family code are discussed in greater detail by David Reiss (chapter 9).

THE INDIVIDUAL PARENT'S CODE

There is good evidence that individual behavior is influenced by the family context. When operating as part of a family, each member alters his or her behavior (Parke & Tinsley, 1987), frequently without awareness of the change (Reiss, 1981). There is also no doubt that each individual contributes to family interactions. The contribution of parents is much more complexly determined than that of young children. Each parenting figure imposes individualized interpretations on the cultural and family codes. To a large extent these interpretations are conditioned by each parent's past participation in his or her own family's coded interactions, but they are captured uniquely by each member of the family (Sameroff & Fiese, 1989). These individual influences further condition each parent's responses to his or her own child. The richness of both health and pathology embodied in these responses are well described in the clinical literature. In terms of early development, Selma Fraiberg (1980) and her colleagues have provided many descriptions of the attributions that parents bring to their parenting. These "ghosts" of unresolved childhood conflicts have been shown to "do their mischief according to a historical or topical agenda, specializing in such areas as feeding, sleep, toilet-training or discipline, depending upon the vulnerabilities of the parental past" (Fraiberg, Adelson, & Shapiro, 1975, p. 388).

Parental psychopathology has long been recognized as a contributor to the poor developmental status of children. Although we acknowledge that influence, we must also be careful to note the effects of the contexts in which parental behavior is rooted, the family and cultural codes. It is important to recognize the parent as a major regulating agency of child development, but it is equally important to recognize that parental behavior is itself embedded in regulatory contexts.

REGULATIONS

Macroregulations   The most extensive regulations in duration are macroregulations, which are part of a culture's *developmental agenda*. This agenda is a series of points in life when the environment is restructured to provide different experiences to the child. Weaning, toilet training, and schooling, for example, may be initiated at different times in the child's course of development, depending on cultural codes. The contrasting beliefs of the Digo and Kikuyu described earlier are examples of such differences in macroregulations. Even in contemporary Western culture, there is variability in beliefs about the earliest point at which a child may be educated, ranging from structuring prenatal experiences to waiting until the child reaches school age to implement educational efforts (Elkind, 1981). Macroregulatory codes provide the basis for socialization in each culture; they apply to the distinct behavioral events that are expected of all members of a culture or subculture. Macroregulations, the most highly articulated and purposive of the regulatory functions, are known to socialized members of each culture and may be openly discussed or written down in the form of laws (such as all children age six and older must be registered for school). Macroregulations may be keyed to universal human characteristics or individual differences: universal milestones such as walking, puberty, or reaching a specific age can be contrasted with unique individual triggers such as level of intellectual, physical, or creative competence. Macroregulations recognize differences between individuals as well as similarities. For example, schoolchildren who pass certain tests may take a different educational track than those who don't; the exams trigger experiential restructurings of the developmental environment.

Miniregulations   The second level of regulations consists of miniregulations, which operate within a shorter timespan. They come into play daily, reflecting the repeated caregiving demands within the family. Such activities include feeding children when they are hungry, changing diapers when they are wet, and punishing them when they misbehave. Miniregulations are susceptible to a wide range of individual variability while still conforming to cultural codes. The family provides the arena for miniregulations throughout much of the child's growth and development. Families may develop and transmit their own codes (Reiss, 1981; Sameroff & Fiese, 1989). Families may carry out culturally mandated caregiving practices, such as disciplining, in different ways that will have different consequences for their children. Deviances within our culture such as coercive parenting can have a detrimental effect on the child's behavior yet be maintained as a form of regulation within the family (Patterson, 1986a). Most family members can agree upon the miniregulations within the family although they may not be able to articulate them spontaneously (chapter 9).

The child's contribution to miniregulations may be seen in instances where the caretaking behaviors of the family are restructured to meet the demands of the child. For instance, a child with autism may present the family with difficulties in routine caretaking; however, adjustments in miniregulations permit the incorporation of the child into daily routines.

Microregulations   The third level of regulation consists of microregulations, which operate in the shortest time frame. Microregulations are momentary interactions between child and caregiver, referred to by others as "behavioral synchrony" or "attunement" (Field, 1979; Stern, 1977). Microregulations are a blend of social and biological codes because, although they may be brought to awareness, many of these activities appear naturally with seeming automaticity. Toward the biological end are intuitive parenting behaviors such as baby talk or a smile in response to an infant's smile, and toward the socialized end are "microsocial" patterns of interaction that increase or decrease antisocial behavior in the child (Patterson, 1986b). The child's contribution to microregulations may be seen in the effects of infant activity on maternal responsivity. Premature infants or infants who have experienced multiple perinatal complications may exhibit a lower activity level overall and require different stimulation from their parents than healthy, full-term newborns (Field, 1978; Goldberg, Brachfeld, & DiVitto, 1980). Such adjustment in parental microregulations is stimulated in large part by the child's behavior (Brazelton, Koslowski, & Main, 1974).

The three sources of regulation are organized at different levels of the environtype. (The use of the prefixes *macro, mini,* and *micro* is analogous to Bronfenbrenner's use of these terms only with respect to size.) Macroregulations are the modal form of regulation within the cultural code. Many cultural codes are written down or memorized and may be passed on to individual members of society through customs, beliefs, and mythologies, in addition to laws that regulate children's health and education. Miniregulations are modal within the family code, in which less formal interactions condition the caregiving behavior of family members. Microregulations come into play at the individual level, where differences in personality and temperament balance with common human behavior in reactions to the child.

During early childhood, the common pathway of these regulations is through the behavior of parental figures, and especially the primary caregiver, in their relationships with the infant. Thus early relationships become central to the development of normative and deviant infant adaptations.

The three levels of regulation are in constant interaction and even transaction. The family develops its caretaking routines influenced by the transactions between the cultural and family codes, that is, between social norms and family traditions. As children develop within the family, they increasingly participate in these transactions, which serve as a foundation for social interaction. Families highlight through rituals the role defined for each child and develop myths that further regulate the child's development. The style of each family member contributes to the way in which the regulations will be carried out in relation to each child.

The operation of the family code is characterized by a series of regulated transactions. The parents may hold particular concepts of development that influence their caretaking practices. Through exposure to different role expectations and listening to family stories, children make their own contribution through their particular style. The child's acting out of roles within the family is incorporated into family stories, rituals, and myths. As the child becomes an active transactor in the family code, his or her behavior may ultimately affect the child-rearing practices of the parents and the creation of the code to be passed down to the next generation.

The Contribution of Developmental Psychopathology

Developmental psychopathology has introduced an important reorientation within psychiatry. The principles of development that apply to the achievement of healthy growth are now seen as the same ones that apply to the achievement of illness (Sroufe & Rutter, 1984). In this view most illnesses are indeed achievements that result from the active strivings of each individual to adapt to his or her environment. The nutrients or poisons that experience provides will flavor that adaptation, for every complex human achievement is influenced by experience. For young children, organized experiences are either provided or arranged for by the family and the culture.

Developmental psychopathology applies developmental approaches to understand maladaptive individual differences in behavior. Whereas developmental psychologists try to understand the continuities between normal and deviant behavior to reveal general laws of development and psychiatrists seek to define the discontinuities between normal and disordered behavior to categorize individuals, developmental psychopathologists combine the two approaches by using general principles of development to explain why some individuals develop disorders that are discontinuous with normal functioning. Thus the scientific program for developmental psychopathology is to explain both the continuities and discontinuities in individual patterns of behavioral adaptation.

The discontinuities of interest are both cross-sectional and longitudinal.

Cross-sectional discontinuities are evident where deviant behavior is seen as qualitatively different from normal behavior. Longitudinal discontinuities are evident when past normal adaptations change into disordered ones or, conversely, past abnormal adaptations are no longer evident in current functioning. Developmental psychopathology is faced with the task of explaining the dynamic processes by which abnormality separates itself from normality.

Within a framework of developmental psychopathology, continuity in development is conceptualized as continuity in adaptive organization across time. Because the contents of behavior change over time, we can expect to see continuity not in the specifics of behavior (Sroufe & Waters, 1977) but rather in the child's ability to function in a personal and social context. What is adaptive at one age will not be adaptive at another. Crying, which is an important social signal for infants' survival, becomes a sign of immaturity and incompetence when used by older children. However, the adaptive organization of older children requires them to develop effective ways of solving their problems and communicating their needs to others. The movement from one level of adaptive organization to another is the result of the transactions among the developmental regulatory systems—the phenotype, the genotype, and the environtype. The genotype permits children (the phenotype) to develop language skills that can be used for communicating their needs. The environtype provides the specific language children will be using and caregiving agents who can respond to their requests.

Sometimes the quality of adaptive organization improves. The development of communication abilities in the deaf is one example. Because of their inability to hear language, deaf infants are unable to use vocal language for other than the simplest communication. If the environtype had no differentiated regulatory system for deaf children, their intellectual outcomes would be generally poor and there would be serious deficits in their social skills. In environtypes with differentiated regulations for deaf infants, their experience is altered to facilitate adaptive outcome. They are given special training in the use of gestural communication in a context in which these signals are understood and responded to. Dyslexia is another case in point. Children who cannot easily understand the relationship between written symbols and sounds have great difficulty in learning to read. The commonly used phonics system, which produces accelerated reading ability in most children, produces no learning in such children. If the environtype is triggered by this developmental problem, new regulations can alter the mode of teaching reading to these children. By substituting whole-word learning for phonics, many such problem children can learn to read.

In each of these examples, if the environment were not coded to be sensitive to individual differences in children's quality of functioning, no regulation would occur and we would see continuity of poor adaptive organization from early childhood to later phases of development. Our clinical judgment might be that there is something wrong with the child instead of with the regulatory systems. What must be understood is that no child learns language and reading without a context in which there is an organized language system and methods for teaching reading. Even children who learn to read "by themselves" do so in an informal learning context in which it is clear from adult behavior that there are links between the written word and spoken language. Although for large numbers of children the environment is uniformly coded, it is not necessarily set up for every child's development. In this sense, developmental problems are *never* in the child alone but always in a relationship between a child with unique characteristics and a context that does not provide the necessary regulatory experience to allow the child to move to more advanced levels of adaptive organization.

Using this framework, how would we understand the transition from adequate states of adaptive organization to inadequate states, that is, from good to bad? In cognitive development, the case is clear: in environtypes where there is little to learn, little learning will take place. Where the child's learning opportunities are limited, intellectual advancement will be limited. The washout effect in the case of Head Start children who were initially well advanced is a sad example (Zigler & Trickett, 1978). Once these children were returned to their usual environtype for further schooling, limited learning opportunities generally reduced their level of cognitive adaptation to the local norm.

In social and emotional development, changes in adaptive organization are less clear because we do not have adequate theories of how social and emotional behavior change over time. For social behavior, one dimension of development is the increasing number of settings in which social interactions take place, from the caregiving dyad to the extended family, peer groups in schools, and work sites that comprise Bronfenbrenner's (1977) social ecology. From the perspective of developmental psychopathology, we will be asking how the adaptive organization of social behavior that is established in the early dyadic relationship translates into the adaptive organization of social skills in other settings. Research on the consequences of anxious attachment relationships at the end of the first year for subsequent peer interactions has demonstrated how variations in regulation of the infant by the environtype produce variations in later social competence (Sroufe, 1983).

In emotional behavior, developmental changes in adaptive organization are even less well specified. One dimension that has been defined to some extent is the child's increasing ability to regulate arousal. T. Berry Brazelton (1973)

31

has made the infant's ability to modulate states of arousal—that is, to become alert in interactive situations or to self-quiet from states of high arousal—a centerpiece of adaptive functioning. The role of caregivers in soothing distress, enhancing alertness, or eliciting smiling is a regular feature of early development and part of the regulatory aspect of the environtype. A shift to better adaptive organization occurs when an infant who is hypersensitive to stimulation is treated very delicately by the caregiver until the child can develop his or her own ability to control sensory input. On the other hand, a shift to worse adaptive organization can be seen where parents constantly tease a well-organized infant into high states of arousal and do not permit the child to experience self-regulation (Fraiberg, 1982).

A shift to worse adaptive organization in which emotional and social development are meshed has been identified by research on the ontogeny of antisocial behavior (Patterson, 1986b). As a consequence of inept parenting—an inadequate environtype—children who are trained to use coercive social interactions within the family use the same nonadaptive patterns in interactions with peers in settings outside the family. Instead of being able to use experience in these new settings to enhance social skills, the children are locked by their antisocial behavior out of contexts in which further development could occur.

In each of these examples adaptive organization is based less on the maintenance of a stable set of behaviors than on the maintenance of a dynamic balance of emotional states that permits social interactions in settings where learning can take place. The etiology of behavioral pathology must be understood within these dynamic developmental systems. The study of the adaptational process emphasizes the constructive aspect of development in which each individual comes to terms with opportunities and limitations of experience to produce a uniquely integrated outcome. The study of the linkage between a child and his or her experience contains the recognition that no individual can be understood apart from the relationships in which he or she lives. The analysis of the environtype emphasizes the many levels of influence that potentially regulate the adaptational process.

The perspective taken by developmental psychopathology offers a powerful alternative to nondevelopmental approaches because principles of process are integrated into an understanding of behavioral deviancy. Whereas traditional views have seen deviancy as categorically inherent in the individual, developmental views place deviancy in the dynamic relationship between the individual and the internal and external context. The success of this approach will be determined by whether it illuminates the importance of early relationships for the current and future mental health of the child.

Chapter 2

The Infant's Relationship Experience: Developmental and Affective Aspects

Robert N. Emde

Most families regard infancy as a hopeful time, as a new beginning, when parents can participate in the rapid growth and social awakening of someone separate and loved yet part of themselves. The fact that there are many troubled families in which this positive experience does not occur or is thwarted is a topic of direct relevance to developmental psychopathology. But before we consider pathology or deviance, it is wise to grasp what is expectable or normative.

The Early Caregiving Relationship in Biological Perspective

Normative experience necessarily has its roots in the biological adaptation of our species; we are used to thinking of principles of organization, regulation, and change as being prominent in an individual's development. But the most salient feature of infant experience has to do not with the individual's state of adaptedness but rather with the caregiving relationship. The pediatrician-psychoanalyst Donald Winnicott (1965) dramatized this paradox some years ago by stating "there is no such thing as a baby." Winnicott meant that the health care provider cannot regard the infant in isolation from the mother. An infant cannot survive and develop without the intimate, committed, and consistent care of a parenting figure. Moreover, appropriate care involves satisfaction not just of physical needs but also of emotional needs (Bowlby, 1958; Emde, 1980a; Mahler, Pine, & Bergman, 1975; Spitz, 1965). Today most developmentalists would see the satisfaction of needs in terms of an interpersonal matching of regulatory systems in development—the infant's and the caregiver's—but the essential point is the same: in thinking about early experience we must think about the caregiving relationship. That relationship frames all individual experience, and the facilitation of infant development is virtually synonymous with the facilitation of the caregiving relationship.

Biology takes a lifespan approach and studies patterns of behavior that are universal or species-wide. Thus, it behooves us to consider the infancy relationship experience in the context of other life relationships. Several kinds of relationships are salient at different times in development, although they are sometimes confused in discussions. The *parent–child relationship*, for example, is not limited to childhood; it is a relationship that links a specific parent and a specific child throughout the lifespan. Because of psychological processes of internalization (wherein interactive experiences become represented; see chapter 3), this relationship in fact lasts beyond the death of the parent and through the lifetime of the adult daughter or son. Moreover, interactions characteristic of the parent–child relationship change dramatically as a function of development. In infancy, responsibility and power are asymmetrical, with a strong predominance in the parent; these functions tend to be symmetrical in adulthood, but may be asymmetrical again when the offspring engages in taking care of an elderly parent.

Other lifespan relationships include those among *siblings*, among *peers*, and in adulthood among *marital partners* and *work colleagues*. These other relationships assume more importance beyond infancy and are discussed more fully in later chapters (especially chapter 8).

Parental behaviors are normally activated in caregiving even though the infant cannot yet understand them. At the outset, the infant cannot share intentions and the infant does not know that he or she is in a relationship. Much has been written recently about the newborn's organized capacities and "competence" (Brazelton, 1973; Haith & Campos, 1983; Osofsky, 1987; Stone, Smith, & Murphy, 1973). Still, the infant can be competent in performing his or her role only if the caregiver is appropriately responsive (Ainsworth, Bell, & Stayton, 1974; see chapter 4).

Functional Aspects of the Parent–Child Relationship

The early parent–child relationship is characterized by caregiving in a number of interdependent domains or functional aspects. Each functional aspect of the relationship is strongly biologically prepared and has complementary components in the parent and in the child. Table 2-1 lists these functional aspects.

ATTACHMENT AND BONDING

Considerable research has been done on the functional aspect having to do with the specific affiliative tie of the infant to the mother or father. Two separate literatures have used somewhat different terms to refer to this tie— one from the side of the child (referring to it as *attachment*) and the other from the side of the parent (referring to it as *bonding*). Thus, from the infant's side, *attachment* refers to the specific affiliative tie of the infant to the mother or father, which generally begins soon after six months of age. Once cumulative everyday experience has resulted in the infant's developing an internal working model of an attachment figure, separation from that figure is painful and loss can be devastating (Bowlby, 1973, 1980). From the parent's side, this affiliative aspect of the caregiving relationship is usually referred to as *parental bonding* (Klaus & Kennell, 1982), which can be thought of as the parent's affectionate, warm, and loving commitment to the infant. Such a commit-

TABLE 2-1
Functional Aspects of the Caregiving Relationship

Child	Parent
Attachment (security-exploration)	Bonding (emotional availability and commitment)
Vigilance	Protection
Physiological regulation	Provision of organized structure; responsiveness to needs
Affect regulation and sharing	Empathic responsiveness
Learning	Teaching
Play	Play
Self-control	Discipline

ment can, of course, begin during pregnancy or soon after birth. From an ethological perspective, attachment and bonding represent two complementary affiliative aspects of the caregiving relationship; from the individual's standpoint, they are separately organized subsystems of human social development with corresponding potentials for activation that occur at different times in the lifespan.

The separation of these subsystems is highlighted by a particular form of disorder. Some troubled parents who abuse their infants experience the activation of a developmentally inappropriate affiliative subsystem in the process of caregiving. Instead of the developmentally appropriate parental-bonding subsystem being activated, they may experience the activation of the attachment subsystem (with a corresponding representational model of an earlier attachment figure and an earlier model of self that may want to be assuaged and may feel frustrated). Normal caregiving is thus disrupted by parental "ghosts in the nursery," as Selma Fraiberg put it so memorably (Fraiberg, Adelson, & Shapiro, 1975). Our later discussion of representational processes in infantile experience will add a further theoretical framework to this speculation (see chapter 3) and will provide a basis for understanding the cross-generational transmission of patterns of attachment (see Main, Kaplan, and Cassidy, 1985; Ricks, 1985).

Research has shown that the emotional availability of the infant's caregiver—including sensitivity and responsiveness to needs—is associated with the outcome of secure attachment in the one-year-old (see chapter 4). Secure attachment is observed not only in the one-year-old's positive greeting of the caregiver after a brief separation, but also in the toddler's ability to explore a new environment in the caregiver's presence, the "secure base" effect (Ainsworth & Wittig, 1969). Some researchers have characterized this aspect of the infant's relationship experience in terms of attachment-exploration; and, as we will later review, the concept has led to research linking early secure attachment to social competence in the preschooler.

As important as the attachment-exploration link is, however, we must remind ourselves that it concerns only one functional aspect of the caregiving relationship. Other aspects are equally important for the infant's experience.

VIGILANCE AND PROTECTION

Vigilance and protection are complementary components of another basic aspect of caregiving. These qualities are preeminent in conditions of poverty, violence, or environmental disaster, when the caregiver must protect the life and safety of the infant and the infant must be vigilant to survive.

PHYSIOLOGICAL REGULATION

The physiological regulation of the infant's needs is an aspect of the infant's experience that must assume priority in all caregiving relationships (not just in special conditions) because the infant's survival, physical health, and development depend on it. Caregivers must provide food, fluid, warmth, and a suitable sensory environment within the limits of the infant's homeostatic requirements.

AFFECT REGULATION AND SHARING

Affect regulation and sharing on the infant's side are enabled by *empathic responsiveness* on the caregiver's side. Although communications of affect mediate all aspects of the infant's relationship experience, the regulation of affect is especially important for adaptation; the infant must be guided to avoid the extremes of excitement, distress, and withdrawal. In addition, the parent's empathic responsiveness facilitates the infant's affective sharing and the reciprocal, positive, pleasurable features of social development.

It used to be thought that all aspects of the caregiving relationship were secondary to the satisfaction of physiological needs, especially hunger. But abundant clinical and experimental evidence now exists to counter this view. Infant attachment and exploration can vary independently of the regulation of physiological needs. Interferences with the development of attachment can occur even when physiological needs are met (see Bowlby, 1973, 1980, 1988, for a review). A similar statement can be made about the relative independence of two other aspects of the caregiving relationship, namely play and learning/teaching.

PLAY AND LEARNING/TEACHING

Play and learning/teaching are to some extent dependent on other aspects of the infant–caregiver relationship: the needs for protection and physiological regulation must be sufficiently met before play and learning/teaching are activated; attachment and parental bonding serve to enhance both play and learning/teaching. But it is useful to consider these as different functional aspects of the caregiving relationship. We might even postulate a hierarchy of motives reflected in these other aspects, similar to that proposed by Maslow (1971) for adults and by Sandler and Joffe (1969) for infants. Hierarchical or not, the motives underlying human play are different from those underlying attachment/bonding and learning/teaching. Play in later infancy is not necessarily associated with security of attachment, and fathers and mothers tend to play with their infants at different times and in different ways.

SELF-CONTROL AND DISCIPLINE

Finally, self-control on the infant's side and discipline on the caregiver's side are included as a functional aspect of the relationship that becomes prominent beginning early in the second year. Parental concerns with regulating discipline and socializing the toddler according to the dos and don'ts of the household (Emde, Johnson, & Easterbrooks, 1988) enable the toddler to exercise increasing self-control in the midst of conflicting opportunities and demands.

Biological Preparedness for Social Interaction

Our views of the human infant have changed rather dramatically as a result of the last two decades of research. We no longer view the infant as primarily passive or undifferentiated. We no longer view the infant's social interaction as a reactive consequence of drives or physiological needs. Instead, we view the infant as coming to the world with biologically prepared active propensities and with organized capacities for self-regulation. These are manifest in patterned cycles of sleep and wakefulness as well as in a highly complex organization for physiological homeostasis. But even more important, the infant comes to the world with a biological preparedness for participating in social interaction. It seems that our evolution has guaranteed that the infant can participate in the caregiving relationship with sufficient competence for the biologically prepared self-regulatory capacities, insufficient for life on their own, to be completed by the caregiver through meaningful social interaction (see Sander, 1975). The infant has built-in capacities for initiating, maintaining, and terminating social interactions with others. Some of these capacities are present at birth, including propensities for participating in eye-to-eye contact; for being organized and soothed by human holding, touching, and rocking; and for showing prolonged, alert attentiveness to the stimulus features of the human face and voice (see reviews by Ainsworth, Bell, & Stayton, 1974; Emde & Robinson, 1979; Papousek & Papousek, 1981). As Hanuš and Mechtilde Papousek point out, much of the behavioral activity and integrative capacity of the young infant can be thought of as a preadaptation for the dynamic circumstances of human interaction. These capacities include those of orienting to new stimuli, processing sequential information, generating patterns of motor activity, and engaging in cross-modal perception (or "amodal" perception; see Stern, 1985).

The parent is also prepared for social interaction in caregiving. A variety of parenting behaviors are performed automatically, seem to be species-wide, and therefore are presumed to be biologically based (Papousek & Papousek, 1979). Parental behaviors that the Papouseks include in this category are those that minimize transitory states and maximize either wakefulness or quiet sleep and those that support visual contact by means of special postures. Such behaviors also include exaggerated greeting responses, imitation of the newborn's facial and vocal expressions, and the use for interactional episodes of simple repetitive structures that nearly match the infant's requirements for learning. Parents' baby talk has also been seen in this light (Snow, 1972; Stern, 1977). A further biological preadaptedness for social interaction in both infant and parent is indicated by recent research on behavioral synchrony. Infants and parents mesh their behaviors in delicately timed mutual interchanges during social interaction. The dynamics of synchrony have been examined from the point of view of behavioral states (Sander, 1975), through microanalyses of looking and arousal (Als, Tronick, & Brazelton, 1979; Brazelton, Als, Tronick, & Lester, 1979; Stern, 1977), and through the microanalysis of voice and movement (Condon & Sander, 1974).

The fundamental activity and biological preparedness of the human infant has still another feature, which has to do with the centrality of affect in the relationship experience: infant experience is monitored according to what is pleasurable and not pleasurable. From the outsider's viewpoint, affective activity shows us there is a preadapted organized basis for guiding behavior. In early infancy, an infant's affective expressions are used to guide caregiving actions. The mother hears a cry and acts to relieve the inferred cause of distress. She sees a smile or hears cooing and cannot resist maintaining a playful interaction. Later, the infant makes use of affective monitoring for guiding behavior in uncertain situations, whether the caregiver intervenes or not. The affective expressions of caregivers and others are sought out to resolve the uncertainty and regulate behavior (for example, happy or interested expressions would encourage approach; fearful or angry expressions would discourage approach). From the infant's viewpoint, we presume that affective activity is also central. Our ideas about the role of affect in organizing the continuity of self and the relationship experience will be presented later in this chapter.

Another example of the biologically predisposed activity of the infant is evident in our understanding of the course of development itself. Again, our views have changed. We now appreciate that there are regulated developmental trajectories (chapter 1). From a biological point of view, development gives the appearance of being goal oriented and, with respect to species-important developmental functions, there are multiple ways of reaching goals, a principle Ludwig von Bertalanffy (1968) referred to as developmental "equifinality." As Arnold Sameroff (1981) has pointed out, children who are congenitally blind (Fraiberg, 1977), congenitally deaf (Freedman, Cannady, & Robinson, 1971), without limbs (Decarie, 1969), or have cerebral palsy all go through infancy with different sensorimotor experiences; still, all typically develop object permanence, representational intelligence, and self-awareness in early childhood. Strong developmental functions are also characterized by self-righting tendencies that give evidence of strongly regulated biological systems. In other words, a fundamental property of infancy is manifest in a strong tendency to get back on a developmental pathway after deficit or perturbation (see Waddington, 1962; Sameroff & Chandler, 1975). Further, illustrations of this tendency are provided by observations wherein a change in environment has corrected severe retardation in infants who had been environmentally deprived (see examples in Clarke & Clarke, 1977).

We have also learned that the developmental course of infancy is not linear. There are normative times of qualitative change or transformation, sometimes referred to as times of biobehavioral shift. These have been noted to take place at two to three months, six to nine months, around one year, and at eighteen to twenty-one months (Emde, Gaensbauer, & Harmon, 1976; McCall, 1979; Kagan, Kearsley, & Zelazo, 1978). These transformations have also been thought of as indicating stage boundaries in cognitive development (Uzgiris, 1976) as well as important shifts in socio-emotional and perceptual-motor development (Campos, Barrett, Lamb, Goldsmith, & Stenberg, 1983). The widespread nature of such behavioral changes has led to the hypothesis that they reflect regulatory shifts in the central nervous system.

Developmental Transformations and Affect

Affective changes are salient in developmental transformations. René Spitz (1959), who pioneered in his observations of early transformations and incorporated these observations in his theory of ego formation, felt that affective changes were the primary indicators of a new level of organization. We have found that affective changes are clearest at the concluding phase of a shift and have therefore speculated that they provide an incentive for developmental consolidation (Emde, Gaensbauer, & Harmon, 1976). Thus, maturational events may inaugurate a group of developmental changes, and the affective changes (such as the onset of social smiling, the onset of stranger and separation distress, euphoria with walking, and the "subduedness" mood that Mahler, Pine, and Bergman [1975] described later in the second year) may reflect adaptation in providing for integration at a new level of organization. Integration is enhanced because of social feedback (what is attended to by parents and reinforced) and because of internal feedback (what is experienced as new, interesting, and pleasurably mastered). Both kinds of feedback provide the infant with incentives for engagement with the world at a new level and, hence, promote a wider world of being and interaction. This expanding universe can be seen in the following review of some of these changes.

FIRST-YEAR SHIFTS

At two months a developmental transformation occurs following a gradual increase in time spent awake, which has been under way since birth. The distribution of wakefulness changes, with more during the day and less at night. Further, the quality of wakefulness changes: less of it is complicated by fussiness and—as some observers have put it—it becomes used in a new way for increased exploratory activity with toys and people (Dittrichova & Lapackova, 1964). Correspondingly, enhanced learning has been demonstrated in many laboratory experiments. After two months the infant can learn in a variety of ways, can accommodate and change behavior in a social situation, and can adjust to what is familiar, thereby completing learned activities so that exploration of the new is possible. Jean Piaget, in his scheme of cognitive development, notes that at about two months the infant becomes increasingly involved in activities "designed to make interesting spectacles last" (Piaget, 1952; see also review in Emde & Robinson, 1979).

New parents often state that beginning around two months their baby seems more human and less like a doll. The affective changes that appear quite dramatically at this time give parents pleasure and incentives for continuing to be with the baby. These include (1) enhanced eye-to-eye contact, (2) social smiling, and (3) social vocalizing. Enhanced eye-to-eye contact around two months has been both described in the naturalistic setting (Robson, 1967) and documented experimentally (Haith, 1977). The social smile blossoms at about two months. Although smiling has developmental antecedents, there is a shift from endogenous (state-related) smiling to exogenous (externally elicited) smiling at this time, and the response becomes predictable and social (Emde

41

& Harmon, 1972). Social vocalization, or cooing in response to the face of another, begins within two weeks after the flowering of the social smile. Altogether, parents now begin to think of their baby as playful. When they approach during wakefulness there is apt to be back-and-forth smiling, vocalizing, and looking, which make an affirming, fun-filled encounter—an exchange that is a welcome addition to the routines of caregiving. The enhancement of social reciprocal functioning at this age has been documented in the studies of Daniel Stern (1977).

At seven to nine months there is another major shift. Leading up to this, the infant sits up and begins to crawl. With self-produced locomotion the infant's world changes again. In the realm of cognition the infant shows a beginning of understanding means–ends relationships and of intentionality in the sense of anticipating an event independent of action (that is, the onset of Piaget's stage IV of sensorimotor development). Further, out of sight is not out of mind. The infant can playfully remove a cloth covering an object that was seen to disappear under it. There is a related advance in emotional capacity. An infant can now demonstrate expressions of fear in advance of avoidance and pleasure in advance of approach (Sroufe, 1979b). There is now play in addition to playfulness. Simple games begin with peekaboo and give-and-take with balls or favorite toys. Freud and Spitz have discussed how these games seem to have a theme of withdrawal and return and that they may bear a relationship to the comings and goings of caregivers as well as to the infant's beginning sense of mastery and coping with such experiences (Freud, 1920; Spitz, 1957). This change is also heralded by another shift in wakefulness and sleep-state organization between seven and nine months (Emde, Gaensbauer, & Harmon, 1976).

But there is another change, now well studied (for a review see Horner, 1980), which has special emotional significance to parents. Up to this time, although their baby may have smiled or reacted more pleasantly to them than to strangers, substitute caregiving was relatively uncomplicated. Now things are apt to be different. The baby may cry when mother or father leaves, and there is often distress or even fearfulness when a stranger approaches. A recent experimental study (Fouts & Atlas, 1979) documents the change: while infants at six and nine months experienced mother's face as rewarding, they experienced a stranger's face as neutral at six months and as negatively reinforcing at nine months. After this shift, substitutions in caregiving are more difficult to make but parents feel needed and special. The developmental message is generally compelling: no one else will do.

We have sometimes referred to these nodal transformations in the first year in terms of their social properties, the two-month shift being "the awakening of sociability" and the seven-to-nine-month shift being "the onset of focused attachment." These shifts inaugurate new levels of organization in the infant's social world of experience in terms of what is demanded, what is rewarding, what is expectable, and what is reciprocated.

SECOND-YEAR SHIFTS

The transformations of the second year have not been studied in the same detail as those of the first year. Nonetheless, striking features have been documented.

At twelve to thirteen months toddlerhood begins, with the onset of walking. In terms of cognition, the infant begins to appreciate the independence of entities in the world and their properties. In terms of language, the infant can now comprehend that a word is agreed upon to designate a specific object. Symbolic functioning enters a new domain (see Kagan, 1981; McCall, 1979). The infant can imitate totally new behaviors not previously seen and not currently in the response repertoire. As we would expect, there are also important affective changes. The one-year-old's frequent mood of elation in exploring the world has been observed by many (Mahler, Pine, & Bergman, 1975; Sroufe, 1979b). This is a time when the infant begins to use affect expressions instrumentally or purposefully. Moreover, it has been shown experimentally that when a twelve-month-old gains control over the operation of a potentially fear-provoking toy distress is reduced; this effect is not seen earlier (Gunnar, 1980). Social referencing, the seeking of expressions of affect by significant others in order to resolve uncertainty, becomes prominent at this age. Parents note that smiling and pouting expressions can be used by babies in order to get their way, and that anger is now often directed at a person. Parents begin to attribute responsibility to their infant and therefore become disciplinarians in addition to caregivers. Parents also become concerned about socializing emotions (whether to encourage or inhibit anger or sadness, for example).

Eighteen to twenty-one months is another time of transformation. Mahler, Pine, and Bergman (1975) describe that the child, while energetically exercising growing autonomy, both frequently pushes mother away and tends to cling to her. In terms of cognition, the child is now capable of remembering and imitating sequences of actions and of understanding symbolic relationships between entities. The prolonged one-word phase typically gives way to two-word or multiple-word utterances at this time. In terms of affect, this is when willfulness increases, when the intentional use of "no" expressions begin, and when there are increased temper tantrums. There may be, as Mahler and her

43

group have pointed out, swings of mood and even evidence of sadness—mood changes that they relate to the beginnings of the "rapprochement crisis" (Mahler, Pine, & Bergman, 1975). In observed interactions with mother there are apt to be "shadowing and darting away patterns"; the earlier "emotional refueling" interactions with mother tend to be replaced by a deliberate search for or avoidance of close bodily contact. It is as if the toddler is keenly aware of his or her separateness and the obstacles to mastering the world on his or her own. Obviously, this brings forth further changes in the child's social world. Caregivers react to these affective changes in a variety of ways, which often reflect their own developmental experiences with separation-individuation. Some may feel proud and encourage autonomy; others may feel uneasy and protective.

The Role of Affect in Organizing Experience

Affect organizes experience. We have just discussed how affective change promotes the integration of experience related to developmental transformations. Accordingly, affective change provides incentives for new levels of functioning, both on an internal psychological level and on a social interactive level. Affect also provides a sense of coherence over time and a continual orientation about what is familiar. It can be said that there is an affective core to self-experience, providing both a sense of continuity during times of developmental change and a sense of empathy with others (Emde, 1983). If this is true, then there must be a strong biological preparedness for affective organization and its communicative aspects throughout our species. Research evidence supporting this inference is now substantial. Cross-cultural research in adults indicates universality in both the expression and the recognition of discrete emotions, namely for anger, fear, sadness, disgust, and interest (Ekman, Friesen, & Ellsworth, 1972; Izard, 1971). Observational and experimental research in infants indicates that these patterned discrete emotions are not only present in the young infant but used in caregiving (Campos, Barrett, Lamb, Goldsmith, & Stenberg, 1983; Sorce & Emde, 1982; Izard, Huebner, Risser, McGinnes, & Dougherty, 1980). Furthermore, measurement studies indicate a similar organization of emotional expressions in infancy, childhood, and adulthood (see review in Emde, 1980b).

There is also a day-to-day and less abstract way in which affect organizes experience and gives a sense of coherence. It can be said that the infant behaves in order to "feel right" (Stern, 1985). Everyday experiences of curiosity, interest, pleasure, and boredom are motivating, as are everyday doses of distress from which the infant seeks relief. Moreover, affective monitoring in the everyday sense has a dual aspect: it occurs not just within the child but reciprocally between child and caregiver; in other words, monitoring occurs within the relationship experience. Emotions are fundamentally social, and it is likely that in the interpersonal sphere emotions have evolved to ensure the more sustaining aspects of affiliation feelings, often known as social bonding or attachment (Emde, 1980b; Hamburg, 1963; Myers, 1967).

The very fact that such a rich array of emotional signals are present early in infancy and are used in caregiving (for example, see Izard, Huebner, Risser, McGinness, & Dougherty, 1980; Klinnert, Campos, Sorce, Emde, & Svejda, 1983) indicates the existence of a functional system of extreme developmental importance for cuing needs and for learning about social interaction and play. The infant's relationship experience is characterized not only by an emotional infant but by an emotionally available caregiver who has a corresponding emotional sensitivity and responsiveness to infant cues.

The reciprocal emotional availability of another is also important in a recently identified aspect of emotional development known as social referencing (Campos & Stenberg, 1981; Feinman & Lewis, 1983; Sorce, Emde, Campos, & Klinnert, 1985; Hornik & Gunnar, 1988). Soon after six months of age, an infant who is confronted by a situation of uncertainty often seeks out emotional information from a significant other person in order to resolve the uncertainty and regulate his or her behavior. An experiment on the "visual cliff" can be considered paradigmatic. The visual cliff is a glass-top table that was originally designed by Walk and Gibson (1961) and used by Campos, Hiatt, Ramsay, Henderson, and Svejda (1978) for studying depth perception and the onset of fearfulness. In our experiments the apparent cliff edge is adjusted to the threshold of the infant's depth perception, namely, 30 cm. An infant crawls across the glass surface to explore, encounters the uncertain drop-off zone—where a checkerboard pattern appears under the glass—and looks to mother's face. If mother displays happiness or interest, the infant will cross; if she displays fear or anger, the infant will not cross (Sorce, Emde, Campos, & Klinnert, 1985). Social referencing has been experimentally demonstrated in a number of situations of uncertainty, including an approaching toy robot, a small collapsing playhouse, a stranger's approach, and unusual toys. Social referencing experiments have demonstrated that especially from nine to eighteen months the infant actively uses emotional signals in significant others.

As has already been noted, the mother's emotional availability, as judged from her sensitivity and responsiveness in the home setting in the middle of the infant's first year, has been found to predict the infant's security of attachment as observed in the strange situation at one year. In other words, the mother's emotional availability has enabled the infant's continued emotional development within the relationship, so that the infant can cope with separation experiences, engage in positive reunion with the mother, and be confident enough to explore the environment in the mother's presence. Enhanced exploration in mother's presence has been described in terms of the "secure base" effect (Ainsworth & Wittig, 1969), and in terms of mother being the "beacon of orientation" for exploration (Mahler, Pine, & Bergman, 1975). Experimental observations in fifteen-month-olds have also demonstrated this effect, showing that the exploration and play of the toddler were influenced by whether mother was reading a newspaper or not (Sorce & Emde, 1982).

We might now ask how affects organize the infants' knowledge of the relationship experience itself. Stern (1985) has pointed out that early infant relationship experiences are represented in memory as an average or as a prototype of many similar experiences. From this point of view, a retrieved memory of the relationship experience may never have occurred "just that way." This line of thinking also suggests the special influence of affect in the storing of some prototypes. Some specific relationship experiences elicit immediate affective reactions which contain within them innate, stereotypic physiological response patterns; thus the latency of the immediate affective reaction is fixed with respect to the stimulus or the incentive event. In this manner, an affective response to a stimulus that is repeated in relation to a fixed point of reference gets averaged into a prototype. Specific affective prototypes will then gain salience and will rise above the variability of other aspects of everyday experience. The analogy is to the electrophysiological technique of the average evoked response (AER). In that technique, the response to a repeated stimulus that would otherwise be hidden in background activity of the EEG is summated and given salience by virtue of its known fixed interval of response in relation to the stimulus. This model fits with our knowledge of the strong biological preparedness for immediate emotional responses to particular stimuli, not only in terms of distress and pleasure, but also in terms of discrete emotions, such as Charles Darwin (1872) and Silvan Tompkins (1962–1963) have described. In addition, the model fits in with something else we know. Positive emotional reactions tend to be more variable than negative emotional reactions in relation to specific stimulus events—there is less immediacy and less stereotyping in responses to pleasant stimuli. Consequently, one would expect that positive emotional prototypes would be more general and less salient; positive emotional signals would be broader and less sharply peaked, whereas negative emotional signals would be sharper. This model is in line with the clinical view that psychotherapeutic work usually deals with the reexperiencing of negative emotional prototypes, which are far more specific than positive emotional prototypes.

In a more general sense, clinical observations have indicated the importance of emotional availability in the caregiver–infant relationship. Where emotional availability is present, a range of emotions is expressed by each partner; there is a clarity of emotional signaling, and there is a balance of emotional tone in favor of interest and pleasure as opposed to sustained distress. Under such conditions, clinicians are likely to conclude that behavioral development is probably on track. On the other hand, when behavioral development is not going well, emotional availability is apt to be compromised and behavioral interactions of the infant and caregiver are apt to be marked by a restricted range of emotional expressiveness; less clear signaling; and a predominance of disengagement, distress, or avoidance in interactions. Under these conditions, clinicians may also see a "turning off" of affective interactions and, in extreme cases, sustained sadness or depression (see Emde, Gaensbauer, & Harmon, 1982; Gaensbauer & Harmon, 1982; Emde & Easterbrooks, 1985).

When emotional availability of the caregiver is not optimal, the organizing role of affect in its dual aspects (the simultaneous monitoring of emotional signals from oneself and from others) can lead to developmental problems. If there is too much pain in the child's experience, for example, there may be a defensive exclusion of information, as John Bowlby (1973) has pointed out so poignantly. Under these conditions, especially when caregivers disconfirm the child's painful experience (for example, by communicating that the child is not rejected and is not supposed to express unhappiness), there can be a constriction of experience. This kind of development is especially problematic after semantic memory and language develop and it has been connected to the dichotomous establishment of a "true" versus a "false" self (Winnicott, 1965). Prelinguistic defensive behaviors involving avoidance and the warding off of painful affects have been discussed by Spitz (1961), Fraiberg (1980, 1982), Sroufe (1983), and Gaensbauer and Harmon (1982). Moreover, painful affects and conflict avoidance have become more salient as a result of recent research concerning variations in information processing and the representations of attachment experiences (Bretherton & Waters, 1985; Main, Kaplan, & Cassidy, 1985).

Implications for the Child's Future Relationships

At this point we might ask, which biological and affective aspects of the infant's relationship experience are carried forward in development? Are there significant continuities? These questions are guiding current research and theories, but some answers are already apparent. First of all, temperament, which may be thought of as individual differences in the organization of emotional sensitivity and responsiveness (see Campos, Barrett, Lamb, Goldsmith, & Stenberg, 1983; Goldsmith & Campos, 1982), shows evidence of heritability in infancy and throughout childhood (Plomin, 1986). But the lion's share of the continuing influence on behavior is environmental; recent behavioral genetics research points to the importance of the specific family environment for each child (as compared with its shared aspects). These findings are quite compatible with our emphasis on the infant's relationship experience.

What seems plausible, then, is that the infant's biologically organized affective core becomes exercised within the infant–caregiver relationship and gains a varying quality of shared meaning with significant others. Through processes of internalization the affective response system becomes biased in accordance with the availability of the caregiver and the infant develops a sense of effectiveness and cumulative mastery experiences.

As research on the development of attachment documents (Ainsworth, Blehar, Waters, & Wall, 1978; Bretherton & Waters, 1985; Maccoby & Martin, 1983) and as our observations confirm, the child normatively comes to experience security when parents are available. This security is manifested by a balance of interest, curiosity, and exploration of the environment in the presence of caregivers (Emde, Gaensbauer, & Harmon, 1982). During the second half of the first year, parents increasingly guide their infant's activities so that the infant is able to fulfill parental goals, and parents give approval to desired behaviors (Kaye, 1982). Children experience mastery not only in relation to their own goals but also in relation to goals promoted by parents. This is an aspect of shared meaning that tends to be repeated.

Positive emotions play an important adaptive role. Mutual referencing and the sharing of positive affect between infants and caregivers were typically observed in a normative study conducted during the beginning and middle of the child's second year (Emde & Easterbrooks, 1985). In one sense, child and parent appeared to share the joy of mastery which, at least in part, resulted from the child's striving to do what parents did and approved of (that is, fostering imitation and identification processes). But shared meaning also results from progressive differentiation and from the internalization of a sense of reciprocity with others and of rules for social interchange that involve fairness, turn-taking, the appropriateness of context, and ownership. Moreover, a sense of empathy for another's distress or joy, along with prosocial inclinations, grows out of such exchanges.

Throughout we have stressed the importance of emotional availability in the early caregiving relationship. Positive emotions such as interest, joy, and surprise deserve emphasis as a regular feature of this availability. They become a reservoir in the affective core of self as a result of salutory infancy experience. Even more than having pleasure in life, positive emotions generate from within the affective core an interest in the expanding world and an encouragement of sociability.

An important question remains. What happens when there is not an appropriate range of emotional availability in the early caregiving experience? What happens to the child's affective self? It appears that a *deficit of emotional availability* in the early caregiving relationship is associated with a restriction of experience and with a risk for the later development of narcissistic personality disorder. On the other hand, an *inappropriate excess of emotions* in the early caregiving relationship—notably with hostility, rejection, and maltreatment—may be associated with warded-off affects and a risk of neurotic conflict structures of the sort found in parenting disorders of the next generation. Moreover, an increased risk of other kinds of personality disorder also seems likely.

We also believe that, in optimal circumstances, the relationship experience in infancy lays the groundwork for the beginnings of moral judgment. If all goes well, by three years the child may develop a sense of "we" that contains an executive sense of the significant other's being with the child in a positive sense and that gives an increased sense of mastery, power, and control. Thus, in one study, it was found that in the parent's absence internalized rules carried with them a sense of the "other"; to the extent that the rules were activated in a new social context, they carried with them an autonomous sense of the "we." When the caregiver was absent from the room, a mild temptation was given by a tester's puppet, which asked about playing with a prohibited set of toys. A number of children told the puppet, in one way or another, "Didn't you hear my mommy? I better not play with those toys. We better not either" (Emde & Buchsbaum, in press).

George Klein asserted that psychoanalysis had need of a theory of a "we-go" to correspond to its theory of ego (Klein, 1967). The child's developing sense of "we" and the interpersonal world of shared meaning has become a focus of research attention among developmentalists and psycholinguists (Bretherton, 1985; Bruner, 1982; Kaye, 1982; Brenner & Mueller, 1982; Rommetveit, 1976; Stern, 1985). This work, which has its origins in the social psychology of George Herbert Mead (1934) and of Lev Vygotsky (1978), is receiving new appreciation in the context of the infant's early relationship experience and positive emotionality.

It is too early to know if the three-year-old's "we-go" or what might be better called an "executive we" is characteristic more of optimal or of normative development. It is too early to know if individual differences in the "executive we" could mark a significant or sensitive indicator of risk for later problems. It is also too early to know if the "executive we" can serve as a buffer or bias against future stresses. But from a theoretical psychoanalytic standpoint, a fundamental motivating characteristic of repetition is the seeking of the familiar in a new relationship and the recognition of oneself as being with the other in that relationship (Sander, 1985). It would therefore seem that variations in the "we sense," and its absence, will assume increasing importance for our inquiry. From all indications, positive emotions and the availability of one or more caregivers are crucial in the development of what goes forward.

To summarize, the affective self, strongly prepared biologically, becomes biased with tendencies toward certain emotional responses, depending on early experiences in the caregiving relationship. Subsequently, additional influences result from specific relationship experiences that become internalized as shared meaning becomes more complex in the midst of intentions, negotiations, and counterintentions (chapter 3). If early caregiving experiences have included enough positive emotional exchanges and an emotionally available caregiver, there may be a new level of shared meaning in the three-year-old. An internalized executive sense of "we" will then be brought to new interactions and new relationships with peers and adults.

What are the conditions under which analogous experiences are reinstated later in life? Although much more research is needed, there is every reason to believe that there are important individual differences with respect to the affective core of self, its biased response tendencies, and early forms of internalized shared meaning. There is also reason to believe that such individual differences persist in development, exerting a pull on other relationship experiences throughout the lifespan. Indeed, one wonders if the infant–caregiver relationship experience does not have an influence on these early motivational structures of a unique sort, one that is pervasive and resistant to later environmental change.

Louis Sander (1985) has phrased the matter in a developmental systems language that is compelling for psychoanalysis.

Each infant-caregiver system constructs its own unique configuration of regulatory constraint on the infant's access to awareness of his own states, inner experience and initiatives to organize self-regulatory behavior. These configurations then become a repertoire of enduring coordinations or adaptive strategies. . . . These strategies set the conditions in the system by which infants can re-experience a knowing of, or recognition of themselves. . . . The organizing logic of initial experience, which confirms continuity by re-creation of individual uniqueness is a repeated process, which ultimately describes that individual's life span trajectory. (p. 29)

Most repetitions occur in the context of social relationships. When one considers that what is re-created is a relationship experience, Sander's statements indicate a pervasive social referencing process, biased by infancy experience, which is influential throughout the lifespan. According to Sander, through the mechanism of self-awareness of inner states one recognizes oneself in the context of the other. One re-creates situations for continuity and familiarity—with or without smoothness or pain and with varying degrees of openness to new experience and to new possibilities. Thus the individual creates and re-creates new relationships. Moreover, the affective context of new relationships is important, and throughout the lifespan internally represented relationships from early childhood will influence other relationships.

What about the maladaptive instance? In that case, specific new relationships are characterized by rigidity and a lack of openness to new possibilities. To the extent that internalized emotionally based structures from infancy are involved in such maladaptive repetitions, we might say that there are two types of new maladaptive relationships. In one type, there is a search for *recognition* and awareness of self in a familiar context, as Sander put it. This repeated search is presumably related to a deficit of emotional availability in the caregiving experience. The affective core of self has been biased toward uncertainty and caution. In a second type, new relationships are characterized by repetitions based on attempts at the *mastery* of an excess of painful emotions experienced in caregiving. Such mastery repetitions are along the lines proposed by Freud (1920) in his model of overcoming helplessness. The idea that repetitions stem from early caregiving experiences has strong roots in clinical literature (for example, see Anders & Zeanah, 1986; Call, Galenson, & Tyson, 1983; Spitz, 1965) but requires further research. Only with more knowledge can we understand the relationship conditions of later life under which repetitions are activated and under which maladaptive repetitions can be overcome.

Chapter 3

The Representation of Relational Patterns: Developmental Considerations

Daniel N. Stern

Clinically, relationships develop their own predictable patterns. This predictability of pattern forms a large part of what is characteristic about the relationship. These repeating patterns can be normal, problematic, or frankly disturbed. A first question concerns where to place or locate the relational patterns that involve the contribution of at least two people. The answers to this question are crucial.

Where Does a Relational Pattern Reside?

We have come to recognize that relationship patterns, normal or disturbed, come into being only during the interactions between two or more people. Even in the extreme but common case where a single individual plays out a relationship pattern in physical solitude, we assume the presence in the person's mind of an interactive partner who is contributing to the pattern via the individual's memory of patterns that have at one time been overtly enacted by two partners.

We assume that at some original period in the formation of any relational pattern there was a predictable sequence of observable interactive events and that the sequence could be confirmed by an observer outside the interaction. It is in this sense that relational patterns reside in the dyad or family and not in the individual. We are placing the origins of relational patterns in objective reality, that is, something that actually happened between two people and that, at least theoretically, could be independently validated. This assumption is not universally accepted and stands in opposition to certain psychoanalytic traditions. Sigmund Freud first proposed that many neurotic symptoms in adults resulted from actual early traumatic seductions or seduction attempts: that is, they were based on a reasonably accurate perception of an actual event perpetrated by an adult on the patient as a child. He later turned this proposal inside out, abandoning the seduction theory and suggesting that the seductions never happened, that they were instead wished for and fantasized events. The origin of the relationship event was removed from interpersonal reality to fantasy, that is, to subjective reality. Where then did the fantasy come from? For Freud, such fantasies ultimately had a phylogenetic origin—in the case of seduction fantasies, the Oedipus complex. They were, in some unspecified way, innate psychic endowments resulting from experiences of the species or race and unfolding in the course of development. Such fantasies were not solely, or even primarily, the product of a real interactive event. Rather, the particular nature of the fantasy was determined in large part by a psychobiological contribution that was thought to exist outside objective life events and to reside somewhere in human biology as manifested in the psychic domain. From this point of view, the origin of a relational pattern owes less to actual interactive events than to the inherent tendencies of the human mind in processing nonspecific interactive material.

In considering early development, Melanie Klein has taken this position even further (Klein, 1952). She has suggested that the nature of object relations from the infant's subjective viewpoint is largely a result of the ontogeny of fantasy life, with no significant determining input from the behavior of the actual mother. The same fantasies would unfurl in the same order, no matter who the parent. From this perspective, subjective relational patterns reside in the individual from the very outset.

We are taking the opposite point of view here, namely, that the nature of object relations or relational patterns is largely the result of the history of actual interactions with the mother. Of course, the interaction as subjectively experienced is construed or constructed by the infant, but not with significant distortions due to an inherent ontogeny of fantasy. From this perspective, relational patterns at the outset reside outside of any one individual and are constituted only during the interaction between two or more individuals. They are mutually derived even though subjectively constructed. They are both objective events and subjective experiences.

Assuming that interactional and relational patterns emerge between and reside in two individuals, what then provides the source of continuity for these mutual patterns? How does a mutually derived pattern get re-created at each encounter so that it becomes characteristic? These problems lead to our second question.

What Gives Relational Patterns Continuity?

An individual's history and memory provide the answers. The memory of past interactions serves as a guide for present interactions, and the conduct of present interactions (along with past ones) serves as a guide for future interactions. In other words, mental representations of repeating interactive events assure the patterning and its continuity.

Memory, in the form of mental representations of interactive events, is the repository for continuity. However, we are dealing with the memories of two individuals. Each individual may have experienced, or interpreted and encoded, a given interaction quite differently based on various asymmetries, the most important of which in the parent-infant dyad is age. Nonetheless, the two separate memories must be sufficiently related one to the other so that each can serve as a reliable guide to the other's behavior in the given interactive situation. This leads us into the third set of questions. How shall we conceive of representations of the history of interactions and relationships? What are their units? How are these units positioned and in what hierarchies?

What is a Representation of Interactive History?

Because the representation of interactive history is the main engine and mechanism of repetition and continuity, a consideration of its nature is critical. But, first, a few words about the nature of relationships are in order. Relationships are made up of interactions. Relationships are the cumulative constructed history of interactions, a history that bears on the present in the form of expectations actualized during an ongoing interaction, and on the future in the form of expectations (conscious or not) about upcoming interactions (see Hinde, 1979; Bowlby, 1980). The relationship is not only a larger unit than the interaction, it is of a different conceptual order. The interaction, as a unit, is usually defined from the perspective of observable, objective behavioral events, whereas the relationship is mainly construed as a more abstract representational unit. The relationship, however, is made up of the observed interactions as interpreted. For the purpose of considering the infant's representational world of interpersonal relations, I will try as far as possible to keep straight which of these two levels I am writing about and will suggest some possible mappings of one onto the other. The task, then, in conceptualizing the representation of relationships is to decide what units of interpersonal experience become organized in the formation of such representations and how the organization is accomplished.

Units of the Representation and Their Organization

FORMAL ORGANIZATION

We can conceptualize units of interaction in a hierarchy (figure 3-1). Proceeding developmentally, each successive unit is inclusive of the former units. These units begin with a lived (L) specific interactive moment, an *L-Moment*. This L-Moment is then encoded in memory to form a specific episodic memory, an *M-Moment*. Many specific episodic memories of similar M-Moments become organized to form a prototype. This prototype is a representation of a set of M-Moments that can be categorized together to form a generalized moment, which is a representation of the set of M-Moments. This representation is called an *R-Moment* and makes up the next unit in the hierarchy. Similarly, there are lived sequences of moments called *L-Scenarios*. These, too, become specific episodic memories, *M-Scenarios*. Many similar M-Scenarios become organized and generalized to form a representation, an *R-Scenario*. In a previous publication (Stern, 1985), I referred to RIGs, which are the *r*epresentations of *i*nteractive experience as *g*eneralized. In the present account, the R-Moment and the R-Scenario together correspond to the more inclusive and less specific RIG. The RIG can be used as a shorthand term for either or both of these representational units.

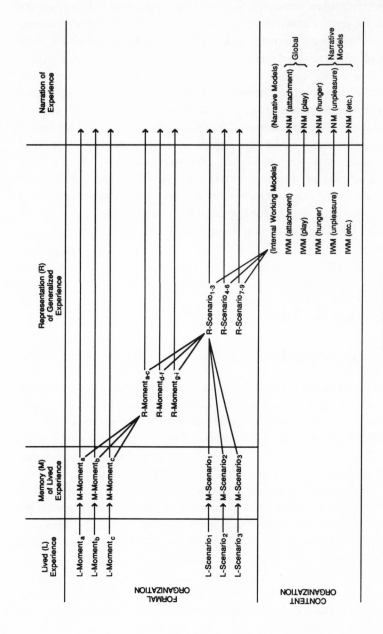

FIGURE 3-1

Schematic Organization of Units in the Representation of Interpersonal Experience

The L-Moment and the M-Moment   The smallest unit for consideration here is the lived specific interactive moment. As an objective event, it is
defined operationally by an observer. One example would be an exchange
between people in which one person directs some action to another and the
other responds or fails to respond, as when an infant raises his arms as if to
be picked up and the mother does or does not pick him up. Or when an infant
smiles at mother, who smiles back. The specific interactive moment is also
assumed to be a discrete subjective experience for the infant. It is important to note that the interactive moment is a hypothetical unit of unclear
size, with undefined boundaries that consists of elements (attributes) whose
interrelationships are not yet established or agreed upon. Nonetheless, postulating such a basic subjective unit seems necessary to an understanding of a
representational world, and much more thought and work on this unit is
needed.

The unit of the L-Moment is not a representation. It is simply a lived
experience in actuality. It is then encoded in memory as a specific instance
of a lived event. It is a singular memory trace of a specific lived moment, an
M-Moment. The degree of correspondence between an L-Moment and its
M-Moment is an open question, certainly in infancy.

The memory of autobiographical experience in this domain of interpersonal
events is episodic memory. Episodic memory, as described by Endel Tulving
(1972), refers to memory for real-life moments or experiences occurring in real
time. Or perhaps, more relevant here, as lived moments subjectively experienced. These episodes of lived experience can be trivial—what I experienced
when I ate my toast at breakfast this morning—or they can be of major
significance in a life—what I experienced when I learned my mother died. For
categorizing and ultimately representing interpersonal lived experience, episodic memory has several advantages. It includes as attributes of an episode
those essential features that concern us most: shifts in affect, arousal, motive,
cognition, perception, and action. However, none of these is in itself a basic
unit. The basic unit is the episode as lived, as subjectively experienced. An
episode appears to enter into memory as an indivisible unit—a singular moment of experience—and it is recalled from memory as a single indivisible
unit, although that is not to say that one cannot access the memory via one
of its attributes alone.

The R-Moment   We are suggesting that L-Moments enter memory
as M-Moments, which are then organized into functional categories at the
level of representations, R-Moments. The construction of these R-Moments
will concern us now. There are two reasons why such representations are
necessary. First, in the course of a short interaction the infant develops a

57

blueprint of how the interactive event is supposed to occur. A set of "still face" experiments suggests that by around three months the infant becomes upset when a normally occurring (expectable) interactive moment is violated. The experiment consists of placing a three-month-old in an infant seat facing the mother, who engages in typical social interaction with the infant using the play of her voice and facial expressions to engage him. At a signal, the mother stops moving her face and freezes it. She becomes silent but continues to gaze at the baby. The infant becomes mildly upset at this violation of expectable maternal behavior. The presence of an expectation is inferred by the infant's response to the violation of normal routine (Tronick, Als, Adamson, Wise, & Brazelton, 1978). Other, more anecdotal, evidence exists to suggest that infants may form some kind of representations of repetitive social interactive moments during the first six months of life and certainly during the second half of the first year (Stern, 1977, 1985). It is clear that very young infants can form expectations of repetitive events using experimental stimuli (Haith, Hazan, & Goodman, 1988; Hayne, Rovee-Collier, & Perris, 1987).

The second reason the infant needs to form separate organizing representations of many of these expectable social interactive moments is mental economy: either the infant will need to have a memory system that has recorded each and every previous interaction as a specific instance and then work upon this vast array to create expectations, or the infant must be able to form general categories of interactions and then create expectations on the basis of generalizations rather than multiple specific instances. Some current thinking suggests that the infant quite early begins to form categories of lived moments that are relatively invariant (Bornstein, 1981; Hayne, Rovee-Collier, & Perris, 1987; Resnick & Kagan, 1983). Each new instance of an interactive moment will simply confirm or slightly reshape the generalization and then no longer have to be held in memory storage. The constantly reshaped generalization will suffice.

The choice, however, is no longer exclusively between a representational system that preserves all past memory traces and works with these in some computational way and a system that is constantly creating and reshaping dynamic prototypes and discarding the separate memory traces. The recent description of the distributed model of memory as proposed by James McClelland and David Rumelhart (1985) offers another possibility. In this model, each memory trace affects the activation patterns of the brain and is thus conserved. No prototypes or generalizations are formed and separately stored as representational "structures" somewhere. Instead, the cumulative pattern of activation throughout the brain, contributed to by each separate memory trace, serves the generalizing function. Debate between these positions is currently very active (Palmer, 1987).

58

Yet there is another possibility to consider. Some prototypes appear very early in life and are thought to be innate or predesigned. For instance, infants have the ability from the first months of life to distinguish between different colors and to categorize them just as adults do. This early categorizing ability seems to depend upon the infant's capacity to recognize prototypic examples of certain colors (Bornstein, 1981). May such examples of predesign also exist in the infant's world of interpersonal stimulation and perception?

Whatever the model used by infants—and it may be different for different subject matter—infants give ample evidence of the very early formation and efficient use of functional categories in most domains of their experience. For the rest of this chapter, I will refer to categories, prototypes, and representations without knowing whether they actually exist as distinct brain structures or even as mental structures; however, we know with certainty that the functions to which they refer exist from infancy on, and we know in general descriptive terms how models of moments or events are constructed from individual, specific examples to form prototypic or generalized events. In brief, suppose the infant is engaging in a specific interaction for the first time. No representations are yet available. After the second and third time, the infant will begin to identify the invariant aspects of the interactive event or moment. We are now aware that the identification of the invariant features of an experience is one of the infant's central mental tendencies that leads to a progressive categorization of experiences. This categorization leads to the formation of prototypes, which may be defined as mentally constructed R-Moments of experience that best represent the constellation of invariant features that make up many remembered, lived moments. These R-Moments are small, coherent chunks of generalized interactive experience storing sensations, goals, affects, actions, and perceptions by both self and other in a short temporal-causal sequence.

The formation of a prototype of a facial visual pattern provides a good example. Mark Strauss (1979) showed a group of ten-month-old infants a series of schematic line drawings of a human face. Each face was different in the size and placement of the eyes, or position of the ears, or length of the nose. At the end of the series, the infants were tested to ascertain which drawing would be chosen to "represent" the whole series—as measured by which drawing would appear to the infant the least novel and the most familiar. Using this criterion, the infants chose a drawing they had, in fact, never seen but which represented the mathematical average of all the facial-feature sizes and positions previously seen. The infants appeared to be performing a running averaging process in the course of watching the series of drawings and came up with a prototype that well "represented" the entire sequence—even though the picture chosen as the prototype did not exist in the original series. (These results could be explained by any of the models discussed above.)

It is in this fashion—or something like it—that we imagine the infant constructs R-Moments. For interactive R-Moments, however, the elements need not be visual features (eyes, nose, and so on); the elements probably are a heterogeneous set of features occurring in the domains of motor action, perception, cognition, affect, sensation, and motivation. Furthermore, they are a set that belongs together as an invariant constellation. For instance, consider the infant initiating a smile toward mother while they gaze at each other. The infant will experience his or her own motor acts of smiling and whatever arm and leg movements go with it. He or she will experience the proprioceptive feedback from these movements and the quality of feeling joy. He or she will experience a surge in arousal and an intention or goal. At the same time, as part of the same moment, the infant will see the mother's face and that she is gazing back, potentially engaged, and the infant will expect her face to break into a smile if that is the usual consequence. Some additional attributes of her behavior may become invariant features of the moment.

Thus, this often repeated interactive moment consists of many invariant features from different domains and, importantly, emanating from two different people. We assume that after repeated instances the infant will have identified the invariant features of attributes and created a prototype constellation that represents this particular interactive R-Moment.

The notion of an R-Moment owes much to other work describing the infant's categorization of repeated events, but the nature of the categories formed is different. Work such as Mark Bornstein's is concerned with categories of nonsocial events. Katherine Nelson and Janice Gruendel (1981), on the other hand, have been concerned with children's lived sequential events that are closest to life scripts (Shank & Abelson, 1977), such as what happens at birthday parties or at bedtime. Nelson and Gruendel have described how young children form generalized event representations (GERs) of these sequential events. A GER is formed by generalizing the invariant features of an ordered event flow and placing them in their correct sequence, such that a model or representation emerges of a characteristic or prototypic "birthday party" or "going to bed." The small units that make up these GERs are mainly events between the subject and objects or events in the world at large (such as blowing out the candles on a cake, or being read a story or sung a song) or between the subject and a nonspecific character playing a known or knowable social role (the guest at a party, and so on).

The R-Moment and the GER are both products of the general principles of functional category formation. These principles have emerged in the recent past from promising work in the cognitive domain of category formation, generalization, and representation (Posner & Keele, 1968, 1970; Rosch, 1978; Bornstein, 1981; Resnick & Kagan, 1983; Hayne, Rovee-Collier, & Perris, 1987). The R-Moment is distinguished from any other constructed category not by the general principles involved but by its size and the nature of the events to be categorized and represented and by the general situations in which those events occur. The R-Moment is concerned with those microinteractive sequences of social behavior between infant and caregiver that regulate affect, arousal, motivation, attention, intimacy, and attachment (Stern, 1985).

The R-Moment has several distinct aspects. First, the features of the experience to be categorized come from two partners. Second, the features or attributes (the potential invariants) of the event consist of shifts in affect, arousal, motive, and specific states of consciousness, as well as motor acts, cognitions, and perceptions of self and other. This universe of attributes includes the entire array of the features that make up subjective autobiographical experience. The R-Moment concerns the mutual attempts to regulate a dyadic system that comes into being only in the interactions between intimates. And, finally, it is an event of short duration—split seconds or several seconds—that contains a single but coherent chunk of experience.

It remains to be seen whether it is worth calling categories formed in this special domain of human interaction by a specific name, such as the *R-Moment* above and the *R-Scenario* below. However, it is highly possible that the laws regulating functional category formation in this domain may have some distinctive features. For example, in the GER referred to by Nelson and Gruendel, shifts in affect, states of consciousness, arousal, and motive are not necessarily present as attributes. Accordingly, maintaining a separate name—R-Moments—for the categories formed in this interpersonal domain of regulatory interactions seems reasonable, on a provisional basis.

The notion of an R-Moment being a category of certain episodic memories, M-Moments, raises some problems. The various attributes that make up an episodic memory or M-Moment (affect, motive, action, and so on) are essentially equal, since the entire lived experience is encoded as the unit. (To be sure, on any occasion one attribute may be subjectively more salient than the others, but all are always present.) However, there is also a long tradition that assumes that some attributes of experience are intrinsically more salient when it comes to defining clinically important subjective experience as well as the memory or the representation of such experiences. For instance, in classical psychoanalytic theory the level or change in the frustration or gratification of drives (that is, the building up or discharge of psychic energy) is the most salient experiential attribute of a lived event. Variations on this viewpoint give to hedonic evaluation (pleasure or unpleasure) privileged status as an attribute. Robert Emde (1980a, b) has argued for the invariable importance of the affective attributes. In self-psychology, the level of empathic failure and repair most determines the salience of an interactive event for later clinical purposes (Kohut, 1977). Jean Piaget would have stressed the sensorimotor components.

Klaus Scherer (1986) has proposed a theoretical system in which each event is processed in a temporal sequence: first its degree of novelty, then its hedonic evaluation, then its attainability, and so on. In this system, each attribute of an experience is privileged only in the temporal position it occupies. But that is no small matter: Scherer further suggests that at different developmental phases different attributes are more relevant—for example, novelty very early in life, hedonic evaluation later, and so on. Similarly, many psychoanalytic thinkers have suggested that the salience of an attribute will be importantly influenced by the "developmental phase-specific" relevance of the attribute or event (Pine, 1981).

These different positions on salience are not theories of how interactive events become represented; they are rather points of view concerning which lived events with which attributes will be salient enough to be noticed, registered, and thus available for inclusion in the formation of representations. To represent these interactive events we have only the processes of identifying the salient invariants, forming generalizations or prototypic moments, and categorizing moments into representations.

For the present, we will take the position that no single attribute—such as cognition, affect, or arousal—has more salience or a more privileged position all the time in the formation of R-Moments. The advantages of leaving this question of salience open, for the while, are several. First, in the field at large, the empirical evidence does not yet exist to answer our questions. In fact, much of the current evidence suggests that different attributes of experience may be processed separately and in parallel (recall our mention of distributed memory models). Second, we need an approach to the problem that is flexibly responsive to the fact that infants occupy many different "moments" in a day or hour (Pine, 1981). At different times they are in very different states of consciousness (drowsy or very alert), at different levels of arousal, in different phases of build-up or consummation of physiological motivational systems, in different moods or states of affect. Even during moments of strong motivation and high affect and arousal, which are central to most psychodynamic thinking, the infant does not stop thinking or perceiving, so that cognitions and perceptions are necessarily yoked to these other attributes, and vice versa. However, we must also account for the more numerous moments of interaction when the levels of affect, arousal, and physiological motive are relatively low and the infant is manifestly engaged and occupied with cognitions, perceptions, or motor actions.

In brief, at different interactive moments, different attributes may appear to have and may in fact have more salience. But overall none is privileged, and all are always present in the lived (L) moment and in the formation of R-Moments. In this fashion, the representational world of interactions consists of ordinary daily events, both those our theories mark as important and all others. Both types of events tend to occur over and over—often dozens of times a day, every day, for months—so there is enormous opportunity for the infant to identify and represent the expectable interactive moments that make up feeding, changing, playing, teaching, and going to sleep.

Several major issues raised by the above discussion should be mentioned at this point, although they need not be addressed here. How does distortion enter the representational world, if it does? By distortion do we mean discrepancies between interactive events as observed by an outsider and lived moments as subjectively experienced? Or is the distortion between L-Moments and M-Moments, or between either of these and R-Moments? Why do certain L-Moments remain as vivid, specific ("traumatic") memories rather than being assimilated into R-Moments?

We can readily imagine "distortions" emerging in at least two ways that differ from what has already been described. (1) Because a prototype is an abstraction of reality, it may represent something that never actually happened. Thus, to be guided by a prototype as a representation will result in behavior that is historically (statistically) well founded but gives rise to errors of conservativism (Bowlby, 1980). (2) If a specific memory has resisted assimilation into a prototype (for whatever reasons, perhaps its traumatic nature), this memory will be a guide to further action that is not based on the majority of categorizable experience. Accordingly, as a guide it will be open more to errors of riskiness.

L-Scenarios, M-Scenarios, R-Scenarios　　Beyond the L-Moment and its representation, the next larger hierarchical unit worth postulating en route to the relationship as represented would be sequences of interactive L-Moments. The script (Shank & Abelson, 1977) would be the model for this kind of unit made up of different interactive events in an invariant sequence. A simple example would be this: (1) infant approaches mother; (2) mother orients and readies her body to receive approach; (3) infant raises arms to be picked up; (4) mother picks up infant; (5) infant nestles head in mother's neck; (6) mother adjusts position appropriately. Such an interactive sequence might occur in a limited number of different circumstances, for example, part of a reunion sequence after an absence or as a consequence of fatigue, pain, or fright. We can call this unit a (lived) *L-Scenario*. Its episodic memory can be called an *M-Scenario* and its representation can be called an *R-Scenario*.

As in the case of R-Moments, a distinctive term—*scenario*—has been chosen to represent relationships. It may be that after more research is done in this area it will be determined that scenarios and scripts are indistinguishable. At this point, however, until scripts explicitly include states of consciousness and shifts in affect, arousal, and motivation as well as cognitive and motor components, the term *scenario* will be used as the representational repository of all these distinctive features.

The R-Scenario will form when several similar M-Scenarios are available in memory to be organized, that is, it will form according to the same principles that governed the formation of the R-Moment from many M-Moments, only now a larger unit is involved. We use the term R-Scenario to distinguish it as a form of personal interactive autobiography from the script as a form of general event representation.

The individual R-Moments (such as the raising of arms to be picked up) that in sequence make up an R-Scenario can occur in several different R-Scenarios (such as raising arms to be picked up to play or to be cuddled during a reunion). However, the combination and sequence of R-Moments constituting a single R-Scenario would always be unique.

Our knowledge of infants' representations of moments in sequences is still limited. Infants probably have fairly well developed R-Scenarios for many play sequences, especially ritualized play (games), feeding, diaper changing, and being put down to sleep. More information on infants' knowledge of these scenarios and at what age they learn them is needed. Future experiments based on the violation of expectations may provide a source of such information.

The structure of an R-Scenario probably derives from two sources: the generalization of many M-Scenarios and the infant's store of R-Moments. This is shown schematically in figure 3-1. It is reasonable to speculate that developmentally the R-Moment will appear before the R-Scenario because it is shorter and requires minimal memory of sequence.

CONTENT ORGANIZATION

So far, we have discussed only the formal relationships between the proposed representational units of R-Moments and R-Scenarios. We must now address the organization of these representations into content categories.

Internal Working Models   The internal working model (Bowlby, 1980) is the representation that permits the infant to form expectations and evaluate the interactions that regulate his attachment system. The internal working model (IWM) operates at a level of unawareness and is a "presymbolic guide to action," interpretation, and feeling. For our purposes, the IWM is a unit of representation that organizes selected R-Moments and R-Scenarios in terms of specific contents. Traditionally, the internal working model has been largely reserved for the motivational content of attachment; however, it is equally applicable to any of the major motivational systems: play, physiological regulation, self-control, or other activities that require mutual regulation (see chapter 2). Internal working models may also exist as content categories for affects—for example, happy, sad—or as content categories for major hedonic evaluation, such as pleasant, unpleasant or good, bad. We conceive of the internal working model as an organization of selected R-Moments and R-Scenarios that belong together within a content category. At this point, it seems necessary to postulate several separate internal working models and empirically test their coherence and interrelatedness. Ideally, all the major different functional aspects of the relationship experience as described in chapter 2 will need separate internal working models.

The internal working model as a reorganization by content of the various R-Moments and R-Scenarios is schematized in figure 3-2. Note that a single R-Moment could contribute to two different R-Scenarios scripts. The R-Moment of infant raising his or her arms to be picked up and being picked up could occur in a reunion script or in a "pick up to play" script. However, the combination of R-Moments constituting a single R-Scenario would be unique. The same applies for the relationship between R-Scenarios and internal working models.

In figure 3-2, R-Scenario$_1$ is made up of R-Moments (a, b, c) that are not part of the sequence of any other R-Scenario. R-Scenario$_2$ and R-Scenario$_3$, on the other hand, share an R-Moment (f) in their sequences. And R-Scenario$_4$ and R-Scenario$_5$ share two different R-Moments in their sequences (j and k). Similarly, in the diagram, the two internal working models share one sequence between them (R-Scenario$_3$). This sharing of elements will facilitate the infant's association between different representational units. Also, an internal working model can consist of a group of R-Scenarios, two or more of which may be contradictory. This would produce an ambivalent working model and may help explain certain types of insecure attachment patterns.

The issue of several concomitant internal working models raises the question of where to place John Bowlby's internal working model, which is generally used by attachment theorists. I believe the term is used in two different senses. First, it is used as a rather general term to refer to the currently active

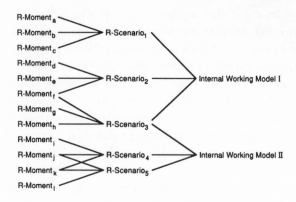

FIGURE 3-2

Schematized Possible Relationships between Representational Units

representation that best explains ongoing behavior. In this sense, it can refer to the level of the R-Moment or the R-Scenario or the ensemble of these that makes up the internal working model. There is no problem with such a general usage of the term: in fact, it is highly useful—especially clinically—to account for the influence of mental structure (at whatever level) on current behavior, in part because of its lack of specificity. At times Bowlby uses the term in this general sense (Bowlby, 1980). I have reserved it for an organization of R-Scenarios, but it could be also used at less elaborated levels.

Second, the term has historically arisen in close association with the emergence of attachment theory (chapter 2). In this association it has come to mean the entire network and hierarchy of representations, which are organized by the activation or deactivation of the attachment motivational system (Bretherton, 1985). When used this way, the internal working model becomes synonymous with the working model of the regulation of attachments and we are left without an equivalent term or concept for the internal working models of play, hunger, curiosity, learning, and so on. Not only do different working models exist for different motivational systems, but even within the same motivational system different models may exist for different caregivers—father versus mother versus siblings. I am reserving the term *internal working model of regulation* for the entire set of R-Moments and R-Scenarios that regulate a separate and major motivational system such as attachment or curiosity or hunger or play.

Narrative Models   The narrative model is the story or account of the internal working models of regulation as told to oneself or to another. This is, in part, the verbal rendition of the nonverbal internal working models of regulation, but there is not a simple correspondence: the narrative model puts the nonverbal working models into a larger context.

The narrative model of regulation never corresponds with the working models of regulation for several reasons. First, the internal working model is nonconscious, nonverbal, private, and made up of subjectively experienced events. The narrative model is generally conscious, verbal, narratable, social, and made up of referents experienced via words. There is much room for slippage and lack of overlap between a working and a narrative model of the same regulatory system. It is essential to note that the emergence of a narrative model sometime during the third year (Peterson & McCabe, 1983) in no way makes the internal working model of regulation obsolete or inoperative. The two coexist in relative harmony or disharmony throughout life. For instance, we frequently see patients who maintain a positive, idealized narrative model of their mother as a figure of secure, stable, warm attachment. However, an examination of their operative working models shows a different picture, far less positive and mixed with ambivalent expectations and feelings. It is often the case in clinical practice that much effort is spent in bringing these two models into closer harmony. (See Main, Kaplan, & Cassidy, 1985; and Stern, 1985, for greater detail on this point.)

Second, the narrative model can include elements or features that never were a part of the individual's direct experience but came secondhand, so to speak, from the direct experience of others. These elements may include family stories, myths, lies, and secrets. At the level of the internal working model, all input to the model comes from the direct historical experience of the individual. With the formation of the narrative model, a process of co-construction is possible, bringing together both the historical experience of the individual and the separate historical experience of others. The mechanisms whereby the direct experience of other individuals is transmitted to and grafted onto the narrative model of another individual are not well understood, but David Reiss (chapter 9) puts forth some of the most compelling and eloquent material to bear on these issues. Reiss proposes a number of family and group practices and unwritten traditions that may become activated when an individual is within the group. These practices and traditions then serve as the source of memories and continuity of behavior for the individual, even though much or all of the original historical experience behind these group traditions was never available to him or her as direct experience.

The notion of a narrative model may permit us to understand how some of these group phenomena work. Certain of them are transmitted largely in narrative form. The transmission is achieved through what is narrated and how it is narrated, especially the inconsistencies, the lack of coherence, the missing pieces, the premature terminations of story line, and so on. These peculiarities in narration must constitute a primary means of transmitting and activating important information about the unspeakable and unthinkable. (The narrative model will play a less important role in the transmission of family scripts, rituals, and paradigms, which remain nonverbalized.) Thus, some family traditions can elaborate on an individual's narrative models and in so doing determine the continuity of his or her behavior in a group or family setting. Likewise, narrative models can include aspects that are not present in working models.

The narrative model is different from the internal working model in providing a different kind of regulation. When relationship events are told, the telling itself may act in multiple ways to regulate and even alter the experiences related. This is commonly assumed in psychotherapy but may also prove to be of major importance in the developing child's capacity to regulate his or her daily experiences (Nelson, in press).

The final reason that the narrative model is distinct and larger, hierarchically, than the internal working model is that a single narrative model can include more than one working model. For instance, when a person is describing his or her narrative model for attachment, whole pieces of an internal working model for curiosity learning or play or physiological motivational systems may get mixed in. This intermingling is probably the rule, and the exact nature of the intermingling will result from the individualized history of the associations among the separate motivational systems.

In this chapter, I have proposed a formal organization and a content organization of representational units. R-Moments and R-Scenarios are the formal units. Internal working models and narrative models are the content units that are made by reorganizing the formal units. Specifying the units of representations and placing them in hierarchical order, even provisionally, may have worthwhile theoretical, clinical, and research implications.

Theoretically, we need to envision how the representational world of relationships is structured and how the structures are formed. The greater the emphasis we place on the importance of the relationship as the locus and engine of disturbances, the greater this need becomes. Our outline of representational units and their ordering is a step in this direction.

Clinically, the representation of relationships has always been crucial in psychoanalytic work, but it has rarely been operationally defined. In this light, the recent work of Mary Main, Nancy Kaplan, and Jude Cassidy (1985) is relevant because they have attempted to work with defined and systematically analyzed representational structures. They have shown that the nature and quality of a woman's representation of her own mother will predict the type of attachment pattern (driven by the internal working model) she will have with her own child. The evidence suggests that it is the coherence versus incoherence or adequacy versus inadequacy of the new mother's internal working model of her own mother, rather than whether her mother was a good or bad mother, that most determines her attitude and behavior toward her own child.

How are we to conceptualize coherence? There must be separate parts to the model that can or cannot go togther well. Inge Bretherton (1985), assessing the adequacy of the internal working model, speaks of the coherence between the specific event schemas (R-Moments and R-Scenarios, in our terms) and the more global representations (working and narrative models of regulation, in our terms). The schematization offered here is more specific in describing and identifying the constituent parts of the representations and thereby possibly more precise in considering the cohesion or adequacy of a model.

The present outline also permits different types of incoherence. There can be incoherence or conflict residing in the coassemblage of R-Moments or R-Scenarios, and there can be incoherence or conflict between the nonverbal internal working model and the narrative model. Different clinical consequences may result from each of these.

Finally, such a schematization may prove helpful in framing developmental research questions for the future. Once we have postulated different units of representation that become progressively organized into larger units, a host of developmental questions arise. What are the ages at which the different units can be identified? What individual or illness-related variability exists in these timetables? Will the timetables for the formation of internal working models for the different motivational systems be the same as for attachment?

Questions about process also arise. Is the categorizing process that forms the successive levels of organization the same for each level? Is there one overall categorizing process, or are there many? How is conflict built into representations? Does it occur between levels (for example, if the internal working model is at odds with the narrative model) or within levels (as when mutually exclusive R-Scenarios are assembled into one internal working model causing ambivalence)? Perhaps we now can begin to pose such questions with greater clarity.

Chapter 4

Relationships, Self, and Individual Adaptation

L. Alan Sroufe

> The process out of which the self arises is a social process which implies interaction of individuals. . . . Selves can only exist in definite relationships to other selves. No hard-and-fast line can be drawn between our own selves and the selves of others, since our own selves exist and enter as such into our experience only in so far as the selves of others exist and enter as such into our experience also.
>
> —George Herbert Mead (1934)

The basic thesis underlying this book is that most problems in the early years, while often manifest poignantly in child behavior, are best conceptualized as relationship problems. This position immediately suggests a number of inter-related issues. In general, what justification is there for attributing such a powerful influence to social relationships? Second, if it is the relationship that is disordered, why is the disorder so strongly manifest in infant and child behavior? And how do what begin as disorders in relationships become disorders in individuals, even when they are no longer in the context of that relationship? All of these questions may be approached by considering what is perhaps a more fundamental developmental question, namely, what is the role of social relations in the emergence and formation of the self or individual person?

In this chapter we will present a beginning conceptualization of the self, describe the developmental process by which the self emerges from early relationships, and explore the implications of variations in the self for individual patterns of adaptation. In brief, it will be argued that self should be conceived as an inner organization of attitudes, feelings, expectations, and meanings, which arises from an organized caregiving matrix. That is, the dyadic infant–caregiver organization precedes and gives rise to the organization that is self. The self-organization, in turn, has significance for ongoing adaptation and experience, including later social behavior. Distortions in self-organization are influenced by distortions in prior dyadic organization, and subsequent problems in individual behavioral organization (adaptation) are most clearly manifest in distorted social relationships. The self is a social creation, and it is defined, maintained, and transformed with reference to others. For these reasons social relations are viewed as having such fundamental importance in both normal and pathological development. The answer to the question of how a relationship disorder comes also to be an individual disorder is the same as the explanation of how individual personality is formed within relationships. Each personality, whether healthy or disordered, is a product of the history of vital relationships.

An Organizational Perspective

As outlined by Arnold Sameroff in chapter 1, behavior, development, and personality may be viewed within a systems or organizational perspective. Behavior is examined not simply in terms of what the person does or how frequently but in light of how any given behavior is organized with other behaviors and with respect to context. Similarly, development is viewed not simply as the addition of new capacities but in terms of the changing organization of capacities according to the principle of hierarchical integration. Existing capacities and levels of organization are subordinated and integrated into new, more complex levels of organization. Finally, personality no longer is viewed as a collection of static traits or dispositions. It is not a thing or a collection of things that persons possess in certain degrees; rather, it is the organization of attitudes, feelings, expectations, and behaviors of the person across contexts (Block & Block, 1980; Breger, 1974; Loevinger, 1976; Sroufe, 1979a).

The following everyday example may be used to illustrate some of the implications of an organizational viewpoint: A twelve-month-old infant sits playing with a variety of toys on the floor of a laboratory playroom. Her mother sits a short distance away. As the child examines various objects in front of her, a large puzzle piece (a brightly colored carrot) captures her attention. She grasps the carrot with widened eyes. Then, in a smooth motion, she turns and extends it toward the mother, smiling broadly and vocalizing. Mother returns her smile and comments about the carrot.

The significance of this sequence is not in the simple showing of the toy, which would be as commonly manifest toward strangers as toward mothers at this age (Rheingold & Eckerman, 1973), but in the total organization of the behavior. In the first place, one notes the *integration* of the toy show with the other behaviors. (Showing of a toy accompanied by both smiling and vocalizing is rarely directed toward strangers by twelve-month-olds.) Second, one notes the *sequential organization* of the behavior. The child recognizes the object and then directly (as if the sequence has become automated or unitized) shares her delight with the mother. The *meaning* of this organized pattern of behavior ("affective sharing") is fundamentally different from the meaning of toy shows to a stranger ("affiliative gestures"), which are not organized with respect to exploration and mastery of the object world in the same way. In hundreds of cases, one would rarely see an infant in the course of intensive exploration turn and affectively share a discovery with a stranger.

The behavior pattern also reveals the *hierarchically organized* nature of development. One sees the incorporation of earlier visual and object manipulation skills, prelinguistic communication skills, and early attachment behavior (looking, vocalizing, maintaining proximity) into intentional social behavior, all mediated by affect.

One may also look at this example in terms of a changing organization in the dyadic social relationship. First one sees a change in the way the dyadic system meets the infant's need for security. In the early weeks of life caregivers physically hold infants as a means of comforting. Later, by four to six months when the infant is on the caregiver's knee *en face,* the "holding" is with eyes and voice (Brazelton, Koslowski, & Main, 1974). Then, by twelve months, as in our example, looks, shows, vocalization, and the sharing of affect are sufficient for the maintenance of psychological contact. In toddlers, such contact may be maintained even when visual contact is blocked (Carr, Dabbs, & Carr, 1975). Second, qualitative change is noted at each point in terms of the increasingly active role played by the infant. By twelve months it is no longer always caregiver picking up and holding the infant; the infant maintains contact as well. We will return to this point later.

The emerging self and individual differences in personality are also best captured in organizational terms. There are indeed individual differences in the quality of affective sharing among infants and in the tendencies to seek and be reassured by physical contact. But even more important are the timing, flexibility, and organization of such behaviors with respect to context. Similarly, in older children one might assess general level of activity or exuberance or capacity for planning and restraint; yet far more informative would be assessments of the child's organization of such capacities with regard to context. The "ego resilient" child is the child who may be spontaneous and exuberant on the playground when circumstances permit and controlled and planful during classroom instruction when circumstances require (Block & Block, 1980).

When personality is viewed in organizational terms, the formative importance of early social relations with primary caregivers becomes apparent. Others, of course, evoke and respond to behaviors of the infant. But beyond this, relationships provide the framework and context within which behaviors are organized. When one asks, organized with respect to what? in the case of the infant's behavior the answer clearly is, *the caregiver.* Finally, as will be a major thesis of this chapter, the relationship is itself an organization (Sroufe and Fleeson, 1986), from which the self emerges.

The Emergence of the Self

THE DYADIC SYSTEM

Accounting for the emergence of the self presents a basic developmental problem. Self as an inner organization of attitudes, expectations, and feelings cannot be conceived of in the newborn, whose cortex shows little dendritic elaboration and little interconnection with midbrain emotional structures (Minkowski, 1967; Schade, Meeter, & van Goeningen, 1962); yet to posit the self simply as emergent at some later period (something arising from nothing) is a nondevelopmental solution. Louis Sander (1975) has pointed the way to a developmental approach to this problem by postulating that organization exists from the outset, but that the organization resides in the infant–caregiver *dyadic system.* The developmental account, then, traces the origins of the inner organization (self) from the dyadic organization—from dyadic behavioral regulation to self-regulation. From an organizational matrix constructed around the infant, to organized patterns of behavior that make room for increasing participation of the infant, to a "dim recognition" of "his own role in determining action", the "stage is set" for "the 'disjoin' of the self-regulatory core" (p. 141).

The view that the self is a social product has, of course, been widely held. It is a cornerstone of the theoretical positions of George Herbert Mead (1934) and James Mark Baldwin (1897). Baldwin wrote that the self "is a pole or terminus at one end of an opposition in the sense of personality generally, and that the other pole or terminus is . . . the other person" (p. 15), and further that the child is "at every stage . . . really in part someone else" (p. 30). Soren Kierkegaard (1938) poetically summarized the idea of self as a social product:

> The loving mother teaches her child to walk alone. She is far enough from him so that she cannot actually support him, but she holds out her arms to him. She imitates his movements, and if he totters, she swiftly bends as if to seize him, so that the child might believe that he is not walking alone. . . . And yet, she does more. Her face beckons like a reward, an encouragement. Thus, the child walks alone with his eyes fixed on his mother's face, not on the difficulties in his way. He supports himself by the arms that do not hold him and constantly strives towards the refuge in his mother's embrace, little suspecting that in the very same moment that he is emphasizing his need of her, he is proving that he can do without her, because he is walking alone. (p. 85)

The idea of the social origins of self also has been prominent in the work of infant theorists such as Heinz Kohut (1977), Donald Winnicott (1965), Margaret Mahler (Mahler, Pine, & Bergman, 1975), and Mary Ainsworth (1973). Winnicott's famous statement, "There is no such thing as an infant," was meant to capture the basic embeddedness of the infant in the caregiving context. Mahler described a "symbiotic phase," a period of infant–caregiver interconnection that paves the way to individuation. Finally, Ainsworth and Bell (1974) make the same point as Sander when they argue that an infant *can be competent only to the extent that there is a caregiving environment that is alert and responsive to the newborn's reflexive signals.* By responding to the young infant's fluctuating states and primitive signals, the caregiver imbues them with meaning and makes them part of an organized behavioral system. If one wishes to describe an organized relationship between organism and surroundings in the newborn period it can be done only in the context of a responsive caregiving environment. Thus, self, as organization, can be conceived of only within the caregiving relationship system in the early months of life.

74

THE DEVELOPMENTAL PROCESS

Sander (1975) and others have outlined a series of phases in the evolution of the dyadic organization toward the inner organization of self. These phases are not tasks to be completed; rather, they represent ascending and ongoing issues (see table 4-1). When this developmental process approach is embraced the self is viewed as *emerging* rather than as *emergent* at any given age (see Sroufe, 1977, pp. 144–145, for a discussion of this distinction).

Phase 1: Basic regulation   In the first two to three months of life the caregiving system establishes "phase synchrony between mother and infant in regard to the periodicities of relative activity and quiescence" (Sroufe, 1977, p. 137). Infant state and caregiver intervention become coordinated. As Sander concludes here: "One of the features most idiosyncratic during the first three months is the extent to which the infant is helped or compromised in beginning to determine aspects of his own regulation. . . . [For the caregiver] trial and error learning gives way to ideas of what 'works' and to the feeling of confidence that she knows her baby's needs and can specifically meet them" (p. 137). Such physiological regulation may be viewed as the prototype for later psychological regulation, which is characterized by coordinated sequences of behavioral interactions. Such coordination, which is a hallmark of Phase 2, marks the primitive beginnings of inner organization of experience.

Phase 2: Reciprocal Exchange   Chained interaction sequences become a dominant feature in the second three months of life. Basic state regulation is achieved, the infant is awake and alert more, smiling and cooing are common, and the infant actively participates in social interaction. Several investigators (including Brazelton, Koslowski, & Main, 1974; Stern, 1974) have described the coordinated, give-and-take, dancelike quality of caregiver–infant interactions during this period. However, in the strict sense, "coordination" or "reciprocity" here is in part illusory. The appearance of give and take, with each responding to the other, is largely created by the caregiver's respon-

TABLE 4-1
Stages of the Emerging Self

Age	Stage
0–6 months	The preintentional self
6–12 months	The intentional self
12–24 months	The separate (aware) self
24–60 months	The self-monitoring self
Adolescence	The self-reflective self

siveness to the infant. Careful study has shown that there is a dramatic asynchrony in the conditional probabilities of responsiveness; the caregiver makes adjustments to fit the infant's action, but the infant at this age has little capacity to adjust his or her behavior to fit changes in caregiver behavior (Hayes, 1984). To be sure, sequences exist in which the infant does A, mother does B, infant does C, and mother does D. Within such an established sequence the infant does respond to the mother's behavior. C occurs commonly only following B. But the infant cannot readily follow a new lead of the caregiver, whereas the caregiver commonly follows new leads of the infant (for example, A, B, E, F).

Thus, the caregiver crafts an organized system of coordinated behavioral sequences around the infant. Although the infant cannot achieve such organization independently or by design, during this phase he or she can *participate* in such a highly organized system. The organization is not yet "represented" or internalized schematically (the infant cannot fill in the missing parts). The infant does have action schemes, of course, and therefore is able to follow through on an interactive sequence once started, as long as the caregiver keeps it on track.

Although this higher level of organization remains in the hands of the caregiver, it is of great importance to the infant for two reasons. First, the countless repetitions of such highly organized sequences lay the groundwork for a more initiatory role in the next phase. Second, these sequences commonly culminate in exchanges of obvious pleasure and delight (Sander, 1975; Stern, 1974); in one scheme this phase is referred to as the "period of positive affect" (Sroufe, 1977). As Sander puts it, "The affect of joy or delight becomes established as the criterion for precision in the matching of interpersonal reciprocations" (p. 145). Such shared affect represents a reservoir of positive feelings that will be coordinated with the infant's representation (scheme) of the caregiver as it consolidates in the second half year.

Phase 3: Initiative   In the third three months we see the beginnings of "goal-directed schemes" and "a first *active* bifurcation in the direction of the child's initiative: toward her and away from her" (Sander, 1975, p. 138). Fully freed from the twenty-four-hour state regulation issues and with budding intentionality, the infant can direct activities, both those designed to elicit caregiver responses and those that explicitly elicit caregiver prohibitions. The infant now initiates the games orchestrated by the caregiver in the earlier period and in other ways plays a more active and creative role in maintaining and continuing coordinated exchanges. Now the infant can follow and embellish the caregiver's lead, as, for example, when in response to the caregiver's smile the infant smiles and reaches to the caregiver's face (Greenspan, 1981).

Clearly there is movement toward genuine reciprocity in this phase, and behavior is directed through inner imagery and goals. One sees the emergence of organized greeting sequences (bouncing, smiling vocalization with arms raised) in this phase (Vaughn, 1978), which reflect the rise of intentionality and goal-directed behavior. One sees also a dramatic rise in aversive responses to strangers and in specific affects such as anger (Stenberg, Campos, & Emde, 1983), surprise, and fear (Hyatt, Emde, & Campos, 1979; Vaughn & Sroufe, 1979). These developments point to a coordination of affect and cognition (the emergence of affectively toned schemes), marking the beginnings of an inner organization of experience (Sroufe, 1979b).

The changes in the caregiver–infant dyadic system are so dramatic during this phase that it can well be argued that for the first time the term *relationship* may appropriately replace the concept of organized interaction. This is nicely illustrated by classic research on the effects of hospitalization (Schaffer & Callender, 1959). Two distinct patterns emerged, depending on age. For infants older than seven months, a classic picture of protest to the period of hospitalization was seen: "Protest during the initial hospitalization, negativism to the staff, intervals of subdued behavior and withdrawal, and a period of readjustment after return home, during which [there was] a great deal of insecurity centering around mother's presence" (p. 537) (see also Heinicke & Westheimer, 1966). Infants younger than seven months showed none of these reactions. "The reactions of the older group indicate clearly that it is the break in the relationship with the mother that formed the core of the disturbance" (p. 537). By seven months the infant has begun internalizing the organized caregiving context. When the infant begins to initiate behavior intentionally based on the known organization, substitute patterns of care will not do. Earlier, hospital staff may stand in stead for the mother, providing stimulation for the infant, general experiences with chained interactions, and shared affect. The transfer back to the mother's care likewise is readily accomplished. But by seven months or so the particular system is being internalized. The organized caregiving matrix begins to become part of a core of emerging inner organization. A particular relationship and a self are emerging.

Phase 4: Focalization   The increasingly active role for the infant and increased mobility lead to visible changes in the organization of his behavior around the caregiver in the final months of the first year. The caregiver takes on the role of the "home base" (Mahler, Pine, & Bergman, 1975) or "secure base" (Ainsworth, 1973), and the infant centers his expanding exploratory activities around this base. The infant ranges away from the caregiver, drawn by curiosity concerning novel aspects of the environment. But should the baby become fatigued or threatened or otherwise encounter something beyond his capacities (and if the appropriate internal affective signals arise) a retreat to the caregiver or a directed signal brings assistance, reassurance, comfort, and a return to organized exploration. At other times in the course of exploration positive affect arises and routinely is shared with the caregiver. Affect, cognition, and social behavior are smoothly coordinated and organized with respect to the caregiver. Sander uses the term *focalization* to capture how the caregiver has moved to the center of an expanding world. Goal-directed behavior with respect to the caregiver becomes prominent. The infant selects from a repertoire of capacities a signal or behavior suited to the response she intends the caregiver to make (arms raised to signal a desire to be picked up; showing an object for comment). Moreover, should one initiation fail, an alternative is selected as the infant *persists* toward her goal. Both goals and expectations become more specific. Clearly, all of this reflects a new level of organized complexity and must portend advances in inner organization as well.

John Bowlby (1973) describes the emergence of "working models" during this period. A central feature of any child's working model of the world is "his notion of who his attachment figures are, where they may be found, and how they may be expected to respond" (p. 203). By the end of the first year the infant will have developed clear expectations concerning the "availability" of the caregiver. *Availability* in Bowlby's usage includes both the child's expectation that the caregiver will be accessible (present) to satisfy needs and that the caregiver will be responsive. Such models are rooted in the history of interactions over the course of the first year and are viewed by Bowlby as "tolerably accurate reflections" of the infant's actual experience. From the coordinated exchanges orchestrated by the caregiver early in the first year and the caregiver's responsiveness to the infant's intentional signals of need and desire in the second half year the infant learns that the caregiver likely is available and that when the caregiver is available organized behavior may be maintained or reachieved if lost. Such working models will be revealed in the quality and organization of attachment behavior with respect to the caregiver. An infant that expects a caregiver to be responsive will explore confidently in his or her presence, will signal needs intentionally, and will respond quickly to the caregiver's interventions (expecting them to be effective).

Thus, a new level of organization has emerged by the end of the first year, and the flexibly organized, goal-directed quality of the infant's behavior suggests considerable inner organization as well. *The infant responds to new situations in light of his or her past history and purposefully selects behaviors with respect to goals.*

Is this, then, our emergent self? Although a number of compelling arguments could be made in support of a positive response, a process orientation would suggest tracing further the emerging inner organization. The working model of the infant at this time may be better described as a model of the relationship than of the self (Bowlby, 1973; Main, Kaplan, & Cassidy, 1985; Sroufe & Fleeson, 1986). That is, major expectations the infant has concerning her own actions have to do with likely responses of the caregiver (and, to a varying degree, of others). If she gestures she will receive a response; if she seeks contact she will get it; if she signals a need it will be addressed. Her actions are part of these expectations but the expectations are centered on the caregiver's responsiveness. Moreover, under stress the infant has great difficulty maintaining organized behavior without the caregiver's assistance. It is only later that the child will firmly recognize (be aware of) her own potency as an independent center of action and will be able to deal with stress and frustration more on her own.

To be sure, however, the self is nascent here. Numerous theoreticians have suggested that it is from the attachment relationship that the particular organization of the individual emerges (Ainsworth, 1973; Bowlby, 1973; Erikson, 1963; Greenspan, 1981; Mahler, Pine, and Bergman, 1975; Sroufe & Waters, 1977). From the sense of trust comes the sense of trustworthiness (Erikson, 1963); or in Bowlby's (1973) words:

> In the working model of the world that anyone builds, a key feature is his notion of who his attachment figures are . . . and how they may be expected to respond. Similarly, in the working model of the self that anyone builds a key feature is how acceptable or unacceptable he himself is in the eyes of his attachment figures. . . . The model of the attachment figure and the model of the self are likely to develop so as to be complementary and mutually nonconfirming. Thus an unwanted child is likely not only to feel unwanted by his parents but to believe that he is essentially unwantable. (pp. 203–204)

Phase 5: Self-assertion   With the flowering of intentionality and with increased mobility (at about fourteen to twenty months) the toddler more actively pursues his own goals and plans, at times even when these are *explicitly* counter to the wishes of the caregiver. "Guidance of behavior on the basis of the pleasure of realizing *inner aims* can take precedence at times over the more familiar pleasurable reinforcement of finding a coordination with the parental caretaker" (Sander, 1975, p. 141). The child now initiates separations both physically and psychologically. He explores away from the caregiver (Mahler's "practicing"), inevitably engaging objects more on his own. And he operates on the basis of his more autonomous plans. Still, of course, such moves away are balanced by continued bids for reciprocation with the caregiver, and maintaining this balance is forecast by the quality of the earlier relationship.

Securely attached infants are as toddlers able to function more autonomously, while still drawing upon the caregiver when challenges exceed their capacities (Matas, Arend, & Sroufe, 1978; Londerville & Main, 1981; Sroufe & Rosenberg, 1980). This is a critical transition toward the emergence of self-awareness and inner organization, which includes a concept of self as action. Through independent action and through the pursuit of inner plans (even which at times conflict with maintaining previous patterns of coordinated behavior) comes the beginning of the sense of being an independent actor.

It should be noted that these changes mark a redefinition of the attachment relationship, not its termination. Autonomy and attachment are not opposites. The attachment relationship provides the springboard for autonomy, and the development of autonomy brings about a transformation in the child–parent attachment. Nonetheless, attachments endure even as autonomy increases.

Phases 6 and 7: Recognition and Continuity   With the rise of symbolic capacity at eighteen to thirty-six months the toddler can move to a new level of awareness. Behaving autonomously fosters a dim recognition of self as actor, but recognizing that the caregiver is aware of her plan and is, for example, in opposition to it (a recognition greatly assisted by language) brings the "realization that another can be aware of what one is aware of within oneself, i.e., a shared awareness." Sander assumes that this marks the beginning of awareness of a self-organizing core within—"actually a core that from the outset has been operative in the service of regulation at the more biological level but is now in a position to be accorded a new priority in the guidance of behavior" (Sander, 1975, p. 142).

This new level of awareness enables the infant to move toward what Sander has described as *self-constancy*. Drawing upon Jean Piaget's concepts of object constancy and operations, Sander describes a process wherein the child "perturbs" the dyadic harmony and reachieves it through her purposeful actions and the caregiver's continued cooperativeness. Deliberately acting contrary to her understood perception of the caregiver's intention and yet being reassured that the relationship can be reinstated and remains intact ("reversibility"), the child gains a sense of constancy of the relationship *and* of the self-organizing core.

> The intentional disruption of previously reinforcing and facilitating exchanges with the caretaker disrupts the toddler's newly consolidating self and body representational framework. Reexperiencing his own coherence, again at his own initiative or by out reach from the caretaker, provides a situation from which self constancy as an inner structure can be established. . . . Self as active initiator or as active organizer is thus "conserved." (p. 143)

80

Parallel to this development is the emergence of mirror self-recognition (Amsterdam, 1972; Lewis & Brooks, 1978; Mans, Cicchetti, & Sroufe, 1978) and "I do it" and "do it myself" assertions early in this phase (Breger, 1974), and the emotions of shame, pride, and guilt as the phase proceeds (Sroufe, 1979b). The beginnings of perspective taking and the roots of empathic response are also seen (Radke-Yarrow, Zahn-Waxler, & Chapman, 1983; Hoffman, 1979; Flavell, 1977) as the child moves toward what Bowlby calls a "goal-corrected partnership." The child can recognize the caregiver's intentions as separate from his own and can coordinate his behavior in terms of these goals of the other. There is coordination as before, but now it is the coordination of two autonomous and interdependent beings, each recognizing the other. With each new level of self-organization, there is a changed relationship organization, and with reorganizations of the relationship, the self emerges and is transformed.

Self as Inner Organization

From our developmental/organizational viewpoint, then, the emerging of the inner organization that we will call *self* is properly viewed in relationship and process terms. Exactly when one chooses to posit that a self has emerged is partly semantic. Some might argue that there is rudimentary representation and some regularity in experience, and therefore "self," even in the first half year (Stern, 1985). Others may require intentionality and plans, self-recognition, self-monitoring, or self-reflection, all of which occur at later developmental periods (see table 4-1).

In the first six months there is limited memory capacity and limited evidence to suggest that experiences are carried forward. In this sense, the concept of self as an ongoing, organized core seems challenging to justify. On the other hand, in the usual case, there is sufficient regularity in the dyadic organization to ensure basic patterns of repeated experience—sequences of motor behavior, tension regulation, and affect. And *these* regularities commonly *are* carried forward to the next phase, when the infant plays a more active role in the regulatory process. Regularities in the interaction become regularities in the relationship and in the self.

By the end of the first year the infant's behavior is based much more on her appraisal of both external *and internal* parameters. Her immediate and past experiences, as well as her ongoing affective state (mood) provide the context for behavior (Sroufe, Waters, & Matas, 1974). Behavior is goal-directed, and goals reflect a characteristic inner organization. She recognizes the role of the other in maintaining constancy in affective experience and behavioral organization and acts to utilize that other. Some would argue that this, then, signifies the emergence of the self. Others would point to the lack of awareness of self (including absence of indications of self-recognition) and the rather total dependence of organized behavior on availability of another to suggest that even this degree of inner organization does not qualify as self. Again, however, although the infant may not be *aware* of the continuity of experience, continuity is there. And, in time, from the infant's active efforts in maintaining inner regulation (though centered on another) will come the sense of inner organization that is clearly self.

From this process view of self, it becomes clear that the core of self, the basic inner organization, has to do with regularities in experience—cycles of environmental (or state) variation, behavioral disruption, efforts to reinstate organization, and experienced affect. At first such regulation is clearly dyadic regulation; it is highly dependent on the responsiveness of the caregiver. When the caregiver is available and sensitively responsive, periods of disequilibrium are short-lived and reorganization and positive affect routinely follow environmental challenge or negative state change. These repeated experiences of regulation and positive affect (or the converse in the case of nonresponsive care) represent the rudimentary core of what will become the self. For this reason Robert Emde (chapter 2) has put forward the concept of the affective self.

In time the infant comes to play a more active role in this regulatory process and to recognize the other as part of the regulation. Such increased control, which is paralleled by increases in the intensity of regularly occurring positive affective experiences (Sroufe & Waters, 1976), allows the infant to move toward ownership and sharing of the inner experience. The infant comes to recognize the self as competent to elicit the regulatory assistance from the other and, in time, to perturb and reachieve the inner regulation on his or her own.

> The importance of a stable basic regulation has to do with a context in which the child can begin dimly to recognize his own role in determining action. . . . The emergence of autonomy as here proposed is based on the further differentiation of awareness—especially that of inner perception, which sets the stage for the "disjoin" of the self-regulatory core. (Sander, 1975, p. 141)

What is carried forward, then, into childhood is an abstracted history of experiences of behavioral and state regulation and their affective products within the relationship, a recognition of others as part of regulation, a recognition of oneself as effective or ineffective in eliciting care, and, finally, a recognition of the self as the author of experience. At their core, the complementary working models of self and other have to do not so much with particular actions or thoughts as with expectations concerning the maintenance of basic regulation and positive affect even in the face of environmental challenge. The core of self lies in patterns of behavioral and affective regulation, which grant continuity to experience despite development and changes in context. As Kohut (1977) has put it:

> It may well be . . . that the sense of the continuity of the self, the sense of our being the same person throughout life—despite the changes in our body and mind, in our personality make-up . . . does not emanate solely from the abiding content of the constituents of the nuclear self and from the activities that are established . . . but also from the abiding specific relationship in which the constituents of the self stand to each other. (pp. 179–180)

Empirical Implications of the Organizational/Relationship Perspective

There are two major empirical implications of this organizational/relationship perspective on self: first, emerging patterns of self-organization, as they are seen in the context of primary infant–caregiver relationships, should be related to earlier patterns of dyadic organization crafted by the caregiver; second, these emerging patterns of self-organization should forecast in specific ways later patterns of social adaptation (the child's organization of expectations, attitudes, feelings, and behavior) even outside of the family. That is, the way the child organizes, interprets, and creates experience and the way the child forges new relationships are products of the relationship history. From dyadic organization built through caregiver responsiveness to infant states and signals, to more reciprocal relationship organization in which the infant is an active participant, to a self-organizing child, the inner core of self develops.

RESPONSIVE CARE AND THE EMERGENCE OF SELF

The nascent self may be glimpsed within the dyadic organization of the attachment relationship. The particular quality of affect regulation within this

83

relationship is presumed to reflect the experience-based expectations (and dyadic regulatory procedures) developed through the course of interaction. By the end of the first year interactive experiences have become abstracted into particular models of caregiver availability and responsiveness and complementary models of self (which have little definition outside of this context). Feeling states give rise to behavioral tendencies that are expressed in accord with expectations of likely responses by the caregiver and their consequences. If the infant is threatened and expects that an alarm signal to the caregiver will achieve comforting, the signal will be made. *The organization of these feeling states, actions, and expectations is the emerging self.* Its particular form should be the result of the particular history of dyadic interaction. Where various particular actions (mediated by affect) routinely have particular consequences for ongoing regulation, a particular pattern of inner organization (self) emerges. Should these actions lead to consequences that promote smooth regulation of affect and ongoing commerce with the environment, a well-defined, functional self core (and a secure attachment relationship) results.

The proposition that smoothly organized attachment behavior (smooth affect regulation) emerges from a history of responsive care has been amply documented empirically. Ainsworth (for instance, Ainsworth, 1973; Ainsworth, Blehar, Waters, & Wall, 1978) was the first to show that ratings of the caregiver's responsivity at various points in the first year predicted later quality of attachment behavior in both home and laboratory. Infants of mothers who had characteristically responded to their signals promptly and effectively (which entails availability and sensitivity) cried less at home, explored more actively, and showed fewer undesirable behaviors than infants with a history of insensitive care. In a novel laboratory situation, these infants were assessed as securely attached. They used the caregiver as a base for exploration, exploring comfortably in her presence. They actively initiated interaction or contact following brief separations from the caregiver and were readily comforted when distressed (returning again to active exploration). Thus, an infant who has experienced responsive care becomes, by the end of the first year, an active, effective participant in a well-regulated dyadic system. By virtue of this participation and the attendant experiences of effectance, a positive core of self emerges.

Infants with a history of insensitive care were unduly wary in the novel setting and impoverished in their exploration; upon reunion either they were unable to be settled or they avoided contact with the caregiver, even when markedly distressed. (In addition to low sensitivity ratings, mothers of these avoidant infants had been previously assessed as characteristically rebuffing their infants whenever the *infant* initiated contact; Main & Stadtman, 1981.)

Both groups of anxiously attached infants were unable to return to active exploration following reunion with the mother. Active participation in such systems also influences the emerging selves of these infants.

Ainsworth's core finding—namely, the relationship between quality of attachment in her laboratory assessment and sensitivity of care based on extensive home observation earlier in the first year (usually at six months)—has been replicated by several different teams of researchers (Bates, Maslin, & Frankel, 1985; Grossman, Grossman, Spangler, Suess, & Unzer, 1985; Egeland & Farber, 1984). In each of these studies independent coders assessed caregivers' responsiveness and infants' later attachment, and neither set of coders had knowledge of the other's data.

These data provide critical support for the proposition that the nature of the earlier dyadic organization, which depends on the caregiver's responsiveness to the infant's states and signals, provides the groundwork for the later dyadic organization, which, because it is a joint product of two intentional partners, reflects the emerging core of self. In being part of an organized system the infant comes to participate actively in such a system, paving the way for the emergence of an autonomous inner organization (Sroufe & Fleeson, 1986).

THE EMERGING SELF AS ORGANIZER OF LATER EXPERIENCE

The emerging self is the inner organization of attitudes, expectations, and feelings, which derives from the history of affective and behavioral regulation within the caregiving system. As such, it has implications for the ongoing structuring of experience, by taking the child toward or away from certain encounters with the environment, by influencing the style of engaging environmental challenges and opportunities, and by guiding interpretations of experience. Such subsequent encounters with the environment, of course, feed back on the self as the inner organization is consolidated and undergoes continued modification. There is some tendency for continuity in the inner organizing core because (1) there is an active structuring of later experience by the self, (2) early prototypes of inner organization are not readily accessible to conscious awareness, and (3) there is a tendency to form new relationships that are congruent with earlier models. Because of these organizational principles, according to Bowlby (1973), inner models of self, other, and relationships show some resistance to modification even by the end of infancy, become rather firmly established by the end of early childhood, and become quite difficult to modify after adolescence. This is a sophisticated version of the sensitive period hypothesis.

Although Bowlby's entire conceptualization has not been tested, there is now available substantial data concerning the organizing significance of early working models of self and other into the elementary school years. In studies that draw upon Ainsworth's method for assessing quality of attachment in late infancy (twelve to eighteen months), several groups of children have been followed for various periods of time through early childhood. The following discussion is based on comparisons of two groups: (1) those Ainsworth calls secure in their attachment and (2) those who show avoidant attachment. (It should be noted that all conclusions are based on studies in which all coders and informants were blind to attachment history.)

Infants in the first group show confident exploration of novel environments in the caregiver's presence; they routinely share positive affective experiences; they show active, positive greetings upon reunions with the caregiver when they are not distressed; and they are active in seeking and maintaining contact upon reunion if they are distressed. Moreover, such contact readily leads to comforting and a return to active exploration. Both the shared interaction and the ease of comforting reveal expectations about the availability of the caregiver and the likelihood of maintaining organized, affectively positive behavior in his or her presence. A working model of themselves as potent, worthy, and capable and of others as available is assumed to be carried forward from such a relationship.

In avoidant attachment relationships there is an absence of active greetings by the infant upon reunion and a failure to seek comforting when distressed. As stress is increased in Ainsworth's procedure by having a second brief separation, avoidance is more marked, with a consequent failure of resumption of active exploration. As described above, such a pattern derives from a history of insensitive care and, specifically, rebuff when the infant signals need. The resulting working model portrays significant others as unavailable in times of emotional arousal and self as unworthy.

Self as Potent   The idea that from a model of caregiver as available will emerge a complementary model of self as potent has been supported in several studies based on two samples. At both two years and three-and-a-half years, children who had been assessed in infancy as securely attached have been found to be more enthusiastic, affectively positive, and confident in solving problems (Arend, 1984; Matas, Arend, & Sroufe, 1978; Sroufe & Rosenberg, 1980) than children with histories of avoidant attachment. At five years the securely attached children have been shown to exhibit more curiosity on the Banta curiosity box (Arend, Gove, & Sroufe, 1979).

In other studies children with histories of secure attachment were found to have greater ego strength at age three and a half (to be "self-directed" and "forceful in pursuing goals"; Waters, Wippman, & Sroufe, 1979) and to be more "ego resilient" at four to five years (Arend, Gove, & Sroufe, 1979; Sroufe, 1983). In the Alan Sroufe study composites were made of the Q-sorts of three teachers, and these were compared to a criterion Q-sort of the ideal ego-resilient child (confident and flexible in managing impulses, feelings, and desires). For all sixteen children with histories of secure attachment, the correlations between actual description and criterion were all positive and averaged .50; for eleven children with avoidant histories, nine of the correlations were negative and averaged -.13.

In this same study children who had been securely attached were judged by teachers (blind to attachment history) to be dramatically more independent and resourceful, based on Q-sorts, rankings, and ratings. Teachers' judgments were confirmed by observational data; for example, in circle time those with secure histories less often sat by teachers or on their laps; nor did they seek attention through negative behaviors. They did, however, actively greet teachers and use them skillfully as resources; in turn, teachers rated them higher on "seeks attention in positive ways" (Sroufe, Fox, & Pancake, 1983).

Thus, young children with histories of secure attachment are seen to be independent, resourceful, curious, and confident in their approach to the environment. As we will elaborate later, these children, while assertive, are not aggressive, thus confirming the idea that these two characteristics lie on separate developmental pathways (Stechler & Halton, 1987).

Self as Worthy   In our large-scale study of an urban poverty sample (Egeland & Sroufe, 1981) we have had two opportunities to assess self-esteem. The first was based on a rating made in a "barrier box" situation where the child faced the frustration of an insoluble problem in the caregiver's absence. The rating centered on the child's confidence, ability to maintain flexible organization, and capacity to keep "expecting well." The second opportunity was in the preschool setting mentioned above. In this case the composited Q-sorts of each child were compared to a criterion high-self-esteem Q-sort (Waters, Noyes, Vaughn, & Ricks, 1985). In both cases children with a history of secure attachment were significantly higher on self-esteem. (A simple rank-ordering by the teachers on self-esteem was in accord with this finding.) In addition, based on observer Q-sort descriptions in second and third grades, children with histories of secure attachment were determined to be higher on social competence and lower on anxiety than those with histories of anxious attachment (Sroufe, unpublished data).

Children with histories of avoidant attachment carry forward feelings of low self-worth, isolation, and angry rejection, which they sometimes turn inward. Teachers' ratings in the preschool placed them low on emotional health/self-esteem and confidence. In addition, a depression mega-item was extracted from the composited Q-sort data. The mean for the avoidant group was significantly higher than the mean for the secure group, with five of the ten avoidant subjects being clearly depressed compared to only one of sixteen secure children. Even specific items, such as "appears to feel unworthy; thinks of self as bad," were seen as characteristic for those with avoidant histories and uncharacteristic for those having secure relationships in infancy. Teachers' judgments were corroborated by several sets of ratings, including facial affect (Garber, Cohen, Bacon, Egeland, & Sroufe, 1985).

Self-esteem is an elusive concept, and these findings can perhaps be made more concrete with an example from the Minnesota Preschool Project (Sroufe, 1983). One day in the nursery school several children were dancing to recorded music, a lively and inviting scene. Other children arrived. One child (RA) approached another and asked to dance. The child said no and RA withdrew to a corner and sulked. Another child (RT) entered, approached a potential partner, and also was turned down. This child, however, skipped on to another child, and the second time was successful in soliciting a partner. RT, who had a history of secure attachment, showed no evidence of being "rejected," and her persistent stance led her ultimately to receive further confirmation of her expectation that others are responsive and that she is worthy. RA, on the other hand, *experienced* intense rejection and cut himself off from further opportunities to disconfirm his model of himself as unworthy. He had a history of avoidant attachment. Countless related examples could be provided.

THE SELF AND LATER RELATIONSHIPS

Beyond implications for self-reliance, personal power, inner security, and feelings of self-worth, the relationship perspective makes very specific claims concerning the organization of the self and later personal relationships. Such claims have been pursued in a number of studies.

Others as Available and Valuable   The tendency of children with secure histories to draw effectively upon their preschool teachers as resources, their active greetings, and their sharing of discoveries already have been mentioned. A child with such a history who is ill or injured will confidently turn to teachers for support. In contrast, it is particularly at such times that those with an avoidant history fail to seek contact. A boy is disappointed and folds his arms and sulks. A girl bumps her head under a table and crawls off to be by herself. A child is upset on the last day of school; she sits frozen and expressionless on a couch. Such reactions are typical of preschoolers with histories of avoidant attachment.

At the same time, preschoolers with histories of secure attachment are more engaged and more affectively positive with peers. They more frequently initiate interactions with positive affect and more frequently respond to bids by others with positive affect (Sroufe, Schork, Motti, Lawroski, & LaFreniere, 1984). They expect interacting with others to be positive, and they convey to others this positive expectation. They are higher ranked socially, they have more friends (Sroufe, 1983; LaFreniere & Sroufe, 1985), and they have deeper relationships (Pancake, 1985). Recently, our observations in second and third grade have confirmed earlier findings (Sroufe, 1983; Waters, Wippman, & Sroufe, 1979) of a link between secure attachment history and later competence with peers.

In addition, Jeanne Block and Jack Block (1980) assembled a mega-item for empathy from their Q-sort—items such as "shows a recognition of others' feelings (empathic)"; "shows concern for moral issues (reciprocity, fairness)"; "is considerate of other children (does not try to take advantage of other children)." By summing the item placements for these items (treating the placement in categories 1–9, from uncharacteristic to characteristic, as a score) total empathy scores were derived from our preschool Q-sorts (Sroufe, 1983). Children with histories of secure attachment had significantly higher empathy scores than those with histories of avoidance. The empathy items were on average characteristic for the secure group, uncharacteristic for the avoidant group. From a history of empathic responsiveness, securely attached children have internalized the capacity for empathy and the disposition to be empathic. What was a characteristic of their early relationship has become part of the core self.

Other striking findings concern the fantasy play of children with histories of avoidance. Despite IQs equivalent to those of children with secure histories, the play of these children lacks complexity and elaboration (Rosenberg, 1984). What is more noteworthy is the almost complete absence of fantasy play concerning people. Such fantasies dominate the play of almost all preschool children and were well represented in the play of those with secure histories in our sample. These data reveal sharp contrasts in the working models of the two groups—one world is richly peopled, the other is not. In addition, when injury or illness entered the fantasy play of the secure children ("He broke his leg, take him to the hospital!") there routinely was a positive resolution ("They fixed it"). Such was not the case for children with histories of avoidant attachment.

Relations with Peers and Teachers   One noteworthy finding concerns the frequent hostility, unprovoked aggression, and generally negative peer interactions of children with avoidant histories (LaFreniere & Sroufe, 1985; Sroufe, 1983). Sometimes this pattern alternates with emotional distance, and sometimes the latter stance is dominant. We had the opportunity to watch nineteen pairs of children in repeated play sessions as part of our Minnesota Preschool Project (Pancake, 1985), and two sets of findings were noteworthy. First, pairs in which one or both partners had a history of avoidance were rated significantly higher on hostility and lower on commitment than pairs without such a child. (This prediction derived from the notion that if one partner is disposed to be distant or hostile, such a characteristic will pervade the relationship; it takes two to be intimately and positively engaged.) Second, five of the nineteen total pairs were identified as being involved in exploitative relationships, where one child verbally or physically subjugates the partner in an ongoing way (Troy & Sroufe, 1987). In all five cases the "exploiter" had a history of avoidance; the partner had also been anxiously attached (either avoidant or Ainsworth's resistant pattern). Children with secure histories were not observed to be exploitative or victimized. Either role was open to children with histories of avoidance, presumably because of the confluence of hostility and low self-esteem in these children.

The first four comments from the summaries of a clinical judge for four pairs of avoidant-avoidant or avoidant-resistant partners are presented in table 4-2. These were the only four such pairs observed, and, like all other coders, the judge was blind to histories and all other data. The negative quality of these relationships is apparent. One behavioral example from dyad 3 can illustrate the exquisite "negative empathy" of some of these children. When her partner, NT, complained to LJ of a stomachache, LJ smiled and poked her in the stomach. NT cried out in pain and said, "That hurts," whereupon LJ smiled and poked her again.

Recently we have examined further qualitative aspects of relationships between teachers and children of varying attachment histories (unpublished data). We assumed that teachers would develop characteristic styles of relating to different children and that such styles would be related to the child's relationship history. Teachers have histories, too, but they represent constants, as it were. Thus, variations in the attitudes, expectations, and behavior of a given teacher toward groups of children should reflect the *children's* inner working models of relationships and self as these are brought forward.

The first finding was that teachers do behave in different but characteristic ways toward different children. In fact, intercoder agreement on our rating scales was as high when coders looked at sets of totally different interactions

TABLE 4-2

Observations of Pairs of Preschool Children with Anxious (A) or Resistant (C) Attachment Backgrounds

---

Dyad 1 (A/A, girls)

- This relationship is a vulnerable one—not dependable.
- Poor on "give and take."
- There is some degree of attraction for each other but they are not able to work out their differences well (they bark and snap at each other and usually give up)
- They don't know how to compromise, thus they never really build a mutually satisfying relationship.

Dyad 2 (A/A, boys)

- A very unhealthy relationship, characterized by intense conflict and tension.
- They become locked in steady conflict; neither is capable of altering the interaction into a positive one—they are both highly invested in supporting the negative dynamics.
- They develop an organized pattern of interaction, with TE sometimes approaching SO in a sweet-sounding, coy affective tone, trying to "warm up" to SO, then, as SO responds and begins to cooperate, TE will change his tone to nasty and malicious taunts. This dynamic is repetitive and becomes predictable.
- Both have developed maladaptive coping strategies which are very different; TE is better able to change his affective tone at will and uses it to manipulate SO; SO uses accusations and threats as a way of defending himself and provoking TE; SO is more direct and perhaps more vulnerable.

Dyad 3 (A/C, girls)

- *Very* unhealthy! This pair is intensely involved in a system of mutual provocation that neither can stop; they are highly invested in supporting the negative dynamics.
- The relationship is supported by the predictability of behavior from both—JL maintains her cold, rejecting manner, while TN persists in setting herself up as the victim of JL's rejections.
  JL leads the play (without initiating interaction with TN), TN tends to crawl around her, following her like a puppy, begging for her attention, taunting and teasing her, yet doing it in a sweet and innocent voice.
- As TN moves closer in, JL moves away, and in one instance JL whispers (3 times), "Go over there and play!" TN doesn't move away, rather she tries to redirect her attention (she won't be left alone).

Dyad 4 (A/C, boys)

- This relationship looks immature and impulsive.
- Not a healthy "give and take" relationship.
- Not good cooperation or balanced exchanges.
- Often play side by side but don't connect, sometimes communicate for brief periods via indirect attention seeking (silly sound effects, "in-role" invitations)—they seem to rely on this as a form of communication or cooperation by doing it at the same time, sometimes rhythmically.
- They do interact, but the interaction is not mutually supportive—they get into negatives more often than positives, fall into nonsense talk, taunting, mimicking (both contribute to negative cooperation).

Source: Fury, 1984.

for a given teacher and child as when they made ratings on the same set of interactions (generally agreement was in the .70s).

Moreover, there were clear and notable differences in teachers' behavior depending on the children's attachment history. Teachers expected children with secure histories to comply with requests, to follow classroom rules and standards, and to engage in age-appropriate behavior. They treated them in a matter-of-fact manner. In contrast, children with histories of avoidance were shown more discipline and control, lower expectations for compliance, less warmth, and, at times, even anger. Children with histories of anxious resistant attachment were also controlled more. Yet they were also shown more nurturance and tolerance; that is, teachers, perceiving their emotional immaturity, made more allowances for them, accepting minor infractions of classroom rules and indulging their dependency needs. These ratings were based on independent examination of teachers' behavior by persons with no knowledge of attachment history or other information on the child.

Conclusion

Clinicians have frequently argued that difficulties in interpersonal relationships derive from low self-esteem, which in turn derives from a lack of nurturance or empathic care (Erikson, 1963; Greenspan, 1981; Kohut, 1977; Sullivan, 1953). The inner organization of attitudes, expectations, feelings, and meanings is a product of relationship history with ongoing implications for the organization of socio-emotional behavior. This hypothesis is not new. The organizational/relationship framework, however, has offered a context in which empirical data concerning this proposition could be gathered. Prospective, longitudinal data, based on groupings of early relationships (inspired by Bowlby's model and Ainsworth's organizational scheme), confirm the link between relationship history and the emerging constellation of inner organization that is self. Moreover, there is continuity within the relationship history itself: the nature of the dyadic interaction orchestrated by the caregiver forecasts the nature of the later attachment relationship, which, by virtue of the infant's active participation, is the framework for the emerging core of self.

Avoidant attachment relationships in late infancy reflect a history of insensitive care and rejection, especially in the context of clearly expressed need or desire on the part of the infant. When caregivers are chronically unavailable emotionally, avoidant attachment is virtually guaranteed (Egeland & Sroufe, 1981). At the same time, such a pattern of attachment reveals an internalized working model the infant has developed of the caregiver as unavailable and unresponsive to emotional need. Thus, the infant fails to seek contact as stress is elevated. Reciprocally, this leads to a model of the self as isolated, unable to achieve emotional closeness, uncared about, and unworthy. Care can be sought only in times of low stress (as when avoidant children sit with thumb in mouth on teachers' laps during storytime). The social world is viewed as alien and is treated with anger and hostility. Oftentimes the children behave in ways that elicit further confirmation of their models. They exhibit negative affect and unprovoked aggression, leading other children to reject them. They disrupt classroom routine, exploit the vulnerable, and engage in devious or antisocial behavior (lying, stealing, cheating; Sroufe, 1983), leading even teachers to dislike many of them. Teachers' anger is directed almost exclusively toward these children, and much of the input they receive from teachers is in the form of control. Behaving in terms of the world they have known they create relationships and influence their current environment to confirm their models of self and others (Sroufe & Fleeson, 1986).

One final case example from the Minnesota Preschool Project powerfully illustrates the process of self emerging from relationship history and the ongoing organizational significance of early self-representation. RV experienced chronic rejection and hostility from her mother, which was repeatedly documented. At both twelve months and eighteen months their relationship was classified as avoidant. The interaction with her mother at age two was very angry, and her mother called her a "nasty bitch." By preschool RV vacillated between long bouts of explosive anger and periods of desperate isolation. Nonetheless, one female teacher developed a special fondness for this physically attractive and bright child and stayed emotionally available to her, despite her anger. Late in the term RV reported a dream to this favorite teacher, in which the teacher had, in a fit of rage, thrown her against a wall. The child obviously was shaken by the dream. The teacher, with arm around her, said, "Oh, RV, I would never do that." Astonishingly, RV asked her, "Why?" "Because I like you very much, RV." RV then responded, "Why do you like me?" making it clear that this was a perplexing state of affairs, requiring explanation, not a matter of course.

This interchange allows us a clear look into this child's inner organization— her model of self and other. It also allows us to see the organizing significance of the self. For each child certain material may be more or less readily worked into the existing organization of feelings, attitudes, and expectations. For RV and others like her who have experienced chronic emotional unavailability from their caregivers, it is very difficult to make sense out of another's obvious caring.

There are several reasons that models of self and others are difficult to change (and that there is basic coherence to self-structure over time). First, individuals often tend to select partners and form relationships that promote continued enactment of existing working models, although this process generally remains out of awareness (Sroufe & Fleeson, 1986). Second, individuals (certainly including children) tend to elicit input confirming their preexisting models, be that rebuff or positive feedback. But, in addition, as illustrated by RV, countervailing information often is not recognized as such when it does occur. In these ways early self-structures, created in the context of infant–caregiver relationships, in time become self-stabilizing and resistant to change.

It is not the case, however, that change is impossible. Change may be possible at many points during childhood. For example, as Main and Goldwyn (1984) point out, the advent of formal operations in adolescents makes it possible "to step outside a given relationship system and see it operating" (p. 16). Thus, working models of self and others could be modified, most likely in the context of other significant relationships. Understanding the origins of self in relationships, the organizing nature of self, and processes of social exchange that stabilize this organization will be important for understanding the process of growth and change as well as psychopathology.

Return now to the basic questions that initiated this chapter. First, the literature on outcomes of individual differences in infant–caregiver attachment is quite compelling with regard to the importance of early relationships for individual development. Even discontinuity between early attachment and later functioning in childhood has been found to be associated primarily with changes in the child–parent relationship (Erickson, Sroufe, & Egeland, 1985). Second, from this conceptualization it is clear that relationship disorders would be manifest in infant behavior because the infant is so inextricably embedded within the relationship system. Indeed, the infant can be competent only to the extent that there is a well-organized, reciprocating relationship. Finally, the internalization of a relationship disorder poses no mystery. The nature of the dyadic organization—well functioning or disordered—will be embodied in the self-organization.

PART II

DISTURBANCE

Chapter 5

Relationships and Relationship Disturbances

L. Alan Sroufe

To understand the concept of relationship disturbance, we need first to understand the concept of interpersonal relationships. Although clinicians have argued for some time that dyadic relationships, and even families, have unique properties (Jackson, 1977), it is only recently that systematic efforts to establish a science of interpersonal relationships have emerged (see, for example, Hinde, 1979).

In this chapter I will argue that there are emergent properties of relationships—definable features that transcend the behavior of individuals. Relationships, but not individuals, may be described as synchronous, for example, and an individual may be involved in both synchronous and asynchronous relationships with different partners. Thus, relationships are at a different conceptual level than individuals and may not be reduced to assessments of individual characteristics. If relationships have definable features, it should be possible to establish dimensions and taxonomies of relationships. If particular relationships can be shown to have characteristic properties, then it may be shown that some relationships promote healthy individual adaptation and others compromise individual functioning or are pathogenic—in short, that some relationships are disturbed or disordered. Because relationships transcend individuals, relationship disturbances are at a different level than individual

97

psychopathology. A separate description of relationships may contribute substantially to our understanding and treatment of psychopathology.

Conceptualizing Relationships

DEFINITIONS

As Robert Hinde (1979) points out, a social relationship involves, at a minimum, a series of interactions between people over a period of time. Moreover, there must be "some degree of continuity between the successive interactions. Each interaction is affected by interactions in the past" (p. 14). Without this feature one has only a series of interactions (as with a telephone operator) and not a relationship.

Moreover, in any relationship "the nature of any interaction is a product of both partners, even though it sometimes appears to be under the control of only one" (p. 15). For example, children with anxious attachment histories tend to elicit from teachers either controlling and angry reactions or undue nurturance, depending on the particular quality of the child's early relationship (Sroufe & Fleeson, 1988). But such school relationship patterns also depend upon the particular teacher. Relationships are more than the sum of individual characteristics. As George Herbert Mead (1934) and others have argued, what each person does in a relationship depends upon his or her perceptions, expectations, and past history with the other, as does the person's interpretation of the other's response to his or her action. Humans are cognitive and affective beings, and human interactions center on interpretation and meaning. These interpretations hinge on the history of relationships with the given partner and with other significant persons.

When meaning comes to the fore, the description of relationships must include quality as well as content. Relationships can be described in terms of *what* the partners do together, but full description must also include *how* they do it. Hinde, for example, points out the distinctions between kissing passionately, tenderly, and dutifully. Likewise, caregiver and infant may mold to one another in a relaxed way, or the contact may be intermittent, fitful, and tense. Even when the frequency of caregiver–infant contact is not predictive of later infant development, qualitative aspects of the ongoing interaction are strongly predictive (Ainsworth, Blehar, Waters, & Wall, 1978; Sroufe, 1985).

98

The description of relationships must also include a reference to the patterning of interactions, which is closely related to quality. *Patterning* refers to timing, sequences, and combinational features of the ongoing interaction. *When* does the caregiver pick up the infant? Is the pickup in response to a gesture by the infant? Is there an ongoing tuning or synchronizing of the behavior of each to the other? Does the infant mold to the caregiver or mix molding with stiffening, squirming, and pushing away?

In one case, an infant's distress may be terminated efficiently and smoothly. The caregiver responds promptly to the infant's cry, bending to pick up the infant and conferring meaning to the cry. Reciprocally, the infant leans or reaches toward the caregiver, yields her body to the pickup, and then actively snuggles into the caregiver's shoulder, both arms wrapped around her neck. The caregiver rocks the infant with a swaying motion, gently pats the infant's back, and whispers in soothing tones. The infant settles, relaxes, and returns to play.

By contrast, in response to the baby's wail, a second caregiver bristles, then after some delay picks him up with a jerky motion. The infant's body stiffens and the crying seems to intensify. The infant shifts from side to side and alternates leaning in with pushing away from his mother, whose own irritation and tension show through pats that are too rough and movements that are stiff. The distress persists for several minutes.

These are profoundly different interactions and, if characteristic, reflect aspects of quite distinctive caregiver–infant relationships: a *well-regulated* relationship on the one hand and an *asynchronous* relationship on the other. A complete description of the relationship would, of course, entail observations on the patterning of interactions in a wide variety of circumstances (feeding, play, bedtime, and so on).

Relationships are, at the simplest level, regularities in patterns of interaction over time. Such regularities provide the observable data available to researchers and clinicians. Work by Gerald Patterson (e.g., Patterson & Dishion, 1988) with aggressive children highlights the importance of sequencing and patterning. Patterson compared problem and control families, examining especially the frequency with which an aggressive behavior by the child was responded to by a parent or sibling with a behavior that was likely to induce another hostile response. Such aggressive cycles were five times more likely in the problem families, a phenomenon that illustrates the relationship features of this "individual" behavior.

To comprehend relationships it is also important to go beyond patterns of interaction to infer the functions of relationships and the goals they serve.

These give rise to and maintain regularities in interaction and are often revealed in affect. Distress in the two infants mentioned earlier prompted contact seeking on the part of caregivers and infants. In each case both partners shared the goal of terminating the distress. In the first pair the infant's confident expectation that this goal would be realized in contact with the caregiver is shown in the pickup signal, the active contact efforts, and the rather immediate settling. The caregiver's empathy and self-confidence are seen in her relaxed and tender care; she has soothed her infant readily many times before. The mutual doubts and anger of the other partners are revealed in their clearly ambivalent behavior. The doubts and irritation of each feed the other, presumably because of their history of experiences with dyadic affect regulation.

THE REALITY OF RELATIONSHIPS

Relationships are intangible; they cannot be viewed directly, they cannot be touched, they do not have size. Yet they can be described, and they can be assessed. Relationships may be compared and categorized. Like individuals, each relationship has its unique stamp and yet may be grouped in various ways with other relationships. Relationships often show stability and even more generally show continuity and lawful change when change occurs. That is, there is a degree of predictability in relationships; when a relationship is properly described and examined, predictions of future qualities may be made even in circumstances of change. For example, predictions may be made concerning the mother–toddler relationship from the mother–infant relationship (Londerville & Main, 1981; Matas, Arend, & Sroufe, 1978; Pianta, Egeland, & Sroufe, 1989), even though the specific behavior of the child, and consequently that of the mother, changes dramatically during this year.

As paradoxical as it may seem, relationships manifest a reality that at times transcends observable individual behavior. For example, behaviors shown by year-old infants in a laboratory assessment (vocalizing, looking, seeking proximity) show little stability, even from week to week. And over a period of six months stability is even less; the behavior repertoire is vastly expanded and more flexibly employed. Few infants cling to their mothers following brief separations at eighteen months; most do at twelve months. Yet qualitative aspects of the caregiver–infant relationship commonly are highly stable (Waters, 1978). An infant who shows the ease of settling pattern of our first example at twelve months, after being briefly separated from the mother, may not even be distressed by a similar separation at eighteen months. Therefore, the specific behavior observed would change dramatically. When not distressed the infant in the well-regulated pair does not cry and cling. But it is highly predictable that the same infant who earlier showed relaxed settling now would show joyous greeting and active initiation of interaction upon the caregiver's return. As we will discuss in a later section, the active initiation of interaction when not distressed and the active seeking of contact when distressed are both manifestations of a qualitatively similar pattern of dyadic organization. Both reflect a history of effective dyadic regulation. Both earlier and later patterns reveal the same history of affective sharing, dependable closeness, and confident expectations. Likewise, the ambivalence of the other pair will be revealed at eighteen months, though probably in new ways. Relationships show continuity or coherence even when the particular manifest behaviors of individuals change dramatically.

Moreover, as will be discussed later in more detail, relationships have predictable implications for individual behavior and for other relationships involving a given individual. The social support available to caregivers from spouses and others predicts the quality of their infant care (Belsky & Isabella, 1987; Crockenberg, 1981; Pedersen, Anderson, & Cain, 1977). Mothers' reports of the quality of their own early family relations predicts their style of infant care and the nature of their relationship with the infant (Main, Kaplan, & Cassidy, 1985; Morris, 1980; Ricks, 1985). The infant–caregiver attachment relationship predicts to wide areas of functioning during the preschool years, including competence with peers, curiosity, empathy, and self-esteem (Sroufe, 1983; see also chapter 4). More generally, decades of research have confirmed links between parenting and parental relationship variables and child behavior problems, with an especially strong link between parental disharmony and conduct disorders (Rutter & Garmezy, 1983; Block, Block, & Morrison, 1981; Hetherington, Cox, & Cox, 1978; Maccoby & Martin, 1983; Patterson & Dishion, 1988). The prospective nature of many of these studies makes causal interpretations reasonable. Relationship experiences have consequences for later individual behavior, including social relations.

The validity of relationship constructs, their usefulness to the science of human behavior in general and developmental psychopathology in particular, rests upon the strength of such empirical relationships. Given evidence currently available, it is reasonable to claim that, at least in early development, relationship assessments will prove to have more predictive power than traditional individual measures. This is due most likely both to the integrative nature of relationship assessments (their strength as assessment tools) and to the profound influence of vital social relationships on individual development and behavior.

PROPOSITIONS CONCERNING THE NATURE OF RELATIONSHIPS

June Fleeson and I (Sroufe & Fleeson, 1986, 1988) have outlined four propositions concerning relationships: (1) relationships are wholes; (2) there is continuity and coherence to relationships; (3) individuals internalize whole relationships, not simply roles played; and (4) previous relationship patterns are carried forward to later close relationships. We have already discussed relationships as wholes, with unique properties not reducible to characteristics of individuals, and the continuity of relationships. Various writers have described relationships as characterized by homeostasis (Jackson, 1977), morphostasis (Wertheim, 1975), negative feedback (Hinde, 1979), and self-stabilization (Sander, 1975). And numerous clinical examples of sameness within change may be found in the literature (Cottrell, 1969; Luborsky, 1985). Here we will focus on the last two propositions, because they are most relevant to the problem of how relationship experiences affect individual adaptation. They also illustrate the power of a relationship system perspective.

Internalizing and Carrying Forward Relationships   There is a paradox concerning individuals and relationships. On the one hand, relationships have properties beyond the sum of the individuals. For example, "bully–whipping boy" (Olweus, 1980) or "victimizer–victim" (Troy & Sroufe, 1987) relationships are unique to particular partnerships. Bullies do not bully everyone and victims are exploited only by those wishing to exploit. The relationship depends on the participation of both individuals together and thus cannot be reduced to the characteristics of the individuals considered separately. Likewise, there are reliable features of family interaction that occur only when members are together and often are outside of the awareness of participating individuals (chapter 9).

On the other hand, only individuals exist as physical entities and only individuals have intentions, purposefulness, and motives. Thus, individuals are the carriers of relationships. Moreover, individuals, merely by virtue of participating in salient relationships, must come to represent or internalize the relationship or relationship system. Such representations, although unique, must nonetheless in each case reflect the whole. Such an assumption is necessary to account for the role reversal commonly reported in the clinical literature and for the complex reenactment of past relationships in later relationships, including child abuse (Egeland, Jacobvitz, & Sroufe, 1988).

Numerous empirical studies support the proposition that relationships are internalized. Both Olweus (1980) and Troy and Sroufe (1987) find that those who exploit others have particular relationship histories, most notably parent–child relationships characterized by punitive rejection or emotional unavailability (underregulation). Likewise, those who are exploited have particular histories, one example being maternal overinvolvement. Later peer relationships of children who have experienced responsive care are characterized by mutuality, empathy, and "commitment" (Pancake, 1985; Sroufe, 1983).

Other examples of relationships being carried forward concern mothers who had been emotionally exploited by their own fathers, sometimes sexually. Such mothers have been found to behave seductively with their sons (Sroufe & Ward, 1980) and more generally to be emotionally dependent on their children, to defer to them, and generally to show role reversal or parentification (Burkett, 1985). It is important to note that these mothers do not simply show deferred imitation of their parents' previous behavior. For example, those who were exploited by their fathers do not literally do what their fathers did to them. Rather, they engage in the culturally specified adult female form of cross-gender child exploitation. They have internalized a relationship and not simply a set of behaviors. A wide variety of specific behavior patterns can recreate the complementarities of the previous relationship.

These same principles apply to larger relationship systems such as families (Sroufe & Fleeson, 1988). There is integrity and coherence to the network of relationships that makes up the family, and each relationship within the system reflects the whole. It is this total network of relationships that is internalized and taken forward by the individual. Thus, mothers who are seductive with sons were predicted and found to be hostile and derisive with their daughters (Sroufe, Jacobvitz, Mangelsdorf, DeAngelo, & Ward, 1985). This prediction followed from a relationship system view in which it was assumed that mothers who were seductive with sons likely came from families where father was exploitative of the daughter; mother was absent, distant, or hostile; and mother and father were estranged. The child, now our mother, learned that adults cannot meet needs with adults and that adults try to meet emotional needs through children on a gender-related basis. She also learned certain attitudes toward men, women, and herself, which are reflected in both the seductiveness with her son and the derision of her daughter.

This elaborate structure recently received further support from a study of family interactions involving thirteen-year-olds. A number of cases were identified in which there was an imbalance of emotional engagement or seductiveness involving the cross-gender parent–child dyad. From these child–parent dyadic assessments it was possible to predict both the nature of the parent dyadic relationship (emotional distance) and the degree of "triangulation" in the father–mother–child triad, based on completely independent codings (Sroufe & Fleeson, 1988). Thus, from one dyad, other dyads and triads in the family are predictable. This attests to the coherence of the family relationship system and to the fact that the whole is to some degree reflected in each dyad. And, in particular, it confirms that certain anomalous dyadic relationships (such as parent–child boundary dissolution) are supported by the overall relationship system. In the same way we would propose that disturbed individual behavior is supported by the surrounding relationship network and is integral to that network.

Individuals and Relationships   Individuals participate in social relationships, and in so doing become part of systems which, while "larger" than themselves, exercise an ongoing influence on their adaptation, including other social relationships. Such influences are powerful, and any understanding of individual behavior divorced from relationship aspects will be seriously incomplete—both because of the influences of relationships and relationship history on behavior and because of the prominent role of social relations in evaluating individual adaptation.

Philosophers have made the point that words and sentences are mutually defining, the meaning of one being totally dependent on the other. Without the structure of the sentence the meanings of the words cannot be known; yet within the words and their organization is the complete meaning of the sentence. Even though the words carry the meaning (all of it) they cannot do so out of the context of the sentence:

> It is only in the context of a whole sentence that a word has definite meaning; [still,] the meaning of any sentence must be derivable from the meanings of its parts. Those seem to be, but are not, contradictory. . . . The meaning of a word does not belong to it in isolation, but consists in its potentiality to contribute to a completed "thought." . . . The meaning of the sentence . . . [is] wholly determined by the various "potentialities belonging to its parts." (Scruton, 1982, p. 249)

This mutual dependence of whole and part is characteristic of language. We propose a similar interdependence for individuals, dyads, and relationship systems.

Describing and Assessing Relationships

The adequate assessment of relationships requires both multiple levels of analysis and a diversity of methods. One needs to examine what the members do and how they do it, that is, the content and quality of the relationship. One also needs to consider the functions of the relationship, for example, its service to individual development. Closely related to function is structure. What are the recurrent themes or rules that guide and regulate the relationship? How are members, roles, and rules organized with respect to the relationship functions? Each of these levels is pertinent to understanding relationships and relationship disturbances.

CONTENT AND QUALITY

Hinde (1979) has stressed the importance of attending to both content and quality of relationships. On the one hand, the type and diversity of interactions, their relative frequency and patterning, and their reciprocal or complementary nature are noted. On the other hand, the affective tone, commitment, and attributions of the members also are important. Sometimes what the partners are doing is so atypical as to reveal a disturbance in itself. Often, however, qualitative aspects are the key to assessing relationship disturbances.

For example, breast versus bottle feeding bears little relationship to infant development. More revealing are qualitative aspects of the feeding situation. Are feedings harmonious, characterized by mutual responsivity and shared affect? Moreover, is the feeding initiated and terminated in response to signals from the infant or is it determined at the caregiver's whim (or perhaps used as the only response to distress)? Are transitions to and from feeding and other activities accomplished smoothly?

Likewise, investigators of peer relationships and family relationships consistently have found qualitative aspects to be informative (Fleeson, 1988; Goldstein, 1985; Gottman, 1983; Pancake, 1985; Wynne, 1984). For discussion these features are presented under three headings: (1) motivation, (2) affective tone, and (3) operational style of the relationship.

Motivation   In assessing motivation one is interested in the degree of involvement or commitment of the partners in the relationship, disregarding hedonic tone. The focus is on observable engagement (versus lack of interest or detachment) or signs of salience or investment (ongoing affective engagement, disappointment when the partner isn't available, seeking out the partner, resisting termination of an interaction, and so on). These are powerful variables in assessing the vitality and depth of a relationship.

Affective Tone   An assessment will include affective tone of the relationship as seen in interactions. Hostility, for example, may be reliably coded, and is a powerful variable in studies of peer or parent–child relations (see Goldstein, 1988; Pancake, 1985). Amity, enjoyment, and shared affect are also useful dimensions for evaluating relationships, as are mutual emotional support and finding satisfaction through establishing common ground (a sense of "we-ness"; Gottman, 1983). Taken together, involvement and affective tone have proven to be powerful discriminators of relationship quality.

Operational Style   By *operational* variables we mean more formal, regulatory features of the relationship: (1) the sensitivity, reciprocity, or "meshing" of the members' behavior (what Reiss [1982] calls coordination); (2) the clarity, directness, and pertinence of communication (Goldstein, 1988); (3) the mutual support for and complexity of joint activities (are abilities and talents maximized and enhanced in the relationship?—Reiss's configuration variable); and (4) variables concerning conflict resolution: How flexible are the partners in efforts to resolve conflict? Do they stay engaged and persist through to conflict resolution? Can they tolerate the tension of conflict? Is the relationship easily threatened by conflict? Reiss (1982) proposes a related variable concerned with tolerance of ambiguity ("closure").

Although the dimensions and variables outlined in this section do not exhaust all possibilities, they do prove to be rather comprehensive. Taken together, they specify particular relationships and lead to meaningful groupings; for example, preschool dyads whose members had histories of secure attachment showed more "commitment" (positive investment), more mutual sensitivity, and less hostility than dyads in which at least one member had a history of avoidant attachment (Pancake, 1985), and similar variables in an assessment of family interaction predicted teenagers' ego resilience one year later (Fleeson, 1988). In the work of Michael Goldstein (1988), parent controllingness in adolescence coupled with negative affective tone measure predicted later psychopathology.

FUNCTION

Another useful way to approach the assessment of relationships is to begin with the question of function. When functions of relationships are defined, then assessments may be targeted either at the way in which the functions are fulfilled or at the degree to which the functions are realized. How well do relationships serve the individuals involved? Considerations of function lead to a focus on certain aspects of organization or structure, as well as on stylistic variations.

For example, Sroufe and Fleeson (1988) approach the problem of family assessment by pointing to two major functions of the family: (1) nurturing (rearing) of children and (2) meeting of adult intimacy needs. Families organized so as to fulfill these two functions simultaneously are viewed as well-functioning relationship systems. Families in which either function is not being well served are considered nonoptimal. Often when one function is compromised the other will be also, as when adult intimacy failures lead one or both parents to attempt to meet emotional needs through a child, thus compromising the child-nurturing function.

A major function of all close relationships throughout the lifespan is to create or maintain basic patterns of arousal (or affect) regulation. In the case of infants and very young children, affect regulation is obviously dependent upon a well-functioning caregiver–child relationship, as discussed throughout part I of this volume. The child's capacities for regulation, though continually advancing, are at first quite limited. The degree to which the smooth regulation of arousal is achieved is a critical yardstick for assessing the adequacy of the infant–caregiver relationship. Moreover, various patterns of maladaptation or specific problems of arousal regulation may be the basis for a beginning typology of relationship disorders in the early years.

STRUCTURE

Structure and function are closely related. The organization and patterning of relationships commonly has to do with functions being served; and distortions in organization or patterning are related to compromised functioning.

The structure of a relationship is defined by patterns of interaction—regularities or recurrent themes that transcend the specific behaviors through which they are manifest. Family theorists refer to such patterns as rules, which exist at different levels of generality and are hierarchical, therefore structured (Wertheim, 1975). At the most general level, David Reiss (1981) has referred to the family paradigm, the overall rule that governs family functioning. Classification of relationships or families in terms of rules, rather than particular content, may prove to be quite fruitful for developmental psychopathology, for continuity is more likely to be in rules than in specific behaviors. Rules can be enacted through almost infinitely various behaviors which may change with circumstances, including developmental changes in the child.

Many family rules concern the expression and regulation of feelings and emotion. Expression of anger, for example, may be completely forbidden or allowed only in indirect ways. One may infer such a rule both from the absence of direct expression, even in tense situations, from ritualist (repetitive) patterns of avoidance or indirect expression (walking away or successive redirection of anger at other parties), or from denials of anger when expressed, including smiling as the insult or other hurtful act is delivered. One also may see

107

evidence of rules by observing behavior when the rule is broken. Other members in the system will shame, punish, or correct the rule offender, leading him or her to recant or deny the behavior.

In family therapy situations one often sees the entire family go into operation in concert when one member threatens to break a rule. The mother in a family where father is an alcohol abuser, for example, may begin to express her own feelings of having failed her children. College-age children and father all jump in to say, "No, you did just fine." This behavior reveals the rule that such feelings must be denied, as well as the rule that mother is to be viewed as perfect and father is to be viewed as the bad one. Such reactions serve to maintain the status quo. Different individuals may play different parts and these may change with circumstances, but all are governed by the family rules.

Related to rules are alliances and coalitions between members of groups, roles that individuals play, the degree to which boundaries are maintained between some roles, and the degree to which other roles are interchanged (Boszormenyi-Nagy & Spark, 1973). All of these, too, are relevant to classifying disordered relationships, as will be discussed in a later section.

Each of these aspects of relationship or family functioning—rules, roles, and coalitions—may be useful in assessing relationship disturbance. In Arthur Miller's *Death of a Salesman,* one guiding theme (the family paradigm) was that unrealistic goals may be used to salve disappointments (though, of course, such unrealistic goals led to further disappointments, and so on). Numerous rules supported this general rule, including that one must never question the achievability of the goals and the corollary that honest feedback must be avoided. Hints of directness were strongly punished, with all other members colluding against the individual who threatened to break the rule. There also were coalitions that served maintenance of the system. At one point mother (in father's absence) tells the two sons what bad shape their father is in and demands that they show their love for him. In this way father is pushed outside of the group (though ostensibly mother's purpose is to get care for him) and is "protected" from honest confrontation by the sons. Moreover, demanding of her older son that he give love to the father (do what she is failing to do) represents a crossing of generational boundaries and, paradoxically, obligates the son to maintain his animosity. Although considerable work is required to translate such clinical insights into assessment procedures, there have been successful attempts to capture such phenomena as generational boundary dissolution with rating scales (Fleeson, 1988; Sroufe, Jacobvitz, Mangelsdorf, DeAngelo, & Ward, 1985) and structural analyses of interactive data (Burkett, 1985).

In the case of relationships between very young children and their caregivers, maintaining a consistent patterning or structure to the relationship is quite complex because the child's behavior changes so rapidly; the parent's behavior must change in concert with the child's. For example, a mother who related with inordinate physical sensuality to her two-year-old may engage in peerlike teasing with her three-and-a-half-year-old.

In the early months the structuring or organization of the relationship often is crafted by the caregiver around the child (chapter 4). In time the child comes to play a more active part in the organization and, ultimately, may behave in ways to prevent the structure from changing. For example, parents may use the young infant's nighttime crying as a distraction from marital tension. Later, the child's antics may serve the same purpose. In time, the child may come to anticipate and act deliberately to distract or amuse tense or needy parents. In certain instances, such as the case of Ms. K in chapter 6 (pp. 138–43), the pattern must become increasingly disturbed in order to be maintained, because the child's emerging autonomy would otherwise cause a breakdown of the pattern. Such patterns are of great clinical significance.

Many aspects of early dyadic relationship structure also concern the expression and regulation of feelings and emotion. What feelings are allowed and how and when may they be expressed? Some relationships seem to follow the rule of "no current emotional state is acceptable." Thus, whatever the infant's state the caregiver's goal seems to be to move it away from that state, in a rigidly overregulated manner. Other notably underregulated relationships follow the rule of "you're on your own," with any modulation of affect expression being the responsibility of the infant. Some relationships are, of course, quite inconsistent or poorly structured and, for many, the issues concern not too much or too little regulation but asynchronous or poorly tuned regulation. Specific variations are numerous. During one development period regulation may be lacking, followed by harsh control in response to the young child's poorly controlled behavior. Or the infant may receive little modulating input until arousal is quite high, then be helped or, alternatively, precisely then be stimulated or provoked further. The latter pattern has been associated with later hyperactivity (Jacobvitz & Sroufe, 1987).

Having described various aspects of relationships and levels of analysis, we now turn to the concept of relationship disturbances. We begin with the question of criteria. By what standards do we determine whether a relationship is disturbed or disordered?

Relationship Disturbances

CRITERIA FOR ASSESSING RELATIONSHIP DISTURBANCES

Some of the criteria for determining disturbance or disorder in a relationship or relationship system are parallel to those for determining individual disorder; others are quite distinctive. For example, expressions of "pain" (a presenting problem or complaint), intractability, inflexibility or rigidity, and compromised adaptation in various areas of functioning have all been used as criteria for establishing individual abnormality (Kessler, 1966). Relationships, too, may be characterized by complaint ("We have inadequate sexual relations"; "We can't make him mind"), rigidity, or inability to deal with change. They also may be viewed in uniquely relationship terms, such as the balance between individual and relationship or group needs, appropriateness of boundaries between individuals, and (for families) the way the system serves or does not serve the child with respect to salient developmental issues.

Adaptability and Rigidity Various investigators have considered a dimension concerned with the response of relationships or family system to change (Andolphi, Angelo, Menghi, & Nicolo-Corigliano, 1983; Olson, Sprenkle, & Russell, 1979; Reiss, 1982). Openness, tolerance for ambiguity, rigidity, and adaptability all refer to the degree to which the relationship or system flexibly changes in the face of new demands or challenges. Repeated self-defeating cycles, stereotyped solutions, rigidly applied rules, and intolerance of change would be criteria for determining rigidity in a relationship system. Earlier we pointed out that self-stabilization is required for systems to survive. At the same time, theorists agree that systems must also change, in response to both internal demands (such as development of individual members) and external challenges. A system that can't respond to changing demands likewise will fail (though perhaps through stagnation rather than disintegration). Adaptation is always a balance between stability and change—morphostasis and morphogenesis—and this applies to relationships as well as to individuals.

Relationship adaptability, like individual adaptability, is a difficult concept to operationalize. But as we shall see in later discussion, a developmental viewpoint can be clarifying. Flexible family systems, for example, should be able to accommodate the changing needs of the developing child. Along with a second dimension of emotional distance and overinvolvement, the adaptability dimension is part of a categorical scheme proposed by David Olson (Olson et al., 1979) and others. Families may be described as "enmeshed" (rigid and overinvolved) or "chaotic" (lacking in structure), and so forth.

One criterion that will be developed in chapter 6 has to do with a time dimension. A transient relationship problem, in response to an external stress or developmental change, will be referred to as a *perturbation.* Only when the problem persists for some time and has potential negative developmental implications will it be called a *disturbance,* and only when it is relatively intransient and seriously compromises development will we use the term *relationship disorder.* In large part the criterion of rigidity underlies these distinctions.

Structural and Boundary Distortions   Structural and boundary distortions are criteria that derive specifically from family systems theory considerations. They pertain to the coalitions among family members, boundaries between individuals or generations, and, especially, the role of the child in serving parental needs in contrast to his or her own developmental needs. Theorists such as Murray Bowen (1978) and Salvador Minuchin (1974) emphasize problems that arise when a child's developing self is compromised to hold together an unstable family system. Bowen, in particular, describes a process of "triangulation" that has its roots in relationship problems arising in preceding generations. The parents, each a "pseudoself" due to "fusion" (lack of differentiation) in their own families of origin, attempt to enhance (complete) their self-esteem through their partner. Because they are still entangled with their own childhood families, the two pseudoselves' efforts are doomed. A tension remains (*anxiety* being a relationship term in this scheme), and ultimately one parent turns to the child (a more "vulnerable other") for attempted fulfillment (to seek "a more comfortable togetherness"). The parent's own unresolved needs are projected onto the child, and the child fulfills this role not only out of vulnerability but also because the parent becomes less anxious and more predictable. The other parent opts for an "outside position," which removes him or her from the relationship conflict and enables support for the first parent's involvement with the child. Bowen describes one example in which a mother projects feelings of helplessness and a wish to be babied onto the child, a pattern that we would describe as overregulation: "The anxious parental effort goes into sympathetic, solicitous, over protective energy, which is directed more by the mother's anxiety than the reality needs of the child. It establishes a pattern of infantilizing the child, who gradually becomes more impaired and more demanding" (1978, p. 299).

According to Bowen, Harry Stack Sullivan (1953), and other theorists, infants are attuned to, and respond anxiously to, anxiety in the caregiver. Such

111

anxiety in turn may be perceived by the caregiver as a problem *in the child*. In time, the child comes to play an increasingly active role in this process, remaining the mother's baby (being helpless *for the mother*) and sacrificing development of his autonomous self. As a pseudoself, he too will go forward seeking not an autonomous partner but another pseudoself in the hopes of finding completion. The cycle is repeated.

The most clear manifestation of such a relationship problem is in distorted boundaries. The generational boundary between parents and children is not maintained (Kreppner, Paulse, & Schuetze, 1982); the spousal unit is weakened, and the major coalition is between parent (here mother) and child, with, in this example, father on the outside. (Father may, of course, be seeking togetherness with another child, perhaps a daughter.) The child is not allowed to be a child and to develop a separate sense of self—a "real self." Boszormenyi-Nagy and Spark (1973) refer to this boundary dissolution as "parentification" or spousification. The child is placed in the role of meeting the parent's emotional (and at times even sexual) needs, whereas the parent should be in the service of the child's needs. Although a host of individual problems may ensue from such family patterns, the strongest predictive claims concern repetition of the relational patterns across generations. Thus, all these structural positions predict considerable continuity in relationships.

There is ample clinical support for our structural notions (Satir, 1967; Cottrell, 1969; Bowen, 1980), and support is emerging in research reports. Both prospective studies (Egeland, Jacobvitz, & Papatola, 1986) and retrospective interview studies have linked abusive or exploitative parental histories with various forms of child maltreatment (Main, Kaplan, & Cassidy, 1985; Ricks, 1985; Morris, 1980).

Developmental studies also have linked specific parent–child interaction patterns with parental history. For example, the pattern described by Sroufe and Ward (1980) as seductive (sensual teasing, use of sensuality as a control technique, passionate kissing, or genital touching) is an example of boundary dissolution. This pattern of behavior with toddlers was strongly related to independently obtained histories of "spousification" of these mothers as children (meeting fathers' emotional needs in various ways, including, but not restricted to, frank incest). Subsequent follow-up of toddlers at three and a half showed a similar pattern. Here, in a problem-solving situation, the pair either behaved as peers or roles were reversed with the child seemingly having authority. As one example, the child deliberately makes an error, smiling coyly at mother. Mother says, "What are you doing, you little devil," laughs, and tickles him. The two wind up with both of their heads on the table, giggling together—all in a context where the child needs firm reassurance to solve a difficult task. Follow-up in elementary school showed the boys from such relationship histories to be strikingly overrepresented in a group identified by teachers as hyperactive (see Jacobvitz & Sroufe, 1987).

Recent data by Linda Burkett (1985) support these findings. She looked in detail at parent–child interaction, parental practices questionnaire data, and interview material in comparing cases in which mother had been an incest victim as a child with cases without an incest history (matched for psychotherapy experience, education, number of children, and age). All aspects of the data, independently coded, showed "incest" mothers to be emotionally dependent on their children, focused on their own needs, not supportive or encouraging of their child, and unable to accept normal parental ambivalence. A complementary picture of the child as striving to meet the mother's needs and relinquishing his or her own needs, also emerged. These studies represent strong confirmation of the prediction that boundary distortions will be carried forward and perpetuated. The full implications for individual psychopathology have yet to be traced.

The Concept of Risk   If relationship or family patterns that are associated with later individual or relationship disturbance can be identified, we will have a basis for labeling those patterns as disturbed. Such a criterion is related to the concept of *risk* in distinguishing developmental psychopathology from abnormal psychology, child psychiatry, and related disciplines (Cicchetti, 1984; Sroufe & Rutter, 1984). An individual at risk for psychopathology is an individual belonging to a group of people who, for one or a variety of reasons, have an increased likelihood of showing later disorder, though present behavior patterns may not be viewed as disordered by traditional standards. Even given the absence of psychiatric disorder one may wish to address the predisposing condition. Certain forms of parent–child or family relationships may fit this criterion for risk factor, being associated probabilistically with later psychopathology in the child. In this sense such relationships may be viewed as disturbed even though no individual fits a traditional psychiatric profile in the early assessments. It would seem important to identify and address such relationship patterns.

In risk research, an empirical criterion is used, although the search for links may be guided by theory. One example is the work of Goldstein (1988) on "communication deviance." Particular patterns of family communication (diverse behaviors that lead to a reduction in the shared focus of communication) were found to distinguish some clinic-referred families of adolescents. Based on underlying theory, it was hypothesized and confirmed that such a pattern would be predictive of later schizophrenia in the target child. The argument is that this pattern of family communication compromised an important

113

development issue in adolescence, namely, individuation or emancipation. Such interference with a critical developmental issue can promote later pathology. By this criterion the data seem to support the proposition that communication deviance is an indicator of a family relationship disturbance.

The Developmental Issues Criterion   The way the relationship or family system serves a child with respect to critical developmental issues is thus a basic criterion for evaluating relationship disturbances: how the relationship serves individuation is an example of a general developmental issue. But more specific issues may also be examined. For example, in the attachment scheme to be laid out in the next section, a critical issue is the way the infant–caregiver attachment relationship promotes the infant's exploration of the environment. If the relationship promotes exploration, a key developmental issue for the just-mobile infant, it is deemed to be healthy. If the relationship does not promote the infant's exploration of the world, or in fact interferes with exploration, it is viewed as a maladaptive relationship. Stuart Hauser and his colleagues reason likewise when they speak of adolescent family relationships as "enabling" or not (Powers, Hauser, Schwartz, Noam, & Jacobson, 1983). Here they refer to the way the family system promotes adolescent emancipation. Several studies have empirically confirmed that certain patterns of parent–child relationships in early adolescence (joint decision making, responsiveness to the child's input) promote flexible, autonomous adolescent functioning (Grotevant & Cooper, 1985; Fleeson, 1988). Louis Sander (1975) has proposed a series of issues in early life that may be used to assess caregiver–child relationships (see also chapters 4 and 6 for further elaboration).

CURRENT SCHEMES FOR ASSESSING RELATIONSHIP DISTURBANCES

Ainsworth's Attachment Classification System   Mary Ainsworth's attachment scheme is indeed a system for classifying relationships (adaptive and maladaptive), in this case those between infants and caregivers. In doing the assessment one focuses on infant behavior, but the infant–caregiver relationship is in question. One examines the way the infant adjusts his or her behavior across episodes of increasing stress (a series of separations and reunions), noting especially the shifting balance between exploration of the environment and contact with the caregiver.

Infants are classified according to how their behavior is organized with *respect to the caregiver*. Infants who use the caregiver as a base for exploration and for coping with novelty, who are active in seeking contact or interaction, and who find contact reassuring are said to have secure attachment relationships, and to have had a history of responsive care. Infants who cannot use the caregiver as a base for exploration, who are not readily comforted by contact, and who mix contact seeking with anger are said to have anxious/resistant attachment relationships. Infants who withhold contact, and ignore or avoid the caregiver following brief laboratory separations (with more avoidance the greater the stress), are said to have anxious/avoidant attachments. Like the resistant infants, the inability to derive comforting from renewed contact interferes with exploration and environmental mastery.

In using Ainsworth's procedure to assess caregiver–infant attachment, one does not simply examine amount of infant crying or amount of physical proximity between caregiver and infant. Although these are important, one must examine other aspects of behavior. If there are joyous greetings (Ainsworth's distance interaction scale) and active interaction in reunion episodes following brief separations, the lack of physical proximity has a different meaning than if greetings and interaction are absent or markedly delayed (Ainsworth's distance interaction scale). If contact is mixed with angry pushing away or ongoing petulance or pouting, or squirming to get down only to get back up again (Ainsworth's contact resistance scale), one evaluates the relationship differently than if there is relaxed molding and embracing of the caregiver (Ainsworth's contact maintenance scale). Using these scales, the overall patterning of behavior may be used to classify the dyads into three basic categories (see table 5-1).

The relationship is captured because the infant behaves according to established dyadic patterns. Infants who have developed firm expectations concerning the caregiver's availability are free to explore the novel environment. Should they become threatened, they know (through experience) that the caregiver will respond promptly. Likewise, when upset, they go immediately to the caregiver and settle readily, again based on a history of affect regulation experiences with the caregiver. The history of interactions—the relationship—underlies this smoothly regulated and purposeful infant behavior. By contrast, infants who avoid contact when distressed have experienced a history of rebuff when emotional needs were directed to this caregiver. Infants who cannot be readily settled by contact have experienced a history of inconsistent, chaotic, or ambivalent care. In each case, the organization of attachment behavior—the dyadic regulation of arousal—reveals fundamental qualities of the relationship. And the broadest criterion for evaluating the relationship concerns how well it serves the developmental needs of the just-mobile infant.

That the Ainsworth procedure does yield relationship assessments is supported by a variety of evidence. First, the relationship between an infant and two different caregivers may be distinctive; for example, the relationship may be secure with one parent, avoidant or resistant with the other (Main &

TABLE 5-1
Ainsworth's Patterns of Attachment

Secure Attachment

A. Caregiver is a secure base for exploration
  1. Readily separate to explore toys
  2. Affective sharing in play
  3. Affiliative to stranger in mother's presence
  4. Readily comforted when distressed (promoting a return to play)
B. Active in seeking contact or interaction upon reunion
  1. If distressed
    a) immediately seek and maintain contact
    b) contact is effective in terminating distress
  2. If not distressed
    a) active greeting behavior (happy to see caregiver)
    b) strong initiation of interaction

Anxious/Resistant Attachment

A. Poverty of exploration
  1. Difficulty separating to explore; may need contact even prior to separation
  2. Wary of novel situations and people
B. Difficulty settling upon reunion
  1. May mix contact seeking with contact resistance (hitting, kicking, squirming)
  2. May simply continue to cry and fuss
  3. May show striking passivity

Anxious/Avoidant Attachment

A. Independent exploration
  1. Readily separate to explore during presentation
  2. Little affective sharing
  3. Affiliative to stranger, even when caregiver absent (little preference)
B. Active avoidance upon reunion
  1. Turning away, looking away, moving away, ignoring
  2. May mix avoidance with proximity
  3. Avoidance more extreme on second reunion
  4. No avoidance of stranger

Source: Adapted from Ainsworth, Blehar, Waters, & Wall, 1978.

Weston, 1981; Grossman, Grossman, Huber, & Wartner, 1981). Second, such relationship patterns generally are stable over time, even though manifest infant behaviors change dramatically with development (Main & Weston, 1981; Connell, 1976; Waters, 1978). Third, when the caregiver's circumstances dramatically change (for example, upon a marked reduction in stress), the quality of attachment changes—for example, from the anxious to the secure pattern (Waters, Vaughn, Egeland, & Sroufe, 1979). Fourth, these three patterns of attachment are specifically (and almost uniquely) predicted by earlier assessments of the caregiver's responsiveness (Ainsworth, Blehar, Waters, & Wall, 1978; Bates, Maslin, & Frankel, 1985; Belsky & Isabella, 1987; Egeland & Farber, 1984; Grossman, Grossman, Spangler, Suess, & Unzer, 1985). The secure pattern is forecast by the caregiver's consistent responsiveness to the infant's signals and needs, the resistant pattern by insensitive care, and the avoidant pattern by indifference or explicit rebuff. Finally, the Ainsworth assessments predict not only later infant behavior in other situations but also maternal behavior. For example, mothers of infant–caregiver pairs classed as securely attached later are independently rated as more emotionally supportive and providing a better quality of assistance to their toddlers in a problem-solving situation (Matas, Arend, & Sroufe, 1978). Thus, even though the attachment assessment focused on the infant, behavior of the caregiver was predicted because the *relationship* was being assessed.

There also is substantial evidence that the judgment of maladaptive indeed applies to the avoidant and resistant relationships, in particular—that such a relationship places the child at risk for later problems. The procedure was initially validated against the criterion of exploratory behavior in the home (Ainsworth, Blehar, Waters, & Wall, 1978). Several other studies have now shown that children with histories of anxious attachment later show less enthusiasm and persistence in problem solving; less curiosity; lower self-confidence and self-esteem (assessed in a variety of ways); and *more* emotional dependence on teachers and less competence with peers, based on judgments of observers, teachers, or peers themselves (Arend, Gove, & Sroufe, 1979; Matas, Arend, & Sroufe, 1978; Sroufe, 1983; Sroufe, Fox, & Pancake, 1983). Such relationships also predict various behavior problems in preschool and kindergarten (Erickson, Sroufe, & Egeland, 1985; Lewis, Feiring, McGuffog, & Jaskir, 1984; Sroufe, 1983, 1985), especially passivity or impulsiveness for the resistant group and aggression and antisocial behavior for the avoidant group. At times, those with an avoidant history develop a markedly abusive or exploitative relationship with another child. Finally, there is a clear association between the avoidant pattern and depression as assessed in the preschool by both teachers and clinicians. Thus, in terms of the developmental issues of exploration, mastery, autonomy, initiative, and peer competence, anxious attachment relationships fail to serve the child's development. At the same time, such relationships are predictive of later problem behaviors and, to some extent, even psychopathology. (See chapter 4 for a more complete treatment of these findings.) It seems likely that such relationships also can be viewed as rigid, structurally inadequate, and often, acutely painful. The distress of the child in such relationships is easily seen by clinicians and trained observers.

Wynne's Epigenetic Sequence   Lyman Wynne (1984) has drawn from developmental theory and systems theory to construct a series of relational stages, which are applicable to both dyads and families. The scheme is developmental in the fullest sense of the word because each developmental phase builds upon the outcome of earlier phases in a continuing process of hierarchical integration, while later phases feed back upon and elaborate earlier issues. Constitutional and experiential influences recombine in each developmental phase to create new biological and behavioral potentialities which then help determine the next phase. If the transactions at any given developmental phase are distorted or omitted, all the subsequent developmental phases will be altered because they build upon a different substrate. At the same time, each new phase provides an opportunity to rework the issues of preceding phases.

The sequence, which Wynne refers to as *processes,* appears in the first column of figure 5-1. Potential distortions are listed in the other columns. Drawing from systems theory, Wynne argues that these relationship concepts are at a different level from those of individual psychology and that they refer to the distinctive and unique properties of relationships.

In proposing his four major stages Wynne postulates as central a basic duality in human motivation: "strivings for relatedness to other human beings and a simultaneous striving to develop a sense of personal identity" (p. 298). His idealized sequence of relationship development serves to promote the balance between these strivings.

1. Attachment/caregiving   The starting point for adult relationships, as is the case for the caregiver–infant relationship, is the development of emotional connectedness. Need for psychological contact, comfort in the presence of the other, and discomfort when accessibility is threatened are critical in all ongoing salient relationships (Weiss, 1982). Wynne refers not to intimacy, which can occur only as the relationship evolves, but to the basic orientation toward caring and sharing of feeling. (Attachment deepens, of course, as relationships evolve toward mutuality and intimacy.)

2. Communicating   Communicating is a logical outgrowth of attachment because it is based upon a "shared focusing of attention, leading potentially to shared meanings" (p. 305). As is the case in the development from infancy to toddlerhood, when the child's increased understanding of the perspective of the mother allows her to rely upon signals at a distance and verbal reassurances, so the evolving adult relationship can come to be supported by shared meanings as well as by physical closeness. Communicating

118

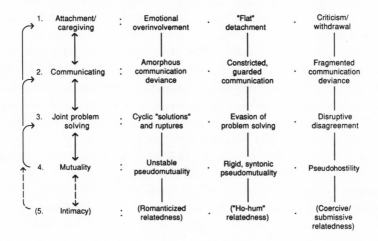

FIGURE 5-1

Major processes and illustrative dysfunctions in the epigenesis of enduring relational systems. The sequence may stop progressing at any stage. Intimacy is not essential for enduring relatedness, but if and when it becomes reliably available, intimacy is a subjective corollary of mutuality.

Source: Wynne, 1984.

depends upon the affective base of attachment; at the same time, through repeated sharings of meaning, attachment deepens and the way is prepared for the more challenging task of problem solving. Should there be difficulty sharing focuses of attention and mutual perspective taking (a "transactional thought disorder"), which likely would happen in the absence of the affective connection of attachment, problem solving would be jeopardized.

3. Joint problem solving   Analogous to Erikson's stage of "industry vs. inferiority," this third stage draws upon and integrates the preceding developments. Difficulties in problem solving frequently bring families to therapy and are the focus of many family therapists. Even so, Wynne argues that a developmental viewpoint should be maintained. "For example, if a family at the adolescent launching stage is still deeply unmeshed and emotionally overinvolved [see figure 5-1] or is still communicating in an amorphous, fragmented or constricted manner, problem-solving will be difficult indeed" (p. 307). Of course, one may well work on communication skills as a way of addressing the problem-solving issue (and any family therapy depends upon family members being emotionally attached). Again, it also is the case that joint problem solving experiences may sharpen communication skills and deepen commitment.

119

4. Mutuality   Mutuality, the outgrowth of repeated successful problem-solving experiences, "involves the processes of longterm relational renewal and reengagement" (p. 308). Members recognize that new patterns of relating are required to deal with difficulties faced. Here the problem to be solved is the megaproblem of whether the relationship should continue and under what conditions. Each partner steps outside and observes the working of the system and may therefore (if choosing to) reenter with a new level of commitment. Without attachment, ongoing communication, and routinely successful joint problem solving, genuine mutuality is not conceivable.

Relationship disorders in Wynne's scheme may be approached in two ways: (1) one examines distortions in sequential patterning, such as couples seeking to achieve mutuality or intimacy (which may or may not emerge after the mutuality phase) without taking the time to build the affective base or the experiential base of shared meanings and joint problem solving; and (2) one uses the scheme as a framework for examining relationship functioning. In figure 5-1 there is an implication of three types of pathological developmental sequences, with the relationship disorder progressing through stages as the relationship develops. For example, in one hypothesized relationship the partners begin with an anxious overinvolvement; each is so demanding of closeness that it can never be given. Out of this a distorted communication process emerges wherein each confuses his own view with that of the other. Because there is no genuine feedback or mutual tuning, problem solving is characterized by cyclic nonsolutions and breakdowns in process. Ultimately, "unstable pseudomutuality" results, "a predominant absorption in fitting together at the expense of the differentiation and identities of the persons in the relation" (p. 298). The process may be continually renewed, but the renewals merely recapitulate the old patterns.

Whether this pattern and the other two patterns outlined in figure 5-1 are genuine types and whether these particular distorted sequences would be revealed by longitudinal study remain to be shown. Other types are conceivable (for example, emotional overinvolvement leading to evasion of problem solving or disruptive disagreement). The point is that this scheme has researchable implications and it clearly is at the level of relationship disorder rather than individual pathology. Moreover, the scheme is suggestive concerning areas of assessment—affective connection, communicating, problem solving, and mutuality. Earlier we cited the work of Goldstein (1988), which indicated that both negative affective tone (attachment) and communication deviance contributed significantly in predicting schizophrenia and schizophrenia spectrum disorders fifteen years after family assessment. This work suggests the power of Wynne's scheme.

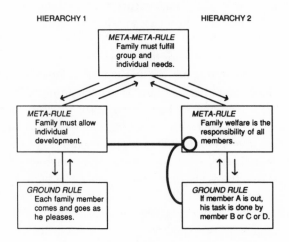

FIGURE 5-2

Structural and dynamic features of systemic rule networks (morphostatic regulation).
Source: Wertheim, 1975.

Dimensional Schemes   Finally, we will briefly mention some of the dimensional schemes that have been proposed. Some, like those of Reiss (1982), Olson (Olson, Sprenkle, & Russell, 1979) and Eleanor Wertheim (1975), have been explicitly aimed at the relationship level. Others, although they initially focused on social behavior or parenting (Maccoby & Martin, 1983; Schaefer, 1959), have evolved toward relationship systems (Humphrey & Benjamin, 1986).

Wertheim's (1975) scheme is representative of the former group. She takes as her starting point that both morphostasis and morphogenesis are necessary for the survival of any relationship system. By proposing two distinct stabilizing (morphostatic) patterns, which may have high or low values, and high or low values on openness to change, there result three orthogonal dimensions, each with two levels, for a total of eight possible combinations or types. "Each type is defined in terms of the degree of its intra- and extrasystemic openness associated with the capacity for change and in terms of its structural integration, the latter referring to an ordered relationship between the system as a whole and its subsystems" (p. 287). Wertheim's first three types closely resemble Reiss's (1982) three empirically derived types.

Determining relationship or family type involves examining the network of rules governing stability and change. A partial example of a well-functioning family is presented in figure 5-2. It should be noted that the existence of the specific rule (in the example, "family members come and go as they please") is mute concerning health or disturbance in the absence of the superordinate rules and parallel hierarchies of rules in which it is nested. It could be part of a system characterized by chaotic disconnection or, as in figure 5-2, a family deeply committed to both family life and individual growth.

The other dimensional schemes have their roots in decades of parenting research. In both questionnaire and observational research certain bipolar dimensions or factors have repeatedly emerged: (1) warmth, support, or acceptance (versus rejection or hostility); (2) permissiveness (versus restrictiveness or overcontrol); and, later, (3) anxious overinvolvement (versus calm detachment). Over the years these and similar dimensions, sometimes in configuration, have been related to child behavior. Following their own summary of this literature, Eleanor Maccoby and John Martin (1983) have offered a new synthesis of this work, emphasizing (1) the frequency of goal conflicts (control issues) and (2) the degree of balance in conflict solutions. Optimal child outcomes are posited to occur when frequency of goal conflicts is low (the parent is supportive of and responsive to the child) and neither the parents' nor the child's goals prevail (parents both demand from and accede to their child and require the same in return). Such concepts could be used as a rubric for assessing parent–child relationships or as a starting point for a typology. Diana Baumrind's (1967) authoritarian, permissive, and authoritative groups, although descriptive of parenting, represent the beginnings of such an effort.

Lorna Benjamin's "structural analysis of social behavior model" is an outgrowth of this tradition. Gerald Wiggins (1974) describes it as the "most detailed, clinically rich, ambitious, and conceptually demanding of all contemporary models" (p. 193). Benjamin's is a circumplex model, with "affiliation" (support) and "dominance" (control) as axes. As in other circumplex, "real-space" models, individuals or parenting styles may be "located" according to the totality of their questionnaire responses or observed behaviors. Variables, and ultimately persons, that are close to one another on the circle are more similar than those that are more widely separated. The special usefulness of the scheme for relationship assessment is that there are both "other" and "self" planes for observational data. The "other" plane represents prototypic parenting behavior—affirming, belittling, helping, neglecting, and so on— whereas the self plane represents behaviors prototypic of the child's role. Thus, one obtains a description of the relationship by scoring both parent and child. Generally, these would be complementary, as with an affirming/understanding parent and a disclosing/expressing child. In addition, the model is well suited for disclosing boundary distortions and other relationship problems. For example, in her study of relationships between mothers who had been incest victims and their five-to-ten-year-old children, Burkett (1985) found that these mothers (compared to controls) focused more on themselves and less on their children and provided fewer affirming/understanding messages and more belittling/blaming messages. They also showed more submission, appeasing, and deferring, which clearly reveal role reversal. The children, in turn, were more other-focused than self-focused (which is quite atypical for children) and showed more leadership in the dyad (more helping/protecting and managing/controlling behaviors). They were lower on trusting/relying and deferring/submitting, and in many ways distanced themselves from their mothers. These data, which were corroborated by independent interview data, strongly suggest disturbance in the relationships between these mothers and children, based on the developmental maxim that maintenance of adult and child roles is critical in middle childhood.

Conclusion

These and other research schemes show considerable promise. It does seem possible to carry out assessments at the level of relationships and to discriminate relationships that are disturbed from those that lie within the range of normal variation. Such demarcations will become more clear with future research. And in the coming years one may expect to see a great deal of work on the consequences of such disturbances for individual functioning in general and later social relationships in particular.

As we next begin to consider the problem of a nosology of relationship disturbances, we can draw from the ideas concerning relationships and relationship disturbances discussed in this chapter. A central concept throughout is the concept of regulation. Regulation is central to the very characterization of relationships, which may be defined as the interregulation of behavior. And the major developmental theme traced throughout this volume is the issue of how dyadic regulation becomes self-regulation.

Moreover, the assessment of relationships centers on the problem of regulation. Following Hinde, we have stressed qualities of relationships, such as patterning and synchrony, that are critical issues of regulation. In discussing functions of relationships, the arousal or affect regulation function was seen to apply throughout child development, from state regulation in early infancy to the individuation issues of adolescence. Even structural aspects of relationships may be viewed in terms of varying organizations promoting particular patterns of regulation.

Finally, existing schemes for categorizing relationship disturbances generally center on regulations. Ainsworth's scheme focuses on the attachment/exploration balance and dyadic regulation of affect (the infant's use of the caregiver as a secure base and as a source of reassurance when threatened or distressed). Similarly, Wynne emphasizes the balance between simultaneous strivings for relatedness and for personal identity. And Wertheim emphasizes the balance between morphostasis and morphogenesis, stability and change. In our beginning effort, too, the issue of regulation is central.

Chapter 6

Clinical Syndromes, Relationship Disturbances, and Their Assessment

Thomas F. Anders

It seems novel to diagnose a disordered relationship; a medical model of nosology typically classifies syndromes or illnesses that are characterized by pathophysiologic dysfunction in individuals. Yet principles of psychiatric classification can be applied usefully to early relationships when one or both partners are exhibiting disturbed behavior.

Attempts to expand and sharpen descriptions of infant psychopathology by clinicians and researchers have not met with widespread acceptance (Greenspan, 1981; Greenspan & Lourie, 1981; Call, 1983). Such efforts, clinically derived and often criticized as not having an adequate empirical base, have tended to focus on the diagnosis of the infant rather than of the relationship. Nevertheless, the absence of an acceptable nosology of infant psychopathology has not slowed the emergence of infant treatment programs in which behavioral symptoms of infants are treated by interventions directed at the parent–child relationship (Minde & Minde, 1986.) The assumption that a disturbed relationship may lead to disordered behavior in the infant is generally accepted.

Given the limited psychological autonomy of infants before three years of age, we feel it is unlikely that psychopathology can be sustained in an individual infant. It seems improbable also that an infant's disturbance is caused solely by an adult's disorder, since, in the absence of the infant, the adult's distress may disappear. Moreover, a disturbance in an infant may be present in relation to one parent and not the other. The conclusion is inescapable: most psychological and behavioral syndromes of infancy disturbance occur in the context of relationships.

A primary objective of this chapter is to stimulate the development of a nosology of relationship psychopathology that can supplement the *Diagnostic and Statistical Manual* (DSMIII-R) of the American Psychiatric Association (1987) for classifying individual psychopathology. Our nosology is only a beginning. It proposes a developmentally grounded assessment scheme for disturbed relationships. Our hope is that it will lead to research criteria that can be tested in both clinical and risk populations.

Rationale: Relationships and Regulation

Relationships are ubiquitous and regulate behavior at many levels of organization. There is a relationship between gene expression and the cytochemical environment that results in mutual regulation; the intrauterine environment and the developing fetus mutually regulate each other; and the young infant regulates and is regulated by caregivers. Regulation implies a dynamic equilibrium of inhibitory and excitatory mechanisms that effect a partnership. Development imposes an epigenetic trajectory of progressively increasing differentiation and complexity on the regulatory process.

Our nosology assumes the primacy of regulation in the maintainance of physical and psychological well-being of both partners in a relationship. We assume that disruption in regulatory function is associated with pathology in the relationship. Since adequate and appropriate regulation is essential to the establishment and maintenance of healthy relationships, regulatory disturbance must be central to disordered relationship patterns. We propose five patterns that can disturb the functional status of relationships: overregulation, underregulation, inappropriate regulation, irregular regulation, and chaotic regulation. Relationship disorders should be assessed in terms of these patterns.

In the caregiver–infant dyad, the assessment of regulation focuses on reciprocity and mutuality in attentiveness and other behaviors. Such regulation occurs in the context of development in both partners and may be influenced by a number of factors: the infant's physical state; the caregiver's social circumstances, including support from the other parent, demands of other children, and the support of extended family and others in the community; and the ability to cope with life stresses. The parents' own past experiences with primary caregivers also affect regulatory patterns (Main, Kaplan, & Cassidy, 1985).

Principles of Psychiatric Classification

John Wing (1973, 1980) has enumerated four criteria of classification for psychiatry: (1) a limited syndrome can be reliably agreed upon; (2) possible links to etiology, pathophysiology, and underlying processes of normal functioning can be hypothesized; (3) uses of pharmacologic and social treatments depend on proper diagnosis; and (4) diagnosis is linked to prognosis. Michael Rutter (1978) adds that a diagnosis must define a condition sufficiently handicapping to warrant clinical attention; furthermore, either the condition should occur with sufficient frequency to merit separate coding or its public health importance should be great enough that its presence must always be noted. Finally, DSMIII-R requires the presence of distress or impairment; the presence of behavioral, physiological, or biological dysfunction; and a prescribed time period of dysfunction. All these criteria, which are necessary for the classification of psychiatric disorder in individuals, can be applied to disordered relationships.

In their wisdom, the authors of DSMIII-R and the ninth edition of the *Manual of the International Statistical Classification of Diseases* (ICD-9) (U.S. Dept. of Health and Human Services, 1980) included "V" categories of classification. ICD-9 defines V categories as "supplementary factors influencing health status and contact with health services." DSMIII-R refers to them as "conditions that are the focus of attention or treatment that are not attributable to any mental disorder." Some V-code diagnoses, such as "marital problem" or "parent–child" problem may indeed refer to relationship disturbances.

Is there a need for yet another nosology, one that classifies relationship psychopathology? We think so. DSMIII-R diagnoses of infancy are, for the most part, inadequate. They neither recognize the importance of developmental stages nor acknowledge the primacy of regulatory functions in early parent–

127

child relationships. DSMIII-R defines only three mental disorders of infancy: autistic disorder, reactive attachment disorder, and rumination disorder. It is questionable in whom the psychopathology resides in the last two conditions when the child is under the age of three.

Moreover, follow-up studies of behaviorally disturbed, at-risk infants have been few and less satisfactory than follow-up studies of infants with physical abnormalities. Without a reliable and valid system of assessment and classification, it is difficult to conduct follow-up research. We believe a nosology of relationship psychopathology holds promise for clarifying the descriptive features of disorder. Through testing hypotheses about outcome the nosology will contribute to a better understanding of early behavioral development, emerging psychopathology, and the opportunities for early intervention.

It is our belief that in infancy, prior to the establishment of the narrative and self-reflective self (Stern, 1985), behavior disorders that are without known organic etiology should be considered relationship disturbances or disorders. We propose that the DSMIII-R V-code category of parent–child problem be defined more precisely and elevated to the status of a set of legitimate diagnoses. Such diagnoses may then be further subclassified as relationship "disturbances" when they describe risk conditions associated with heightened vulnerability for subsequent disorder and "disorders" when they are disabling.

Assessment of Relationships

The diagnosis of relationship disorders requires a comprehensive evaluation of individuals and their relationships. Three areas of assessment are recommended: (1) the current state of the relationship and its history; (2) each of the partners as individuals, including the caregivers' past histories of significant relationships; and (3) the family's socioeconomic circumstances, current stresses, and social supports. The focus of psychiatric assessment and diagnosis in infancy must shift from the individual infant to the infant in the caregiving dyad.

CURRENT STATE

The assessment of relationships must first consider patterns of regulation and regulatory dysfunction. We designate six such patterns: appropriate regulation, overregulation, underregulation, inappropriate regulation, irregular regulation, and chaotic regulation. In general, the younger the infant, the more likely it is that the regulatory pattern will be imposed by the adult. However, as the relationship matures, both partners become more actively involved in perpetuating the pattern.

The regulatory patterns to be described are not always deviant. Deviant patterns are necessary but not sufficient conditions for relationship disorders. There are circumstances in which any one of the patterns may be appropriate. For example, underregulation of a highly sensitive infant or developmentally inappropriate regulation of an ill child are atypical patterns that can be appropriate to a child's needs (see chapter 7).

An *appropriately regulated* relationship is defined by its dynamic properties rather than a particular set of behaviors. Dynamic descriptions focus on synchrony, reciprocity, engagement, and attunement. When a child is uninvolved, a sensitive parent may appropriately increase levels of interaction. However, when a child is overstimulated or overly sensitive, appropriate regulation by the parent may involve a decrease in interaction.

Confusion may arise as to whether the relationship or the caregiver is the subject of evaluation. We feel that, especially during the first year of life, there is asymmetry of responsibility in directing interactions. The child certainly makes contributions through the quality of its responsivity, but the goals of interaction are regulated by the parent. The parent sets the stage by trying to get the child to feed, to play, or to sleep. In this sense, a judgment of the adequacy and appropriateness of the relationship falls primarily on accounts and observations of the parent's abilities and sensitivities, rather than the child's. On the other hand, we feel that a judgment cannot be made out of context. That is why we insist that all three areas of assessment be taken into account, including what the child and parent as individuals bring to the situation, as well as the supports and stresses that may affect the social context of the relationship.

Relationships also must be assessed from the perspective of their affective tone. The range, modulation, and attunement of shared affects need to be rated. Parents may attempt to increase or reduce happiness or excitement, depending on the situation. The appropriateness of affect regulation should be evaluated. To the extent that one or both partners in the relationship can find no happiness or joy in the interaction, a relationship problem is indicated.

In an *overregulated* relationship, most commonly, orchestration by the caregiver is intrusive and insensitive, and the infant has little opportunity to initiate or direct interactions. Either excessive clinging or active avoidance by the infant can be observed in an overregulated relationship.

An *underregulated* relationship lacks inhibition, and mutual involvement is low. Underregulation can manifest itself as a lack of reaction by the primary caregiver to cues of the infant at younger ages and emotional avoidance, withdrawal, or isolation from the infant at older ages. As in overregulation, the child's initiatives are unanswered, in this case not because the caregiver preempts and directs the child's activity but because the caregiver is inattentive.

Inappropriate regulation is a deviant pattern of regulation that cannot be categorized as too little or too much regulation. Timing of responses may not be synchronous with eliciting signals. Alternatively, infants may be given controls that are inappropriate to their age or developmental stage. Inappropriate regulation leads to negative interactions and dysphoric outcomes.

Irregular regulation refers to patterns of interaction that vary in their degree of control and constancy. The caregiver engages in a number of discernible patterns, but only for short periods of time, and may move from over- to under- or inappropriate regulation. The pattern may be *consistently irregular* if the caregiver consistently responds with one style of interaction in feeding and another in play or bedtime interaction. The pattern may be *inconsistently irregular* if different regulatory controls are noted within the same domain of interaction.

Chaotic regulation is an extreme form of irregular regulation in which regulation during interaction is highly variable and patterns are difficult to discern. As noted above, a judgment about the appropriateness of regulation must depend on a developmental assessment of the dyad.

Although many theorists and clinicians have described stages of infant development (Freud, 1952; Erikson, 1963; Mahler, Pine, & Bergman, 1975), Louis Sander (1962, 1975, 1980) has paid particular attention to the dyadic tasks of development (chapter 4). We find his scheme cogent and therefore recommend it for the assessment of relationships. Sander's seven stages characterize developmental milestones of relationships during the first three years of life. They are: (1) initial regulation, (2) reciprocal exchange, (3) initiative, (4) focalization, (5) self-assertion, (6) recognition, and (7) continuity.

According to Sander, infant and caregiver are required to resolve or "negotiate" dyadic issues at each of these stages. Each of the stages requires progressively higher levels of maturity in the relationship, and each builds upon increasing physical, socio-emotional, and cognitive competencies of the infant and sensitivity on the part of the caregiver. The relationship proceeds toward the infant's achievement of psychological autonomy and a self-reflective sense of self.

Evaluations of relationships in the first three months of life, for example, will focus on the regulation of behaviors surrounding physiologic homeostasis—the effectiveness of the partners in establishing a dyadic pattern of regulation that enhances feeding, sleep, and physical well-being. Between three and six months of age, during the stage of reciprocal exchange, interactions should be assessed in terms of regulating reciprocity. Rigid patterns of interaction not responsive to the infant's signals suggest a stage-specific developmental delay. Between six and nine months of age, the phase of emerging initiative, the relationship should foster a process of negotiation that involves the initiation and termination of social and instrumental interactions. Each partner must become sensitive to the other's cues for such beginnings and endings. Between nine and fifteen months of age, focalization emerges. The infant is able to point and to make specific requests and bids for joint attention. The parent may facilitate, inhibit, or be insensitive in responding. Affect signaling, joint referencing, and the attachment relationship per se all enhance the infant's ability to explore new environments and participate in new social experiences.

Finally, in evaluating the current developmental stage and the patterns of regulation, another dimension must be included. The relationship needs to be assessed in different contexts and domains of interaction. The contexts might include feeding, bedtime, bathing, and times of separation. The domains include physiological regulation, social communication, control and inhibition, teaching and exploration, and comfort and security (chapter 2).

PAST RELATIONSHIP HISTORIES OF CAREGIVERS

A caregiver's own past relationship history is an important part of the assessment. One aspect is the parent's remembered childhood experiences, which are carried forward in patterns of caregiving and influence interactions with the infant. Several current research instruments are noteworthy in this regard. Mary Main and her colleagues have developed the Adult Attachment Interview, which focuses on parents' recollections of their own early primary relationships (Main, Kaplan, & Cassidy, 1985). Scoring of this semistructured interview results in four adult attachment types: dismissing of attachment; secure/autonomous attachment; preoccupied by past attachments; and unresolved attachment. These adult attachment categories significantly predict the four infant attachment types (chapter 8) as observed in the Ainsworth Strange Situation (Main, personal communication).

A necessary first step is to elucidate the nature of past relationship histories as derived from Main's Adult Attachment Interview (Main, Kaplan, & Cas-

131

sidy, 1985). However, the adult attachment types that emerge may be insufficiently precise to account for different attachment classifications in multiple offspring. A parent may recollect a coherent set of childhood experiences that characterizes her or him as a secure/autonomous adult attachment type but may have children with different patterns of attachment.

To assess the nature of the parent's specific relationship to each child, a number of new approaches are being devised. Charles Zeanah and his colleagues (Zeanah, Benoit, & Barton, 1987) have developed a semistructured interview that focuses on parents' subjective experiences of their infants. It assesses parental perceptions, expectations, and feelings about each individual infant. Thus, Zeanah attempts to examine parental working models of infants. Daniel Stern and Nadia Stern-Bruschweiler (personal communication), using similar semistructured reflective interviews, are exploring overlapping domains of family relationship representations. That is, they determine what other areas, beyond the parent–infant attachment relationship, are represented as working models, and how a hierarchy of representations might affect a particular parent–infant relationship. How, for example, do the mother's past relationship with her father and her expected and real relationship with her husband affect her relationship with her infant? All of these issues require operationalization if comprehensive clinical assessments of relationship histories are to be realized.

INDIVIDUAL DEVELOPMENT AND PSYCHOPATHOLOGY

A diagnosis of a relationship disorder supplements a diagnosis of individual psychopathology. Specific physical and psychiatric disorders of individuals need to be noted; for example, postpartum depression, even when transient, influences the parent–infant caregiving relationship. Schizophrenia or substance abuse in a parent may also affect the emerging parent–child relationship, although in different ways at different developmental stages.

Illnesses, handicaps, and unique temperaments in the infant need to be assessed as well. A history of early allergy, chronic illness, premature birth, developmental delay, or other unanticipated handicap violates parental expectations and may lead to heightened vulnerability for disturbed relationship patterns (Green & Solnit, 1964). Distorted interactions that stem from individual parental personality or infant temperament and are long-lasting or recurrent will affect the relationship. We urge that individual diagnostic evaluations of each partner be completed and that diagnoses of individual psychopathology be coded concomitantly with the diagnosis of a relationship syndrome.

CURRENT STRESSES AND SUPPORT

The family's current socioeconomic circumstances and stresses must also be taken into account. Both the strengths and the vulnerabilities of the relationship must be evaluated in the larger context of society and culture (chapter 8). Does the relationship fit in with, or conflict with, the cultural values and socioeconomic realities of the family (chapter 9)? To what extent do social networks support the parent–infant relationship? It is at these levels that a parent's sense of competency and fulfillment with the parenting role can be assessed. Stresses that affect the individual or relationship should be coded.

In summary, only after an assessment of (a) the current level of adaptiveness of the relationship and its developmental history; (b) the individual's history of medical, psychological, and relationship status; and (c) the social context of the current relationship can a relationship syndrome be adequately diagnosed and a treatment plan formulated.

Classification of Relationship Problems

In early infancy, the establishment of mutually satisfying, sensitively responsive, and emotionally comforting regulatory interactions that are predictable over time is the developmental aim of primary caregiving relationships. A prerequisite of our nosology is that a relationship disorder must cause significant disturbances in development and disruptions of overall functioning. We have focused on four criteria of classification that define syndromes of relationship psychopathology: (1) symptoms may be expressed by one individual but reflect the relationship and be expressed in relationship tasks; (2) symptoms are problematic and disruptive to the routines of daily living for one or both partners; (3) interactions are assessed as inflexible or insensitive; and (4) the relationship has stagnated or failed to progress along the expected developmental course. It is again important to stress that individual psychopathology in one or both partners may coexist with a relationship disorder.

The principles that guide our nosology require that assessments be developmentally based and that criteria of classification meet the usual requirements of maladaptive functioning. We are not providing a definitive classification scheme with clear and validated criteria. Instead, we hope to stimulate clinicians who evaluate behavior problems in the first three years of life. We

133

therefore propose a spectrum of relationship dysfunction from perturbations through disturbance to disorder.

RELATIONSHIP DYSFUNCTION

In relationships that are developing appropriately, the occasional transient behavior disruption should be viewed as a relationship *perturbation*. Perturbations represent everyday concerns in a normally developing family. Perturbations are limited in duration and occur as partners in the relationship adjust to new developmental challenges or stresses in their environment. In fact, transient environmental or physical upsets may promote growth (chapter 7).

A seven-month-old infant whose sleep patterns are disrupted for six to eight days during and following the family's vacation is exhibiting a relationship perturbation when his nightwaking begins to exhaust his mother and frustrate her sense of competence as a parent. As the sleep behavior returns to normal, the parent is relieved and professional intervention is not needed.

Relationship *disturbances* are risk conditions. We propose that this classification designate repetitive patterns of inconsistent or insensitive interaction that, if persistent, are likely to lead to individual or relationship psychopathology later in development. The patterns of interaction are more fixed than in perturbations but are not pervasive across domains or contexts of interaction. The duration of a behavioral disturbance is usually more than one month.

The six- to nine-month-old infant who refuses solid foods for several months as her mother attempts to wean her and who thus delays the mother's return to work is exhibiting a relationship disturbance. If the feeding problem persists and extends to other domains of interaction, it becomes a relationship disorder. *Disturbance* implies that the relationship is at risk of leading to a disorder and that intervention is indicated.

Relationship *disorders* are characterized by rigid patterns of interaction. We designate this classification for those patterns associated with failures to achieve the age- and stage-appropriate developmental tasks of one or both partners. A guideline is that the duration of disruption will usually exceed three months. Symptoms pervade several contexts, such as the day care setting and the home, or are evident in a variety of interactional domains, such as play and comfort.

For example, consider an infant girl whose growth is retarded below the third percentile without any discernible organic cause. Interactive social skills are not commensurate with her developmental stage. The domains of physiologic regulation (feeding and sleep), play, control, and comfort are all characterized by regulatory disturbance. Admitted to the hospital, the infant's nutri-

TABLE 6-1
Classification of Relationship Problems

Relationship Perturbation
Transient disruptions in environment including minor physical illnesses
Satisfactory family and social supports
Short duration (usually one month or less)
Relationship Disturbance
Pattern of inappropriate or insensitive regulation in interaction
Interaction patterns not rigidly fixed
Regulatory dysfunction confined to one domain of interaction
Moderate duration (usually one to three months)
Relationship Disorder
Pattern(s) of inappropriate or insensitive regulation in interaction
Interaction patterns are fixed and not easily altered
Developmental milestones of one or both partners disrupted
Regulatory dysfunction is more likely to be pervasive across several interactional contexts and functional domains
Long duration (usually three months or more)

tional state, mood, and interactional capacities in these multiple domains improve.

Another example is a three-year-old boy who is aggressive with peers at nursery school and refuses to follow directions from teachers or parents without physical coercion. His mother is unable to leave him at home with anybody else. Symptoms that extend to settings outside of the primary relationship, such as the day care center, may still be considered part of a relationship disorder if the relationship sustains the psychopathology. Treatment must focus on the relationship since treatment of the child alone is not usually effective.

The boundaries between the classification of perturbation, disturbance, and disorder and their links to specific interventions are unclear. There are as yet insufficient data available to provide criteria for sharp demarcation. Nevertheless, we believe clinicians should routinely evaluate the functional integrity of relationships when assessing behavior disturbances in young infants.

As mentioned earlier, an assessment of the severity and pervasiveness, the developmental stage, and the duration of the condition is essential to diagnosis. For example, excessive clinging in a three-year-old at separation from his primary caregiver can be considered disturbed if the child is able to adapt to the unfamiliar setting and interact with minimal inhibition after the separation. A relationship disorder must be considered if the three-year-old remains inconsolable and dysfunctional throughout the time that the mother is absent. The developmental dimension is important because the same behaviors in a one-year-old might be considered more appropriate.

If the parent's sense of competency as a parent or strivings for independence from the caregiving role are thwarted, the parent may exhibit symptoms of depression or may manifest inappropriateness in the relationship. The developmental status of the relationship may be considered disturbed if the parent can find relief in other relationships, and disordered if the parent's other areas of function are compromised. Neither the child's disorder nor the mother's depression should necessarily be considered an individual disorder. In both examples, the symptoms might just as well stem from the interaction and be alleviated by changing the pattern of interaction.

RELATIONSHIP SYNDROMES

We have attempted to define syndromes for which the psychopathology resides in the relationship and not in the individual. We have chosen syndrome names that highlight the dyadic source of pathology. For example, the term *feeding disorder* highlights the interaction more than *eating disorder*. Our syndrome names are examples of a first attempt to characterize commonly observed patterns of behavioral dysfunction in infancy. We propose that relationship syndromes may present as disorders of feeding, sleep (bedtime), affective exchange (temperamental fit), security-exploration (attachment), control, boundary (self–other differentiation), and gender regulation. Other relationship disorders remain to be defined.

Before six months of age disorders of feeding and sleep (physiologic regulation) are most common. They include overeating, poor eating, regurgitation, and upper and lower gastrointestinal disturbances. In the extreme, a feeding disorder may present as nonorganic failure to thrive (FTT). Sleep or bedtime disorders encompass problems of going to bed and remaining asleep. In older children repetitive nighttime rituals, difficulties in falling asleep, fears of the dark, refusal to sleep alone, and frequent nightwaking are common.

Around the first birthday, security-exploration syndromes may appear. The DSMIII-R diagnosis of attachment disorder suggests serious psychopathology in the infant. This label unfortunately misses the emphasis on disorder in the relationship. The security-exploration syndrome is characterized by excessive clinging and protest around separation and reunion with primary caregivers or, conversely, a resistance to interaction and engagement with active avoidance of contact at reunion with the primary caregiver. Curiosity and exploration are inhibited, especially in strange or stressful situations. Our security-exploration disorder, in contrast to disturbance, is the equivalent of the DSMIII-R attachment disorder.

Control syndromes become evident around one year of age. A feeding disturbance may become a control disturbance when hunger, satiety, and homeostatic regulation become struggles over food preferences and feeding styles. Control syndromes may present as temper tantrums, refusal to cooperate, and aggressive outbursts in response to limit setting or requests for compliance. Physical abuse syndromes (again misnamed as a disorder of individuals) may be extreme examples of relationship disorders.

Boundary syndromes, perhaps the precursors of childhood borderline disorders, are more likely to be seen in toddlers, after two years of age, and are characterized by extreme lability of mood and behavior and manifestations of chaotic or disorganized concepts of self. Both parent and infant are unable to differentiate. Each has expectations of the other that are unrealistic and inappropriate. Regulation of the relationship tends to be global and explosive rather than attuned and focal.

Affective exchange syndromes may occur at any age and are characterized by irritability, apathy, withdrawal, oppositionalism, or negativism. At younger ages physical symptoms, especially prolonged and recurrent periods of fussiness and crying, may indicate a problem of affective attunement. At older ages shyness, withdrawal, or negativism may predominate, and the relationship problem may be related to regulatory difficulties of affective signaling and joint referencing. As described previously, the assessment of interactional sharing in terms of affect intensity, modulation, attunement, and range needs to be carried out.

Gender regulation problems may become evident in the second and third year of life, when play patterns, styles of dress, and peer preferences may begin to conflict with parental or family values.

Relationship Disorder: A Clinical Example

As described above, disorders of relationship pathology are characterized by inappropriateness of relationship regulatory functions and deviation from individual developmental trajectories for one or both of the participants. The final section of this chapter provides a clinical vignette of a relationship disorder.

137

HISTORY AND PRESENTATION

MK, a thirty-two-month-old male infant, was referred by his pediatrician for intractable sleep problems. Referring information indicated that the infant lived with his mother and her female roommate and that three pediatricians over the previous year and a half had been unable to alleviate the problem.

MK was born to a single parent at term, after an uneventful pregnancy. He weighed 7 lbs. 6 oz. His mother claimed that his early development was unremarkable. He nursed until nine months, when he was switched to a cup. He accepted solid foods without difficulty. The mastery of motor milestones was unremarkable. Socially he also seemed to develop appropriately. He smiled socially at his mother by six weeks and began to gesture and babble around six months. Language acquisition proceeded smoothly, so that by two years, MK was using two- and three-word phrases.

Mother described MK as an easy baby until the onset of a sleep disturbance at approximately nine months. The sleep problem began around the time of weaning, which coincided with his mother's return to part-time employment. MK had been accustomed to falling asleep while nursing and being put in his crib asleep. He would protest vigorously if his mother tried to put him in the crib awake. At the time of weaning, his mother tried rocking him while giving him milk in a cup. Even left to cry briefly, he couldn't fall asleep alone.

Exasperated, Ms. K began to lie next to her son on her own bed, or let him stay up with her while she watched TV, until he fell asleep in her lap or on the floor, next to her, around 11:00 P.M. The method of lying by him until he fell asleep was used primarily when she was tired; the method of letting him stay up while she watched TV was used when she wasn't. During the day, MK napped without difficulty each afternoon at the babysitter's house.

Ms. K regularly sought advice from the pediatrician. She refused to place MK on hypnotic medication and finally switched pediatricians when hers felt he could no longer be helpful. Although she was concerned about the bedtime rituals, she was not upset. She felt that her child was expressing his strong will, which she did not wish to curb. His daytime behavior and his development seemed trouble free.

Over the next fifteen months, however, the sleep problem worsened. MK began to awaken in the middle of the night and could not be consoled without a repeat of the bedtime ritual. He would not return to sleep unless his mother lay beside him. Soon the awakenings recurred several times each night, after she herself returned to bed.

Finally, Ms. K slept the night next to her son. The nighttime routine now consisted of letting MK watch TV until 11:00 P.M. or 12:00 midnight and fall asleep on the sofa or floor, next to his mother. They would then go to bed together and sleep through the night. Concern expressed to the second pediatrician met with no suggestions that could alter the pattern. The second pediatrician became frustrated with Ms. K's complaints and his inability to be successful and suggested that Ms. K seek psychiatric counsel. Instead, Ms. K sought out a third pediatrician. Though persistently concerned, Ms. K did not define the disturbance as a problem, and maintained that her son's nighttime behavior was an expression of "strong will."

During the months preceding referral to the parent-infant sleep clinic, the problems worsened. Despite his mother's proximity, MK began waking in the middle of the night, demanding juice or milk. In time, wakeful periods became prolonged and his demands more unrealistic. Sometimes, MK demanded "chocolate ice cream," sometimes "peanut butter crackers" and sometimes, "pancakes," and was inconsolable unless he got his way. Ms. K began to lose sleep herself, and felt that she was becoming less functional at work.

MK had started in a pre-nursery day care program. He protested vigorously when separating from his mother each day. He attended five mornings a week and was cared for by his familiar babysitter or his maternal grandmother during the afternoons. He began protesting when left with these familiar people as well. At the time of his evaluation in the parent-infant sleep clinic, temper tantrums and fits of clinging to his mother were part of any attempt at separation from her.

The mother's primary concern continued to be her own loss of sleep and its impact on her job. She was feeling more and more stressed and worried that she would lose her job. She was certain that the day care setting was adequate, and that once she had separated from MK, he settled down appropriately. In fact, napping in the afternoons with the babysitter or grandmother continued to cause no problem.

The parent-infant clinic evaluation consisted of a complete medical and psychiatric evaluation of MK and his mother in the clinic and in the home. Videosomnography in the home recorded MK and his mother sleeping next to each other. As Ms. K had indicated, the couple went to bed around midnight. MK was already asleep. In the middle of the night, MK awoke several times and asked for something to eat or drink. Other than these awakenings, there were no abnormalities of sleep state organization.

Explorations of the mother's past relationships revealed that she had grown up as the younger of two children. Her older sister had been diagnosed as schizophrenic in adolescence and has been in inpatient psychiatric f for much of her adult life. Ms. K grew up in a family of alcoholics where violence between her parents and the disappearance of her father for prolonged periods was commonplace.

Ms. K described difficult personal times during her adolescence, which included running away from home and experimenting with sexual promiscuity, alcohol, and drugs. Her school attendance and performance were marginal much of the time. Nevertheless, Ms. K finished high school and went on to a teacher's college, completing a degree in education. She attributed her personal success in the face of adversity to her "iron will power," an attribute she said was lacking in her schizophrenic sister.

After completing college, she worked in secondary education for several years. During this time she continued to live with and care for her mother. In an attempt to extricate herself from her home setting, she took a teaching job in a foreign country. There she met a man with whom she fell in love. When she announced to him that she was pregnant, however, he demanded that she obtain an abortion. Again as a "demonstration of her will power," she decided to return home and bear the child as a single parent.

At first she moved in with her mother, who still lived in the house in which she had been raised. After the birth of her son, her mother gave this family home to her and took a nearby apartment. Ms. K found a series of female roommate-companions to assist in the care of the infant and in the maintenance of the home. She returned to a part-time teaching position when MK was nine months old. Infant care was provided by a babysitter and the grandmother. At night Ms. K and her roommate shared in the child's care. Roommates changed several times.

MK's mental state was evaluated over several sessions, both at home and in the office. He was a handsome, well-groomed, cherished preschooler. He appeared his age. At first shy and clinging, he gradually warmed up, explored, and played. In fact, when he warmed up, he frequently interrupted and demanded his mother's attention, becoming "hyperactive" and a "show off" if his mother didn't respond. He would climb on furniture and jump down with a loud clatter when she didn't divert her attention from the interview. In a complementary fashion, his mother did not seem able or willing to set limits. She avoided confrontation and let him run wild in his manipulation of situations.

Alone in the office, he first protested his mother's departure, but settled quickly into play and conversation. He responded readily to limits set by the examiner. He was sociable, sensitive, and somewhat precocious. His range of affect seemed appropriate and his language development normal. He seemed to be a bright and engaging toddler. Although not strikingly unusual, his play themes seemed focused on destruction. He enjoyed zooming cars that crashed, and then calling in emergency rescue vehicles. With dolls, he seemed preoccupied with sleeping figures and bodily injury.

ASSESSMENT OF THE RELATIONSHIP

The parent–child relationship of Ms. K and her son is characterized by inappropriate controls, especially around bedtime interactions and sleep. Similar difficulties are apparent in other interactions, characterized by struggles over the child's autonomy and the mother's independence. The issues of separation and reunion during night and day are largely unresolved. The child's socio-emotional development is more characteristic of a one-year-old, and the mother's inability to foster individuation is arrested at about the same level. Sander's phase of self-assertion has not been successfully negotiated. Ms. K's inability to exercise control and set limits resulted from her view of the importance of her child's "will power" in his emerging autonomy, a reflection of her own childhood issue in the same area. When she was a child, having the attribute of strong will was a virtue that allowed her to survive and avoid disaster.

INDIVIDUAL ASSESSMENTS

The child, MK, has developed normally without any major medical illnesses. Physical and cognitive milestones have been achieved normally. Socio-emotional development is currently impaired around the issue of separation.

The parent, Ms. K, experienced a chaotic childhood in which she felt her only salvation was her strong will power. Her relationship with her mother was characterized by dependency and difficulty in separating. Her father was largely abusive or absent. She has related poorly to men all of her life. The birth of her out-of-wedlock son further isolated her from male companions and independent living and tied her more closely to her own mother. In her capacity to foster autonomy by means of her caregiving relationship with her son, her own past relationship experiences have precluded her from being successful.

ASSESSMENT OF STRESS AND SUPPORT

As a single parent, Ms. K is experiencing difficulties. She is unable to keep up at work because of her disturbed sleep, and her social life is restricted because of her child's demands. She is dependent on her own mother and a female roommate for help in child care and house expenses. She lives in a comfortable home, given to her by her mother, in an area too expensive for her. Her social supports are marginal and her financial situation precarious. Her assets are her personal strength, strong desire to succeed, and genuine concern for her son.

DIAGNOSIS

The relationship disorder is diagnosed as a boundary disorder with inappropriate regulation. In addition the mother is diagnosed with a borderline personality disorder.

FURTHER CONSIDERATIONS

The clearest case of a relationship disorder would be that of a mother who, because of her own relationship history, is unable to regulate a relationship with her child. Similar inappropriate regulation might result from parental distraction due to social stress or the absence of social support. In both cases, the outcome for the child might be the same but the treatment of the disorder would be different. In the first case, intervention would be directed to the parent individually as well as in interaction with the child. In the second case, community support would be more appropriate.

In this case, Ms. K's supports seemed adequate. The problem stemmed from inconsistent and inappropriate regulation. Setting limits requires an appreciation of the delicate balance between control and autonomy. The fragmented and incoherent history of parenting experienced by Ms. K as a child predicted an insecure attachment relationship with her son. Psychotherapy with Ms. K and dyadic therapy with mother and son in which consistent limit setting was stressed produced reduction in the sleep disorder and in the separation protests.

Although there is little doubt that this mother and child manifest a relationship disorder, it is interesting to speculate when the disorder might have been a disturbance and when it might have been a perturbation. Difficulties in going to bed and falling asleep and nighttime waking are common infant problems, beginning during the second half of the first year of life and persisting to age three. These common behaviors may come to the attention of a clinician when the mother–infant relationship becomes strained and the mother is unable to impose limits about bedtime behavior. We would consider this an example of a relationship perturbation. Such perturbations are usually short lasting and self-limited, and they respond rapidly to professional advice directed toward one of the individuals.

MK and his mother exhibited these perturbations by one year of age. By eighteen months of age, after multiple unsuccessful attempts at individual treatment by the pediatrician, we would have considered the dyad as manifesting a relationship disturbance. At this point, the interactions around bedtime and waking during the night were atypical and caused distress. The pediatrician still viewed the problem as individual, however, and told the mother to seek psychiatric treatment. This view precluded appropriate treatment and, in fact, caused further frustration for the mother.

The relationship disturbance became disordered at about thirty months, when MK's nighttime difficulties spilled over to the daytime and manifested themselves primarily in difficulties in separation. At this time, too, Ms. K became concerned that she would no longer be able to function efficiently in her job because of her own disturbed sleep. The developmental agendas of both partners had become derailed and the relationship was characterized by a rigidity of interaction that was inappropriate to each partner's developmental needs.

Summary

The rationale for our new classification is based on two facts. First, the data from early infancy research and family studies demonstrate the importance of primary relationships for personality development and for individual well-being. Second, clinicians in well-baby facilities and infant mental health clinics remain dissatisfied with their ability to assess and diagnose disordered behavior.

Our proposed nosology evaluates and classifies relationship problems as disorders of regulation, from a developmental perspective. Our assessment incorporates the past relationship histories of the partners, the current state of functioning of the individuals, and the contextual circumstances that may impinge upon the relationship. We recommend that several domains of interaction be assessed prior to diagnosing a relationship disorder.

Our scheme is based on the assumption that a relationship diagnosis does not necessarily imply the existence of fixed, individual characteristics. Rather, relationship pathology reflects a dynamic balance between individual, developmental, and social forces. Should this balance change, the nature of the relationship problems can change. To the extent that these factors do not change, relationship disorders and disturbances may become internalized as personality problems in childhood and adolescence. Many clinicians interpret individual psychopathology as the outcome of earlier deficits in a child or in a child's parents. From our perspective, such outcomes are mediated by relationships. The identification and amelioration of relationship problems should prevent regulatory disruptions from leading to later individual disorders.

Chapter 7

The Child's Physical Health and the Development of Relationships

Arthur H. Parmelee

The authors of the previous chapters have emphasized the importance of understanding the normal development of relationships from infancy through childhood in order to identify and comprehend the development of psychopathology early in life. This approach is important for all health care providers who give advice to parents in baby and child care services for both health and parenting problems (Korsch, 1966; Brazelton, 1975; Casey, Sharp, & Loda, 1979; Casey & Whitt, 1980). There are few physical problems in infancy and early childhood that do not disturb family relationships and few caregiver–infant relationship problems that do not precipitate some physical manifestations in infants, however transiently. Health care providers sometimes feel they are not as helpful as they could be and desire more understanding concerning health and illness issues in the development of relationships. Psychiatrists and psychologists who have studied and expanded our understanding of the development of relationships have, however, not placed much emphasis on the ubiquitous biological perturbations in infancy and childhood as part of the usual process of relationship development. It is this aspect of relationship development that I will emphasize in this chapter.

In infancy and early childhood, the perturbations of physical development such as feeding and nutrition problems, colds and other minor diseases, and frequent minor accidental injuries are in fact omnipresent. For example, the frequency of illnesses has been studied for all age groups within the home and family, day care centers and schools, and by national health surveys, and there is general agreement among these studies that children from one to three years of age average seven to nine illnesses per year; from four to ten years of age, from four to six illnesses per year; and thereafter through adult life about four illnesses per year. These illnesses are almost all respiratory illnesses, including the common cold. Typically, they spread to all family members so that a family of two adults and two children averages twenty-one illnesses a year and a family with four children averages thirty-eight illnesses. Within a day care center or school at least one child is likely to be ill on any given day. Thus, these mostly minor illnesses are common events for all children from earliest infancy, both as personal experiences and as observed in others (Valadian, Stuart, & Reed, 1961; Dingle, Badger, & Jordan, 1964; Parmelee & Schimmel, 1958; Loda, Glezen, & Clyde, 1972; Vital Health Statistics, 1980; Denny & Clyde, 1983).

As the previous chapters have demonstrated, it is through infants' relationship interactions with their primary caregivers that they learn to define themselves and others and are motivated to interact with the physical world (see also Sroufe & Fleeson, 1988; Stern, 1985.) From an evolutionary point of view, the initial role of the caregiver, as indicated by John Bowlby (1969), is to provide physical protection and nourishment for the helpless infant for its survival. Through these physically protective and nourishing caregiving experiences infants gradually develop attachment relationships with their caregivers and an early general working model of relationships.

Most presentations of the developmental processes of attachment and later relationships seem to assume, however, that the course of physical development of "healthy" infants is uneventful except for those problems created by normal developmental shifts and the infants' unique temperament or environment. The fact is generally overlooked that there are frequent, naturally occurring perturbations of physical development in "healthy" infants and children, such as episodes of spitting of feedings; loose bowel movements; constipation; varying rates of weight gain and food intake; numerous minor diseases, both respiratory and gastrointestinal; and minor accidental injuries that interact with infants' developmental shifts, temperament, and environment in the process of relationship development.

Since parents come to the task of caregiving with the responsibility of keeping their children alive and healthy, it is not surprising that every disturbance of their infants' nutritional processes and physical growth and every

146

minor disease or injury are seen either as an indictment of their caregiving ability or as evidence that their infants are biologically frail and in danger of not surviving. Without strong confidence in themselves and support from family members, friends, and the health care community, parents can easily develop a sense of defeat and fear for the future well-being of their infants. These feelings of inadequacy and concern can significantly interfere with parents' social interactions with infants and consequently with their infants' development of attachment, conceptualization of self, and social relationships with others (Green & Solnit, 1964; Carey & Sibinga, 1972; Sigal & Gagnon, 1975). On the other hand, with the acceptance of these common disturbances of physical development as a normal part of infant life and with successful management of them, parents can develop confidence in themselves as parents and in the physical vitality of their infants and can successfully foster normal relationship development (Parmelee, 1986).

General Issues

DEFINITIONS OF ILLNESS AND DISEASE

One source of some of the difficulty health care providers have in helping parents cope with their children's physical problems in the context of relationship development is a disparity between health care providers' view of health and disease and that of children and their parents. Health care providers, by training, focus on the biological aspects of health and disease (or wellness and illness). In contrast, children and parents focus more on the personal and social aspects of illness and wellness (or disease and health) and have limited understanding of the biology involved (Apple, 1960; Rashkis, 1965; Campbell, 1975; Natapoff, 1978; Wilkinson, 1988). In this chapter I am emphasizing the social aspects of the impact of physical problems on the development of children's understanding of relationships and of self and others. To help separate children's and parents' personal and social point of view of illness from the biological point of view of health care providers, I have found the following definitions of terms useful (Eisenberg, 1977; Engelhardt, 1981). The term *disease* is best used to designate any category of biological pathology that has similar symptoms and recognizable signs in all persons afflicted; the term *health* is then defined as the absence of any disease. The categorization of biological diseases in terms of similarities across individuals has been very

147

important in the provision of medical care. But parents and children, when they don't feel well, do not generally think in terms of biological diseases. They are concerned with their sensations of distress and mood changes. These may or may not be due to an identified disease. I therefore use the term *illness* to designate the feelings of each individual at these times and *wellness* to designate the absence of such feelings. Thus one may have a disease and not feel ill, or one may feel ill and not have a disease. Illness is not an entity defined or determined by the health care system; it is personally defined by each individual. Since parents and children seek help because of their personal feelings of illness, in this chapter I will use *illness* instead of *disease*, even when the existence of disease has been established (Parmelee, 1986).

Parents identify their children as ill through their observations of their children's distress, state changes, apathy or irritability, reduced vigor, and loss of interest in social interactions and in play, and through the alteration in their relationship interactions. Parents recognize that these behavioral changes may be due to fatigue and emotional stresses such as in separations as well as diseases, and they attempt to sort out the possible causes of illness. When they are in doubt they seek help from health care providers. It is important that the health care providers also recognize that illness behaviors are not necessarily due to a disease and that if a disease is present, it is not necessarily the cause of all of the illness behaviors (Carey & Sibinga, 1972).

RELATIONSHIPS AND CHILDREN'S PHYSICAL PROBLEMS AND ILLNESSES

As stated, infants' and children's personal experiences associated with physical disturbances, illnesses, and injuries are discomfort and changes in state and mood. Of greatest importance to them when they feel this way are, therefore, their experiences with physically and emotionally nourishing caregivers. The events that create mood changes in children also generate feelings of concern in their parents, causing increased expressions of emotion and demonstrations of empathy and prosocial behavior (Freud, 1952; Mattsson & Weisberg, 1970). Illnesses are therefore important for infants' and children's conceptualization of social relationships. During their physical perturbations, they learn a great deal about the affective part of themselves and others and about prosocial behavior. They also learn about their biological self, which is temporarily disturbed and restored. The opportunity is provided to integrate this understanding of their biological self with their affective self in this emotional, caregiving context. Thus, the frequent physical perturbations, illnesses, and injuries in infants' and children's lives can have significant positive consequences for their understanding of social relationships when appropriately managed by their parents (Parmelee, 1986).

Although caregiver–infant interactions not associated with physical problems are the most frequent, they are often not independent of those associated with physical problems. The parents' role as protectors and nourishers of their infants is reemphasized by every physical disturbance the infants have, so that these physical disturbances easily color the parents' attitudes toward all of their daily caregiving interactions. The confidence with which parents and infants learn to negotiate their interactions during physical disturbances influences favorably or unfavorably infants' development of attachment and understanding of self and other, as well as the development of later social relationships.

The parents of infants also bring to relationships their own construct of social relationships derived from their childhood and adult experiences and their expectations of themselves as parents (chapters 2–4). These constructs and feelings become part of the behavioral codes of the new family. The newly negotiated family codes may be supportive of the primary caregiver–infant couple but also may interfere, particularly during episodes of physical disturbances in the infant. The family's experiences related to infants, such as pregnancy or delivery complications—no matter how minor—can also increase the family's apprehension during any subsequent physical disturbances in the infants. The nature of these fears about physical problems and illnesses, and the family's expectations of being able to prevent them from happening, further determine a family's style in these matters (Campbell, 1978; Bass & Cohen, 1982).

Major acute physical problems and illnesses during infancy and early childhood are not uncommon; these, and not the frequent minor diseases, are what we generally refer to and remember as childhood illnesses. Measles, chickenpox, and mumps are commonly thought of as the major primary childhood illnesses, but severe respiratory illnesses are the most common, especially in light of the increased use of vaccines for many contagious illnesses. It is more difficult for parents and their children to maintain confidence in themselves and each other with the more severe illnesses. The parent–child relationship can, however, continue to grow during both the acute and the recovery phases of these illnesses, and how parents and children cope emotionally and cognitively with major acute illnesses is, in part, a function of how successful they have been in dealing with the minor physical disturbances that have previously occurred. To some degree, the younger the children at the time of a major acute illness, the more difficult it is for parents to regain their feelings of confidence in themselves as caregivers or in their children's health, since they have not yet had time to firmly establish such confidence through multiple experiences with many minor disturbances. Severe illnesses early in infancy, therefore, may have more prolonged and distorting effects on relationship development and the children's development of self than those occurring later in childhood.

Chronic illnesses and handicaps identified in infancy or early childhood necessarily alter both the developing relationship interactions between parents and their children and children's development of self. Nevertheless, these alterations do not necessarily produce relationship disorders (Drotar, Crawford, & Bush, 1984; Drotar & Bush, 1985). It is, of course, more difficult for parents to feel competent as caregivers when it is known that their children's condition makes them physically vulnerable, and it is also more difficult for children to develop a strong sense of self under these circumstances. With support from relatives, friends, and the health care community, parents and their chronically ill or handicapped infants and children can succeed in developing secure relationships, and children can develop a strong sense of self. Even in this circumstance, minor illnesses, injuries, or transient physical disturbances play an important role in parent–child relationship development. These more manageable problems superimposed on the continuous background of the more severe problem can help parents gain confidence in themselves as caregivers and in their children's basic biological functioning.

THE "SICK ROLE"

In discussing illness as defined by parents and children, it is also important to describe the concept of the "sick role." When individuals are defined by the family or society as ill, they are accorded a sick role in which they are not expected to carry out their usual daily activities or behave in the usual ways. They are expected to make an effort to get well, so the duration of the assigned sick role is limited (Parsons, 1951). It is important for each of us to learn to accept a sick role and let others take care of us at appropriate times, and to allow others the sick role and to take care of them. Each family has its own version of the sick role. An understanding of the sick role begins in infancy and continues through childhood and adolescence and is a part of the development of relationships (Wilkinson, 1988). The nature of the sick role is learned by children during their own experiences with illnesses and by observing as siblings and parents assume the sick role when ill. In this process children experience empathic nourishing caregiving and see it given to others. This becomes an important part of their adult understanding of illness in self and others.

150

HEALTH CARE

Since it is the physical problems in infants and young children for which parents seek help from health care providers, providers necessarily focus on the parents' concerns about their infants' or children's manifest physical problems. This focus is amplified by any prescribed physical diagnostic evaluations and management programs for the problems. These dynamics, unfortunately, tend to reinforce parents' fears about the physical vulnerability of their children and can enhance their concerns about their own competence to carry out their protective and nourishing functions (Carey & Sibinga, 1972). It is, of course, essential to focus on the children's physical problems for the restoration of health. It is also important to understand relationship dynamics at this time, the potential positive and negative effects on the process of relationship development. Those who advise parents must consciously help them work toward regaining confidence in their competence as caregivers and in their children's physical sturdiness. They should help parents refocus their attention on normal relationship interactions. In addition, when the physical symptoms of the child are more a function of a disturbed parent–child relationship than of any coexisting physical problems, it is important not to convert, in the minds of the parents, what are predominantly relationship disturbances into exclusively physical problems. When this happens, the relationship disturbances can be both exaggerated and prolonged long after the physical problem has resolved. Since such situations are not infrequent, it is imperative that parents and health care providers keep in mind relationship disturbances as potential contributors to any physical problem (Carey & Sibinga, 1972; Brazelton, 1975; Bass & Cohen, 1982).

RELATIONSHIP DISTURBANCES AND DISORDERS

Within the context of illnesses and other physical problems, it is difficult to differentiate among normally developing relationship processes, transient relationship disturbances, and evolving relationship disorders. This task, for example, is not always helped by such discriminators as duration or severity of presenting complaints or symptoms (chapters 5 and 6). The duration of a longstanding disordered relationship may be obscured by the fact that it has suddenly been made evident by an acute illness or physical problem that appears to be the cause. The severity or clinical nature of the presenting physical problem may also not readily differentiate a relationship disorder from a transient relationship disturbance. For example, in a young infant, failure to thrive associated with a nonorganic feeding disorder may be due to a transient relationship disturbance that has followed a mild, brief intestinal illness. Such intestinal illnesses are often sufficiently worrisome to panic mothers into overregulation of the feeding situation after the child has recovered from the acute illness. Such overregulation, with the resulting poor weight gain, can be resolved by providing explanations and support for the mother regarding social interactions during feedings. On the other hand, an infant may appear physically well but have a persisting sleep problem, secondary to a long-term relationship disorder between the infant and the mother that is in turn secondary to the mother's disordered adult relationships, as described in chapter 6 by Thomas Anders.

It is the purpose of this book to help present some of the processes of relationship development in order to provide a better understanding of relationship disturbances and disorders. In health care interactions with families, there are many opportunities to make observations of caregiver–child interactions and of the social interactions of the infants or children with others, and to use these observations to attempt to separate relationship disturbances from disorders. Continuing efforts to define the nature of relationship perturbations, disturbed relationships, and disordered relationships is therefore important. The role of health care providers in supporting parent–child relationships during relationship perturbations and in identifying relationship disorders is aided by the development of strong and continuing relationships between providers and families and their children (Brazelton, 1975). Without such provider–family–child relationships, it is more difficult to identify subtle changes in parent–child relationships and to provide the support necessary to minimize relationship disturbances or to make the early identification of relationship disorders possible. The accepted pattern of frequent well-baby and child care visits does provide opportunities for observations and discussions of parent–infant interaction and infant behavioral development, as well as for observation of particular family styles and codes of behavior. In this context, it is possible to develop sufficient rapport with the families to be able to help them minimize any relationship distorting effects, not only of minor physical perturbations, illnesses, and injuries, but of severe acute and chronic illnesses as well.

Clinical Experiences

MINOR PHYSICAL PROBLEMS AND ILLNESSES

Infants   As already stated, parents focus heavily during the first months of their infants' lives on physical growth as evidence of wellness and good health. They measure their success as caregivers by how well their infants eat and gain weight. Most of their infants' behaviors, good and bad, are likely to be attributed to successes or failures in feeding and digestion (Wessel, Cobb, Jackson, Harris, & Detwiler, 1954; Forsyth, Leventhal, & McCarthy, 1985). An infant who does not sleep well or cries a lot when awake is first thought to be hungry, even when gaining weight well. Concerns about minor variations in bowel movements are a part of this constellation, as are burping, flatus, and leg movements that the parents attribute to intestinal gas. This focus of attention on feeding and physical growth is, of course, legitimate, since survival of their infants is the primary concern of the parents. Well-meaning relatives and friends, as well as health care providers, generally reinforce these preoccupations of the parents with physical growth because they also use physical growth as a measure of health and survival. Parents are questioned by them about the infants' weight, appetite, and bowel functioning. Parents are likely to attend to the development of their infants' social behavior only as long as their infants remain healthy and gain weight. It is difficult to convince mothers of happy, sociable infants that all is going well and that they are successful mothers, if their infants are not gaining at the rate they expected or if they have several minor illnesses in succession. Furthermore, when infants become ill with respiratory infections or gastrointestinal upsets, parents, as well as those from whom they seek advice, often judge the severity of the illness, in part, by whether the infants are losing weight. In addition, most physical perturbations and minor illnesses temporarily disrupt infants' biological sleep, wake, and feeding rhythms, which makes it difficult for parents and infants to time their interactions in their accustomed ways. The perturbation can result in parents' overregulation or underregulation of their infants' biological cycles and can disrupt the infants' developing self-regulation techniques (Sander, 1975; Stern, 1985; chapter 6).

It is not surprising, then, that any factors, social or physical, that interfere with physical growth and biological rhythms during this period of early infancy are a threat to parents' confidence in their caregiving ability and in the physical fortitude of their infants. These feelings in turn interfere with their efforts to establish effective social relationships with their infants. Yet, if properly managed by parents, disruptions can be transient and not of consequence to the ultimate development of normal attachment relationships between mothers and infants. Mothers can regain their confidence in themselves as caregivers and in their infants' physical durability as soon as the infants recover. To cope with what parents presume is due to their failure, they need personal emotional strength as well as support from their relatives, their friends, and those advising them on health care.

An example of a common problem is a mother who is unsuccessful in breastfeeding her infant. There are many socio-environmental causes of unsuccessful breastfeeding, such as the mother's physical fatigue when she tries to resume taking care of the household or when she returns to work, or the mother's inexperience with simple breastfeeding techniques. Mothers tend to attribute their lack of success to some physical inadequacy in their breasts or to their infants' inability to suck well. Mothers' feelings of disappointment in themselves and in their infants after breastfeeding failure can then negatively affect their developing relationships with their infants. With reassurance, however, this problem usually creates only a transient relationship perturbation.

Another example concerns infants who early in life regurgitate some of each feeding, whether from the bottle or breast. This spitting is not uncommon, but it is distressing to parents because the volume of food lost always seems to be much larger than it is. Common maternal responses are to overfeed these infants to make up for the presumed lost food, or to frequently interrupt the feedings to burp the infants, or to drastically limit the quantity of the feedings. These overregulations of the feeding situations often agitate the infants, making the spitting worse and prolonging the feeding relationship disturbance.

The frequent crying in the first few months is another example of a common phenomenon that can disturb parents' confidence. If mothers believe that they should always be able to soothe their infants successfully and relieve all their infants' distress, when they fail to do so they can become convinced that they are unsuccessful caregivers. Mothers can, however, cope with this crying very well when they understand it is part of a normal developmental process related to the increasing sensitivity of the infants to their total environment, internal and external. They come to understand that infants at this stage are easily overstimulated but with maturation become able to suppress crying and enjoy environmental stimulation (Brazelton, 1962; Parmelee, 1977). On the other hand, when parents attribute this crying exclusively to physical disturbances, a normal developmental process can be converted into a physical problem that remains, in the minds of the parents, not only as a sign of failure on their part but also as evidence of a physical defect in their infant (Forsyth, Leventhal, & McCarthy, 1985). Again, in their efforts to correct the presumed physical problem, parents often intrude on the infants' normal biological rhythms, and the overregulation results in even more crying.

These are common examples of early physical perturbations that are frequently seen in healthy infants and that can cause disturbances in the normal process of the development of mother–infant relationships. Such problems, however, can be transient when recognized as relationship perturbations and handled in such a way as to restore mothers' confidence in themselves as caregivers and in their infants' health.

After the first few months, infants have more stable biological rhythms and feeding patterns. They sleep longer at night, cry less when awake, and smile and vocalize more easily socially, especially with their parents. They are also more interested in their physical environment and can amuse themselves for significant periods of time, playing with or looking at objects; they can regulate their own levels of arousal more readily (Gesell & Ilg, 1943; Brazelton, 1969; Emde, Gaensbauer, & Harmon, 1976; Dixon, 1987). For parents, this is a quiescent period when parental caregiving is usually physically easier and more successful and therefore reassuring. It is during this breathing spell in parenting that both mothers and fathers are likely to turn the focus of their attention on themselves and each other. Personal and family goals are reevaluated, any marital stresses are discussed, and mothers return to work or ponder when and whether to return to work. This reorganization of the parents' personal lives helps strengthen their capacity to be attentive to their infants' social efforts and needs. It is also a time when the infants are developing a beginning sense of self and other. Parents find it easier in this period to spend more time and energy focusing on emotional and social interactions with their infants and each other rather than on their infants' physical development (Stern, 1985; Emde, Gaensbauer, & Harmon, 1976; Sander, 1975; chapters 3 and 4).

When feeding, sleeping, crying, and physical growth problems continue beyond the first months into this period, parental and family regrouping can be seriously disrupted or indefinitely deferred. Health care providers can help minimize this disruption by focusing on the parents' needs and encouraging them to think about the family regrouping process. Sometimes family regrouping alone will help the infants' feeding, sleeping, or weight gain problems that have continued into this period. This is because the disturbed parent–infant relationships, secondary to deferred, unresolved family tensions, were the primary reason for the continuation of the physical problem.

Later during the first year, there is a return of infants' awakening in the night. Most infants, children, and adults are likely to have periods of awakening or arousing to near wakefulness during the night, but successfully regulate their arousal so that they return to sleep without difficulty (Anders, 1979). Some infants, however, during this awake but drowsy state in the night, have difficulty in regulating their arousal level and do not readily return to sleep. This is complicated by their dawning awareness and concern about separations from their mothers. They arouse themselves to cry out until they are comforted by their mothers, who then provide sufficient external state regulation to help them return to sleep. It is difficult for parents to believe that these awakenings are not due to hunger, since feedings will quiet the infants, though in fact it may be the parental attention and sucking on the breast or bottle rather than the nutrition that restores sleep. Unfortunately, providing parental external regulation often increases the frequency of the awakening, particularly with infants who have not had much previous experience in self-regulating their levels of arousal either during the day or night. Some infants, for example, are always provided external state regulation during the day or night when they are upset, often by an immediate offering of the breast or a bottle at the least suggestion of fussing, and these infants often have the greatest difficulty with nightwaking. It is important for parents to allow their infants to develop a repertoire of self-regulation of state during daytime activities as well as at night, and to not assume hunger as the primary cause of arousal or fussiness or feeding as the only way to reduce arousal. This can be done with other types of caregiver–infant interactions that strengthen relationships and foster the infants' sense of self and self-regulation (Sander, 1975; Emde, Gaensbauer, & Harmon, 1976; chapter 4).

During this period and on through early childhood minor illnesses such as colds and ear infections become more frequent. Since the average frequency of such illnesses is six to nine times per year during the first years of life, within seasonal peaks there will be periods when children are ill every month or more often. Although parents wish these illnesses would not occur and think they should be able to prevent their occurrence, it is impossible to prevent them entirely. They can learn the most effective ways of incorporating the illnesses into the family organizational patterns and interpersonal interactions so that they and their infants grow in their relationships and understandings of self and other, and in empathy and prosocial behavior (Parmelee, 1986). These illnesses affect infants' newly acquired self-regulation skills. Infants cannot effectively control their states when ill, and they become fussy and sleep poorly. They may also lose their appetite. The parents, therefore, necessarily become involved in providing external regulation of the infants to reduce the fussing, help them sleep, and encourage eating. It is difficult for parents to remain confident that their infants will return to their pre-illness level of self-regulation and desire for food. They risk continuing to provide external regulation long after the infants are ready to resume their own efforts. This is particularly difficult when illnesses follow each other at close intervals. Health care providers can help parents accept these physical illnesses as unavoidable aspects of their lives and use them as positive learning experiences for the entire family, including an understanding of an appropriate sick role.

Toddlers and Preschool Children   By the end of the first year and during the toddler and preschool periods, infants' self-management of daytime activities gains in importance along with their self-regulation of state of arousal. They also play a more direct role in controlling the form of their relationships with parents and other adults. They can express their desires and discontent during interactions more vigorously physically because of mobility and verbally because of their increasing language skills. Thus parents' interactions with their children become both very pleasing and very trying because of their intensity. It is difficult to aid their children in exercising and developing their self-regulation while providing external controls when the children's self-regulation fails. For example, infants have increased ability to feed themselves, first with their fingers and then with a spoon, and their insistence on this independent action in eating can become an issue for parents who fear their children's nutrition will suffer (Gesell & Ilg, 1943; Sander, 1975; Stern, 1985; Brazelton, 1974). This parental fear is enhanced by the fact that at the end of the first year infants have their thickest fat pad and most cherubic appearance but normally become slender in appearance in the toddler period and gain weight less rapidly than in the first year (Stuart & Sobel, 1954).

These issues are further amplified by children's frequent minor illnesses. As previously stated, during the acute phases of these illnesses children lose their appetite, strength, and desire for physical activity; feel distressed; and lose some of their ability for self-regulation. They need and want the parental help for comfort and companionable interaction that they may be physically too weak to seek. As they recover, however, they are eager to return to their own self-regulation and play activities, but are not quite ready to do so without frequent parental comforting (Mattsson & Weisberg, 1970). Parents need to know how to make appropriate allowances in their behavioral and disciplinary expectations for their children during minor illnesses, that is, to allow a "sick role" for an appropriate period of time.

This sounds simple, and it might be if children were only occasionally ill. Minor illnesses, however, can occur so frequently they become disruptive to family activities and work schedules and therefore can become very irritating. Since by this time parents may be more confident that their children can and will recover, they can become annoyed with their children for becoming ill.

157

Young children, however, have no understanding of biology and disease and only know that they feel distressed, have a change in mood state, and are unable to carry on their usual activities. They have no easy way of separating these feelings of illness during a respiratory infection from similar feelings generated by some intense emotional event such as a prolonged separation from mother. We in fact recognize this similarity of feeling when we use the term *homesickness* for the ill feelings we have away from home. Minor illnesses, therefore, play an important role in the development of all children's understanding of relationships, since children define illness in terms of alterations of their capacity to carry on their usual relationships with parents, siblings, and friends (Parmelee, 1986).

MAJOR ACUTE PHYSICAL PROBLEMS AND ILLNESSES

Major acute physical problems and illnesses are episodes that are severe enough to need medical supervision of care either in the home or in a hospital but that end with restoration of wellness and health within a few weeks or months. In children, these events cause greater state changes and more prolonged withdrawal from usual daily activities than the minor physical problems and illnesses previously discussed, and they can result in prolonged relationship disturbances or disorders that create physical and behavioral manifestations (Green & Solnit, 1964; Sigal & Gagnon, 1975; Sigal, Chagoya, Villeneuve, & Mayerovitch, 1973).

Examples of major acute physical problems include accidents with fractures, head injuries or internal organ injuries, accidental drug poisoning, near drowning, acute appendicitis, respiratory tract infections (bronchitis, pneumonia, croup, and so on), meningitis, severe and prolonged diarrhea, and acute contagious diseases. Although most children will not have many such events, few children will escape having one or more during early childhood. These events are the ones most commonly referred to when children or parents are asked about past experiences with physical problems and illnesses. By contrast, the more frequent minor physical problems and illnesses tend to fade into the general background of daily life events, as previously stated. Nevertheless, how infants interact with their parents during major acute events is very much a function of their previous interactions during minor events, as is the family specification of the sick role. Although some children will have major acute events in the first year or two of life, the majority of these occur between two and ten years of age (Valadian, Stuart, & Reed, 1961). Most children, therefore, have some previous understanding of relationship interactions during illness and of the sick role in their family.

158

Major physical problems and illnesses, because of the obvious threat to their children's survival, present a major stress for parents. Under these circumstances, how much confidence parents can maintain in their children's stamina and in their own ability to help their children recover will determine their interactions with their children (Green & Solnit, 1964; Sigal, Chagoya, Villeneuve, & Mayerovitch, 1973; Sigal & Gagnon, 1975). In the best of circumstances, they maintain their normal relationships with a minimum of distortion or disturbance. Parents necessarily focus on their children's survival, which includes not only physical care and nourishment from them but also the mobilization of various health care resource people (with whom they must also establish a confident working relationship). The tasks may require a good portion of their emotional resources and energy, at least at the onset of the physical problem or illness, altering their relationships with each other and with family members. When these major physical problems or illnesses are successfully managed at home, usually under medical supervision, parents are likely to feel a strong sense of accomplishment as nourishing and protective caregivers. It is possible for both children and parents to emerge from such episodes with emotionally strengthened and secure relationships (Shrand, 1965).

Frequently, however, these major problems need to be managed in a hospital where additional stresses to parent–child relationships are presented. The parents are no longer the primary providers of physical care and nurturing. This leaves the parents feeling impotent and without a significant caregiving role for their children in this moment of crisis. The primary role of the parents then becomes that of maintaining their children's secure relationships with them and other family members and sustaining the children's concept of self. When parents can take on this role in the hospital, the disruption and stress of the illness and hospitalization can be minimized and normal relationship development resumed more readily after the children are well. Health care providers can play a major part in guiding the parents into this role in the hospital and should emphasize its importance (Solnit, 1960; Shore, Geiser, & Wolman, 1965; Plank, 1971; Oremland & Oremland, 1973; Azarnoff & Flegal, 1975).

The potential for long-term interference with the development of normal relationship concepts as a result of these major acute events is evident. Parents may focus primarily on physical caregiving long after their children are well because they are not confident that the children are indeed well or that the wellness is durable. This is in conflict with the children's needs, since they now feel well and are ready to resume life and social relationships as they were before the illness. With emotional support, parents can avoid these distortions.

Although the health care provider's role is to treat the major acute physical problem or illness and to restore the children's biological health, a personal feeling of wellness is also an important goal. It is therefore important to focus on parent–child relationships during the event crises and during the recovery period, and to help parents and children cognitively and emotionally benefit from these experiences.

CHRONIC ILLNESSES AND HANDICAPS

Chronic illnesses and handicaps, although not common, do occur more often than many of us might expect. The reported incidence in children ranges from 10 to 20 percent (Haggerty, Roghmann, & Pless, 1975; Gortmaker & Sappenfield, 1984; Hobbs, Perrin, & Ireys, 1985). Chronic illnesses and handicapping conditions extend over many years or for a lifetime and therefore inevitably have a significant impact on relationships. One cannot make the assumption, however, that the parent–child relationships are necessarily disordered or that the children invariably have a distorted understanding of relationships or of themselves and others (Drotar, Crawford, & Bush, 1984; Drotar & Bush, 1985; Adams & Weaver, 1986). Nevertheless, it is undoubtedly more difficult for parents, under these circumstances, to easily develop confidence in themselves as caregivers and in the physical durability of their children (Perrin & Garrity, 1984; Cadman, Boyle, Szatmari, & Offord, 1987). Chronically ill and handicapped children are hospitalized often, so it has been important to develop programs within hospitals to help them and their parents adapt to the hospital as well as their illness. This is often most readily done by nonmedical personnel who help the parents understand their children's and their own feelings in this situation, usually through individual counseling— often in the comfortable setting of a children's playroom—or in a parent group. The children themselves are helped through play activities. Older children may be given school tasks of limited amount and complexity by a hospital teacher to help them keep up with their peers at school; the objective is to help these children maintain a strand of continuity with their daily lives outside of the hospital (Plank, 1971; Oremland & Oremland, 1973; Azarnoff & Flegal, 1975; Brill, Fauvre, Klein, Clark, & Garcia, 1987; Cohen et al., 1987).

Even within the context of chronic conditions, minor physical problems and illnesses, as well as major acute problems, play a role in the development of relationships in the same way as with children without chronic problems. The difference is that the minor and major acute problems are superimposed on the background of the chronic problem. For the children who become accustomed to the steady state of the chronic problem, it is the acute episodes that are most likely to influence their feelings and cognition. The acute minor illness episodes suddenly alter their states and activities and therefore disrupt their usual activities and family relationships. These episodes also provide them with temporary distortions of self, followed by complete restoration to their usual state. It is primarily from these frequent acute minor episodes that they learn about illness and wellness and the family concept of an acceptable sick role. Thus, even within the context of chronic illnesses and handicapping conditions, minor and major acute physical problems and illnesses—depending on how they are managed—can have harmful or beneficial effects on children's emotional and cognitive understanding of relationships, prosocial behavior, empathy, and self and other.

Some disordered relationships in children with chronic illnesses or handicaps may result in part from the intense focus of parents and health care advisers on the chronic problem. The importance of providing confident emotional support to children during the acute phases of the minor problems and sanction to return to usual activities as soon as possible can be forgotten because of the underlying chronic problem. Children with chronic illnesses or handicaps are seldom seen in well-child health care programs for the usual discussions of every child's frequent minor physical problems. Instead, they are seen in a variety of specialty programs where only the chronic problem is likely to be addressed; as long as that is under control, not much attention is given to minor issues, though these may be the most important for the children's relationship and behavioral development. These children are helped most when provided continuity of care by an individual who can coordinate, monitor, and interpret all of the specialists' findings and plans and at the same time address their "ordinary" physical and emotional problems (Palfrey, Levy, & Gilbert, 1980; Stein, Jessop, & Riessman, 1982; McInerny, 1984).

Conclusion

Illnesses and other physical problems, whether minor, major, or chronic, provide opportunities for children to learn important information about themselves and others and about relationships. Physical problems provide an opportunity for children to experience, within a social relationship context, distressing physical changes in self followed by full restoration of their normal physical self, except for chronic illnesses and handicaps. Even within the context of chronic problems, children experience recurring minor and major acute illnesses from which they recover and return to their steady state. They learn about empathy and caring for others in distress, and they are granted a sick role period during which they are not expected to carry out their activities in the usual way. In addition to experiencing frequent acute problems themselves, they observe other members of their family—siblings and parents—go through the same sequence of needing to be cared for, followed by a return to the usual daily routines. In this way, children learn how to provide empathic care for others who are ill and gain some concept of an appropriate sick role.

Providers of both mental and physical health care can help parents understand the constructive aspects of physical problems and illnesses for children's understanding of relationships, self and other, and empathy. The many relationship disturbances associated with children's numerous physical problems and illnesses may be regarded as part of normal relationship development, as indeed they are, but this may not always be helpful. It is often important to go beyond the "everything will be all right" approach and examine in more detail the degree of relationship disturbance and how it is resolving and consider the possibility of an evolving relationship disorder. The development of relationships and of self in all children at all age levels is at some time at least transiently perturbed by some physical problems or illnesses. Therefore, the development of relationships is never one of steady, undisturbed progress. The difficult question is how great or prolonged must a disturbance of relationships be before we consider the relationships disordered, and in what ways does this decision differ at each age level? Providing support and direction to parents can help alleviate perturbations and disturbances and, we hope, prevent the development of relationship disorders. A criterion for assessing the future course of a relationship may not be the degree of relationship disturbance during a particular episode of physical problems or illness, but the duration of the disturbed relationship interactions and the nature of the relationship after the resolution of the disturbance. When there is continuity of care of a particular family through early childhood, there is the opportunity to gather over time the necessary details concerning parental and family strengths and weaknesses and interactions with their children in both troubled and quiescent times. Within this context, it is somewhat easier to make clinical judgments concerning relationship disturbances and disorders. We should always emphasize this important aspect of continuity in health care.

PART III

CONTEXT

Chapter 8

Relationship Disturbances and Development through the Life Cycle

P. Herbert Leiderman

The purposes of this chapter are to extend the concept of relationship disturbance in psychosocial development beyond the infancy period and to explore
the possible consequences of early disturbed relationships in preschool and
school-age children. In addition, I will examine evidence on relationship disturbances emerging during later phases of development, particularly emphasizing peer relationships, which become especially salient during this period. The
major issues to be discussed include the vicissitudes of attachment and affiliative relationships in infancy and childhood, the role of internalized relationship representations for maintaining continuity of behaviors, the role of individual and situational specificity in disturbed relationships, and therapeutic
intervention in relationship disturbances. Finally, I will present two cases of
relationship dysfunction involving an adolescent peer relationship and a married couple in order to exemplify the clinical application of the relationship
disturbance construct to problems seen during the adolescent and adult periods of development.

Psychosocial Development: A Synopsis

INFANCY AND TODDLERHOOD

The primary relationship during the infant's first two years, the mother–infant relationship, has been covered in the previous chapters, which have largely focused on urban families in the United States—although they are applicable to a wide variety of societies because of universal requirements of meeting the infant's survival needs. Mothers provide the necessary instrumental caretaking to ensure the infant's survival, and in most Western societies mothers also provide for the emotional and social development of the child.

In the period beyond infancy, when the child is expected to achieve autonomy and to begin integration into a larger social group, we find considerable variation in relationship development among cultures. Knowledge of the variability found in other cultures is particularly important in assessing the range of normal development in our culture in order to avoid false attributions of pathology to less typical relationship behaviors sometimes seen in Western societies (Fuchs, 1976; Mayer, 1970).

In most societies the child by age two or three years is expected to move beyond the natal family to a world that includes other adults and peers (Krappman & Oswald, 1983). Cognitive development, language, and motor skill development provide the basis for moving to wider horizons of communication and exploration. The child's social task is to begin to understand the nature of reciprocity, sharing, impulse control, status differences, gender identity, and role structures. This process in Westernized urban societies occurs more or less under parental and other adult guidance; in more rural and traditional societies the process involves considerable influence from older siblings and immediately older peers—*near peers,* or individuals two to six years older than the child (Leiderman & Leiderman, 1974; Weisner, 1977). The young child, no longer the central focus of parents' concern, must contend with social forces stemming from same-age companions. The child confronts the challenge of dealing with other individuals more as equals than as persons on whom to be dependent.

The transition from infancy to toddlerhood is a major one; in Western culture continued maternal involvement smoothes the passage by carrying forward the previous mother–child relationship as new peer and adult relationships are added. A disjunction is often seen in more traditional societies, where other members of the family play a very large role in infant socialization and nonfamilial individuals play substantial roles in socialization during toddler-

166

hood and beyond. Polynesian and sub-Saharan African societies provide good examples of this phenomenon.

In the Polynesian society described by Richie and Richie (1979), adults expect that the infant under two years old will need indulgent care to survive and thrive. Mothers are readily available and responsive to the child's physical and psychosocial needs and desires. By the time the child is two, mothers expect him or her to move from the lap or mat to the yard (that is, near the family home). Walking and talking are signs of competence, and the child is then expected to move into the social world. The socialization process is carried out in two worlds, that of the family and that of children—peers and near peers. These two worlds are separate though congruent, especially in community and societal values and in the ultimate expectations for achievement.

The East African agricultural society (Kermoian & Leiderman, 1986) is quite similar to the Polynesian except that the infant's relative autonomy from the family begins sooner, at about the time the child begins to walk but before he or she has achieved verbal competence. In this case, the child's caretaker, usually an older sibling or mother's younger sister, is the key figure for socialization, especially for social play but also for some aspects of instrumental care, with the exception of breastfeeding. The infant in this situation has direct experience in the caretaking relationship with a nonmaternal figure at a very young age, and in addition begins peer socialization with an older, larger, stronger, and more competent member of his or her peer group.

CHILDHOOD

The next major transition for children in most Western cultures is school attendance; in more traditional cultures it is entrance into subordinate roles anticipatory of later adult activities. The social goal for the child at this point of development involves extension of earlier relationships to include non-familial adults and children. In modern societies, interaction with nonfamilial adults typically involves a teaching or learning relationship, such as found in the classroom, but also can include "play," exemplified by participation in sports and musical and artistic activities (Bruner, Jolly, & Sylva, 1976). Such shared experiences serve as the basis for the expansion of intimate relationships and provide the opportunity for the development of empathy with other individuals. Nonfamilial adults are important figures for the child because they serve as readily idealized, nonconflictual role models, providing a contrast to the sometimes conflictual role models of parents.

The major social growth at this age also involves the flowering of peer and near peer relationships (Hartup, 1983, 1986). Middle childhood near peer relationships, although reflective of earlier peer relationships, provide even greater opportunities for the sharing of interests and mutual skills. Feelings of solidarity with others are enhanced and a sense of intimacy with members of a social group develops. Dyadic relationships with same-sex individuals is a hallmark of this period. Gender identification is solidified, and highly structured same-sex social relationships become an almost universal norm (Thorne, 1986). Older children frequently serve as the crucial role models for the learning of day-to-day social behaviors. In traditional societies this can include the development of age-graded cohort solidarity—especially following initiation rites—which can continue throughout the remainder of the life cycle (Spencer, 1970; Mayer & Mayer, 1970).

ADOLESCENCE

The transition into adolescence and young adulthood involves major changes in physical appearance and in psychosocial orientation toward the opposite sex. The relationship skills developed in the previous phases continue, now well internalized, though undoubtedly transformed in the course of shifts in cognitive thinking attendant on puberty. Most characteristic of adolescence is the heightened emotional intensity of relationships, seemingly shifting from moment to moment. Mutuality is a desired norm, with merging of interests, skills, and personal styles between members of a pair. Yet dyadic relationships are not the sole concern of the adolescent. Transcending the dyad are new loyalties to social groups, typically based on school, community, ethnic, or religious considerations. Though peer and near peer relationships are most important to the adolescent, parental models retain their prominence, vying for a place in the internalized amalgam of relationships being constructed by adolescents as they proceed through this phase of development. However, there is wide variation in normal adolescent development, from the relative autonomy of teenagers sometimes found in U.S. communities to highly structured peer-centered groups in some parts of sub-Saharan Africa (LaFontaine, 1970), which suggests that universal norms of adolescent development are unlikely to be found.

Relationship Types, Functions, and Pathology
in the Life Cycle

In developing a concept of early relationship disturbance, we have focused in previous chapters on the caregiving relationships and their functions in infancy. What types of relationships would we expect to find in the period beyond infancy (Weiss, 1986)? I propose, in addition to the caregiving/care receiving initial relationship, three types of dyadic relationships that might characterize human relationships beyond infancy through to the period of young adulthood. These are peer affiliation, mentoring, and romantic/marital, covering the period from toddlerhood to school age, adolescence, and young adulthood. Each of these types of relationships involves different social roles, relationship processes, and functions. Though each of these types characteristically arises at different points in the life cycle, the functions associated with each type continue through the life cycle with varying degrees of saliency for each developmental period.

Functions characteristic of these four types of relationships are listed in table 8-1. They include protection/survival, responsibility/security, physiological need regulation, psychosocial need regulation, teaching/learning, play, and empathic intimacy (see also chapter 2; other schemes have been offered by Hinde, 1979; Gottman, 1979; and Kelley et al., 1983). Each of these functions describes an important aspect of a relationship, but not all functions are evident in all types of relationships. The appearance and importance of a relationship function depend upon the stage of development and on the situational (ecological) and cultural constraints impinging upon the relationship (Skolnick, 1986).

CAREGIVING/CARE RECEIVING

In the case of the mother–infant dyadic relationship, all relationship functions are evident, at least in Western societies. The protection provided by the mother ensures the survival of the infant. The mother is alert for dangers to the child; she anticipates or responds to them; and she solicits whatever social supports are available to achieve her goal of infant survival. Such maternal behavior also has the effect of meeting the physiological and psychosocial needs of both members of the pair, which are exemplified in the feeding situation. For example, maternal breastfeeding provides nourishment and emotional warmth for the infant, emotional gratification for the mother, and physical relief for the mother's breasts as the infant sucks. The physical process

TABLE 8-1
Relationships in the Life Cycle

Chronological Age	*Type*	*Roles*	*Process*	*Functions*
Infancy to adolescence	Caregiving/care receiving	Parent/child	Complementary	Protection/ survival Physiological need regulation Responsivity/ security (attachment) Psychosocial need regulation Teaching/ learning Play Empathic intimacy
Preschool to adulthood	Peer affiliation	Peer/peer	Reciprocal	Play Psychosocial need regulation Empathic intimacy
School age to adulthood	Mentoring	Near peer/peer	Complementary Reciprocal	Teaching/ learning Play Empathic intimacy
Adolescence to adulthood	Romantic/mari- tal	Adult peer/ adult	Complementary Reciprocal	Physiological need regulation Psychosocial need regulation Responsivity/ security (attachment) Empathic intimacy Play

of feeding helps to establish and maintain the social bond between the two, though other psychosocial processes such as communication between the pair also are likely to ensure the regulation of psychological needs.

The responsivity of the mother to the infant's physical and psychological needs forms the basis for the infant's attachment relationship, which emerges between nine and eighteen months. A secure attachment relationship is one index of maternal responsivity to her infant. Inconsistent responsivity or nonresponsivity by mothers in the infancy phase may bring about anxious attachment relationships in infants. Anxious attachment relationships are considered a risk factor for later problem behavior in our society, although in other cultural contexts similar behavior may have other meanings.

As the infant becomes older, teaching/learning comes to the fore as an important function of the mother–infant relationship. The goal is to provide the infant and young child with skills designed to encourage autonomous survival and later incorporation into the social community. This teaching/learning relationship is rarely formal, more often occurring as part of adult–child play relationships. Play for the infant and young child provides an opportunity for the rehearsal of later social roles. More important, play provides a relationship of nonpurposive joyful interaction, enabling the appreciation of "the other"—an important step along the way to the development of empathic intimacy.

In urban industrialized Western cultures the assignment exclusively to the mother of the early caregiving relationship, which involves all of the relationship functions, makes motherhood one of the most demanding of all social roles. In more traditional agrarian, nomadic, and hunting-gathering societies, teaching and play may be functions provided by individuals other than the mother. This is certainly the case for sub-Saharan African agricultural societies, where play and teaching frequently are provided by older siblings and peers rather than mother (Kermoian & Leiderman, 1986).

The relationship process during the caregiving/care receiving phase is primarily complementary, involving two individuals in differing roles with different relationship behaviors required. In this phase the mother is clearly ascendant, frequently initiating actions to which the infant responds. As the infant gets older, the asymmetry of the relationship shifts somewhat, so that both the mother and infant are involved in initiating actions designed to ensure continued caretaking and ultimate survival of the infant.

Pathological relationship processes, although occasionally attributable to individual pathology, more frequently reflect deficiencies in the relationship not attributable to either partner (chapters 2 and 6). Regardless of source, the relationship disturbance involves regulatory functions. The young infant has physiological needs to be met for biological equilibrium. Mother must be responsive to the infant's needs so that regulation of biological functions is achieved. Disturbance in regulation involving overregulation, underregulation, or asynchronous regulation can lead to pathological relationship disturbance (chapter 2). The best example in the psychosocial realm can be seen in underresponsive mothers, whose infants frequently develop anxiously attached relationships to their mother (chapter 5). The infant, uncertain of mother's presence or absence, becomes apprehensive about the unknown, restricting his or her exploration and thereby inhibiting the development of future relationships. The specifics of how a pathological syndrome may develop out of other types of faulty relationship regulation await further explication in long-term research endeavors.

PEER AFFILIATION

Characteristic of the toddler, preschool, and school-age period are relationships among peers and near peers, though the security derived from the positive attachment relationship continues to influence other relationships in the toddler phase. Social interaction frequently occurs between individuals relatively equal in age, size, experience, social skills, and psychological needs. Dependency ceases to be a major ingredient of relationships, especially for peer relationships, though it persists for adult relationships. The fundamental interactive process is a reciprocal relationship between equals, supplementing the complementary relationship between unequals found in the infant–mother relationship. James Youniss (1980) has elaborated the comparison of parent and peer influences.

Play, teaching/learning, and psychological need regulation become the major focus of relationship activity. Empathic intimacy begins to manifest itself and is a most important developmental achievement en route to mature sexual and social relationships. Chum relationships become a hallmark of the last part of this age period, generally involving individuals of the same gender. Gender segregation of play groups (Thorne, 1986), almost a universal experience in this phase, provide homogeneous relationships in which intensive peer-engendered socialization can occur. The small groups mark the transition from infant dyadic relationships to toddlerhood and involvement with the more complex relationships of small groups (Lewis & Rosenblum, 1975).

The relationship pathology of the peer-affiliation phase takes the form of absent or inadequate sharing, absence of reciprocal turn taking, excessive dominant or submissive behavior—for example, bullying and scapegoating (Olweus, 1980)—and deficient skills for working in cooperative endeavors. Individuals who are deficient in relationship skills avoid group enterprise and are less likely to be sought after as partners in dyadic relationships, except for those meeting pathological needs.

MENTORING

A variant of the peer-affiliation relationship that deserves mention since it becomes most apparent in the school-age and adolescent period is mentoring. *Mentoring* describes the child's relationship with an immediately older peer or perhaps an older sibling. (The sibling relationship in many ways is prototypic of near peer relationships [Popler, Abromovitch, & Croter, 1981; Dunn & Kendrick, 1982; Dunn & Munn, 1986].) Near peer relationships typically involve children two to six years older than the child, who are immediately ahead in psychosocial development. Most characteristic of the mentoring phase is the use of observational learning that leads to incorporation of skills, attitudes, and values, in the process of identification with a highly valued member of the social group. Teaching and learning frequently occur in informal participation in team sports, shared tasks, and social activities. Empathic intimacy continues to develop, sometimes taking the form of a crush on the mentor. Children's fantasies are prominent, an important ingredient in the rehearsal for the romantic/marital phase of development.

The mentoring phase has been infrequently studied (Cicirelli, 1973; Hartup, 1983) in the child development literature, though it occasions much discussion in the popular literature, especially as part of adolescent and young adult socialization. Many of the nonparental relationships of later life utilize the mentoring processes so prominent in the school-age and adolescence periods (Levinson, Darrow, Klein, Levinson, & McKee, 1978).

The basic processes of mentoring are both reciprocal and complementary, as might be expected for relationships that include something of both parent and peer. Because mentoring relationships contain elements of both parental and peer functions, deficiencies in this type of relationship are less likely to be pathological, since appropriate models of relationship functions can be derived from peers or parents. (One exception might be the socialization of sexual behavior, where mentoring plays such a critical role in appropriate socialization.) Mentoring in the life cycle has as its major purpose the smoothing of the path to relationships paramount in the next phase of development.

173

ROMANTIC/MARITAL

The romantic/marital phase, characteristic of adolescence and young adulthood (see Gottman, 1979), reflects the biopsychological intensification of early dyadic relationships, taking elements from caregiving/care receiving, peer affiliation, and mentoring phases. Physiological and psychological need regulation is typified by the shared sexual and social partnership characteristic of this phase. Responsivity/security, play, and empathic intimacy also are prominent functions of this phase, especially in regard to procreative activities. The roles of the partners are egalitarian, at least in the initial phase of the relationship. The basic processes are both complementary and reciprocal. Cultural norms play a large part in determining the balance of reciprocity and complementarity in sex-typed behaviors, and there is considerable variation within and among cultures.

Relationship pathologies of this phase generally involve a lack of fulfillment of expectations by each of the partners, coinciding with poor communication between the pair. The unrealistic expectations frequently are derived from the family of origin and are superimposed inappropriately in the new relationship.

Genesis and Consequences of Relationship Pathology

The infant–mother attachment relationship is one of the most widely studied dyadic relationships (Parkes & Stevenson-Hinde, 1982). Empirically, the infant to mother attachment relationship is determined in a standard laboratory setting, developed by Mary Ainsworth and her colleagues (1978) and based upon ideas of John Bowlby (1969); the infant's reaction to the presence and absence of mother and to the separation and reunion with mother are evaluated. On the basis of explicit criteria (Main, Kaplan, & Cassidy, 1985), infants can be categorized as having an anxious/avoidant attachment relationship (A babies), an anxious/resistant attachment relationship (C babies), a secure attachment relationship (B babies), and what is sometimes described as having a disorganized/disoriented relationship (D babies).

In studies replicated widely in the United States and in several Western and non-Western cultures (Bretherton & Waters, 1985), the laboratory procedure appears to produce similar distributions in the categories of infant to mother attachment relationships. In a typical U.S. study, about 65 percent of the infant–mother relationships are categorized as secure, about 20 percent avoidant, 10 percent resistant, and perhaps 5 percent disorganized/disoriented. In other societies, the percentages vary. Most different are the proportions reported in a North German sample (Grossman, Grossman, Spangler, Suess, & Unzer, 1985), where fewer B infants and more A infants were found. In an Israeli sample (Sagi et al., 1985), there were a greater than expected number of C infants, and in a Japanese sample (Miyake, Chen, & Campos, 1985) a greater percentage of C infants and no A infants.

If an infant shows anxious, avoidant, or resistant infant–mother attachment relationships at age twelve months, what are the implications for the child's later social relationships? Two separate issues are raised by this question: one concerns the continuity of the infant's relationship with the caretaker over time, and the second concerns the generalization of this early relationship to other figures, such as other adults and peers.

In regard to the first issue, Alan Sroufe and Everett Waters (1977) have shown there is continuity of the infant attachment relationship from twelve months to eighteen months, though the behaviors exhibited by the child change considerably. Because the attachment relationship becomes difficult to measure at later ages, the data on consistency at later ages are not clear. Alternative approaches to measuring attachment by means of Q-sort techniques (Waters & Deane, 1985) and interview techniques (Main, Kaplan, & Cassidy, 1985) have produced evidence that seems to support the notion of continuity of attachment to the same figure over the early course of development where the family situation has been stable.

In regard to the second issue, generalization, Alan Sroufe and June Fleeson (1986) and Ross Thompson and Michael Lamb (1986) have reviewed the argument for the primacy of the infant–mother attachment relationship as paradigmatic for later social relationships of the child. That the infant–mother attachment relationship generalizes to other relationships, such as peer relationships, at four years of age has received considerable empirical support: several studies (Sroufe, 1983; Erickson, Sroufe, & Egeland, 1985) have shown that children who have a secure relationship with their mothers at twelve months show greater likelihood for exploratory behavior and more adequate peer relationships at forty-eight months as judged in experimental nurseries. This finding has been corroborated by several other groups of researchers for both lower-class and middle-class children and for both disturbed and normal children (Egeland & Sroufe, 1981; Waters, Vaughn, & Egeland, 1980; Vaughn, Deane, & Waters, 1985). The major contrary finding was reported by John Bates and his colleagues (1985) for a middle-class sample in Indiana. However, even in this study there was evidence that mother's inadequate responsivity contributed to insecure attachments at twelve months, as had been reported by Ainsworth, Mary Main, and others.

PRESCHOOL, SCHOOL AGE, AND ADOLESCENCE

Studies directed specifically to the continuities of relationship development from the preschool and school-age periods through to adolescence are relatively rare. In contrast, studies of normal personality and behavioral development have received considerable attention (Bloom, 1964; Robins, 1966, 1978; Rutter, 1970, 1980; Dunn, 1980; Olweus, Block, & Radke-Yarrow, 1986). In general, correlations for personality measures between the preschool period and adolescence are fairly low, and those from the school-age to adolescent periods reach moderate to high levels. Measures of behavioral pathology (for example, destructive acts, rages, and tantrums) yield somewhat higher correlations—presumably because they are more objective and easier to evaluate.

Since studies of normal personality development and of behavior pathology do not necessarily provide much information about relationship development or relationship pathology, it is necessary to turn to studies of conduct disorders to gain more information on pathological relationships (Roff, Sells, & Golden, 1972; Patterson & Strodthamer-Loeber, 1984; Patterson, 1986b). Phillip Graham and Michael Rutter (1973), in their study on the Isle of Wight, found that 75 percent of the children diagnosed at age ten with a conduct disorder persisted with the conduct disorder at age fourteen. David Farrington (1978) reported similar findings on the continuity of aggression: 59 percent of those found most aggressive at ages eight to ten were to be aggressive at ages twelve to fourteen, decreasing to 40 percent by ages sixteen to eighteen.

Lee Robins (1978), in a longitudinal study of adult antisocial behavior, concluded that: (1) most antisocial children do not become antisocial adults; (2) most adult antisocial behavior was preceded by similar behavior in childhood; (3) the severity and variety of antisocial behavior were better predictors of adult functioning than were any other types of childhood behavior; and (4) antisocial behavior was better predicted by childhood behavior than by family background and social class.

In a study more relevant to behavior, West and Farrington (1973), in a study of London males, found that delinquency in adults was associated in childhood with aggressiveness, irregular work habits, pursuit of immediate pleasure, and lack of conventional social restraints. Schachar, Rutter, & Smith (1981) attempted to disentangle overactivity from unsociability in their study of conduct-disordered youth. In a reanalysis of the Isle of Wight data, they reported the persistence of situationally overactive (occurring in specific situa-

176

tions) and pervasively overactive (occurring in many situations) behaviors in children from ages ten to fourteen years. Unsociability (frequency of fighting with other children, being not much liked by others, and solitary behavior) also persisted over this same age range though not as strongly as overactivity. These observations provide some evidence for the persistence of relationship pathology from childhood to early adolescence.

Studies of the onset of relationship pathology in childhood and adolescence are not common (Hinde & Stevenson-Hinde, 1986). However, if we use the onset of psychiatric disorders as a proxy for relationship disorders, there is some suggestive evidence that psychiatric disorders can arise anew in these later periods, though they are associated more typically with childhood pathology (see Rutter, 1980, p. 71). Children's psychiatric disorders are frequently associated with family discord and disruption; in contrast, psychiatric disorders arising in adolescence are less strongly associated with contemporary family factors. This finding could be explained by sleeper effects from infancy or early childhood, or might be due to some developing biological process, or might indicate extrafamilial sources of pathology arising out of relationships in the adolescent period. Thus, no conclusions can be drawn about the role of relationship pathology in the development of adolescent psychopathology.

Glen Elder's work (1974) indicates some of the ecological and developmental complexities in studying continuities of behavior and pathology. In a series of longitudinal studies on the effects of the economic depression (1929–1932) during childhood and adolescence on later adult behavior, he reported that many individuals who showed low self-esteem, indecision, and withdrawal from adversity during adolescence later became effective adults. However, economic hardships experienced during childhood and adolescence had their most deleterious effects on young children. The adolescents seemed to use this experience as a way of developing better coping strategies. On the other hand, the effect of ecological factors was demonstrated by the fact that the psychological ill effects of the depression were more evident in the middle-class children than in the lower-class children, presumably because the middle-class children suffered a greater loss in status.

It appears that there are substantial continuities from childhood and adolescence to adulthood for normal behavior, personality, and conduct disorder. Continuity of relationship behavior also seems likely in light of collateral evidence for continuities of emotional expression and psychopathology. There also is evidence that psychological disorder and psychopathology can arise in adolescence and in young adulthood seemingly independent of earlier pathology. The difficulties in studying continuity and discontinuity in relationship development and pathology are considerable. The evidence collected so far suggests that the effort in elucidating these fundamental developmental processes is warranted.

Mechanisms and Processes in Relationship Development

The question of whether continuities and discontinuities in behavior exist is by no means settled (Emde & Harmon, 1984). Given the relatively strong evidence for the continuity of relationship pathology from the early phases in the life cycle through to young adulthood, it is interesting to speculate upon possible mechanisms to account for continuity. The explanation favored by the authors of this book is that the infant or young child has internalized aspects of the mother–infant relationship. This internalized relationship representation—akin to Bowlby's (1969) concept of a working model—is used by the young child to explore and to facilitate his or her exposure to peers, siblings, and others.

Relationship representations are the internalized relationships derived from experience that become part of the cognitive schemata of the individual. They reflect the enduring aspect of the cognitive structure that is called forth under appropriate contextual conditions. The relationship representation is thus a historical residue of a series of prior relationships. It is not merely the relationships reflected in any single interaction, since the behavior in this circumstance is an amalgam of the contemporaneous setting and the historically derived relationship representations.

This postulation of internalized relationship representations appears to account for the facts of continuity. However, it is obvious that the young child has more than one internalized relationship representation. What happens to continuity and generalization if the infant's attachment relationship to mother is not consistent with the infant's attachment relationship to father? Which attachment relationship becomes preeminent in the future relationships? It has been demonstrated in several studies (Main & Weston, 1981; Kotelchuck, Zelazo, Kagan, & Spelke, 1975), at least for two-parent families in the United States, that there is no necessary concordance between an infant's attachment to one parent and his or her attachment to the other parent (for instance, the infant at twelve months might demonstrate a secure attachment relationship to mother and an insecure attachment relationship to father). If other people live in the household, an even more complex picture of secure, avoidant, and resistant relationships, reflecting the variability of each dyadic relationship within the family, might be observed. All of these relationships would presumably have an influence on the child's internalized representation of relationships.

This mixed picture may permit us to understand some of the discrepancies observed in studies of generalization where the relationship to mother may be insecure and yet the relationships to peers quite adequate. In this instance an insecure relationship in infancy does not inevitably lead to inadequate peer relationships. This observation might be accounted for by secure attachment relationships to secondary figures; and these relationships, rather than maternal relationships, may serve as a template for the child's peer relationships later on. It may well be that any secure attachment relationship in infancy is sufficient for the subsequent development of adequate peer relationships. Thus the insecure attachment relationship to mother may be less important for the infant when other secure relationships coexist with it.

It is likely that early attachment relationships are not of equal importance for the infant. A hierarchy of internalized attachment relationship representations might exist, with mothers primary, fathers next, and other figures such as siblings and grandparents following in order. Although any one of these figures might serve as the basis for ensuring later interactive success for the child, those derived from maternal relationships probably have a special prominence. A reasonable conclusion would be that internalized secure attachment relationships fostered by a responsive mother may be sufficient to ensure optimal social relationships later on, but that they are not necessary, since other figures can apparently serve the same function. This conclusion suggests that later social dysfunction might occur only if most or all early relationships are insecure.

CONTEXT CONTINUITY

The stability of attachment relationships and generalizability to other figures over several months to a few years has been demonstrated (Waters, 1978). The question arises, is this stability due mainly to internalized relationship representations, or is it in part due to stability of context? This is a particularly important issue for studies of generalizations from maternal attachment relationships to later peer relationships, where the research with peers is conducted in the presence of a motherlike figure, recapitulating the secure setting of earlier good maternal relationships. The critical test of context will come when the positive internalized relationship representations are shown to manifest themselves in situations quite unlike those that gave rise to the representations originally. Studies across situations, gender, and age of individuals are essential to test the role of context in maintaining continuity of relationships. An approach to this issue can be seen in studies of relationships across generations (see Frommer & O'Shea, 1973; Uddenberg, 1974; Ricks, 1985), which seem to have demonstrated continuity across contexts.

AUTONOMY

What is the basis for assuming that the relationship representations derived from earlier phases in the life cycle are independent of one another? First, peer relationships are egalitarian, reciprocal, and symmetric, whereas adult relationships are more hierarchical and asymmetric. The power relationships are more nearly equal in peer relationships, whereas for parent–child relationships they clearly flow from adult to child. The goals of the relationships differ in that there is a sense of mutual sharing in peer relationships and differential sharing in the parent–child relationship.

Further, these two relationships achieve saliency at different points in the course of the child's early development. For the attachment relationship, the intense affect occurs before the child is a year old, at the time when cognitive structures are crystallizing, especially self–other differentiation. Thus, the affective component of this relationship for a relatively helpless infant is extremely strong. In contrast, the affect associated with peer relationships occurs in the second year, when motor and linguistic competence have achieved considerable development and at a point when the infant has greater control over relationships than is possible in attachment relationships. The affective component is likely to be less intense because cognitive structures for the infant are sufficiently robust to provide a sense of mastery in a novel relationship. The absence of control and mastery in peer relationships—like the absence of control over an unresponsive mother—can lead to dysfunction. However, this circumstance is less likely because peer relationships are more egalitarian and reciprocal. Although control and mastery in peer relationships may be influenced by the control and mastery issues in maternal relationships, they certainly are not always. Differences in how mastery and control influence the affective qualities of relationships may account for some of the differences observed between parental and peer relationships.

Second, there is considerable clinical evidence that disordered parent–child relationships are not isomorphic with disordered peer relationships, though disordered parent–child relationships are frequently associated with disordered peer relationships (see Hartup, 1986; Sroufe, Fox, & Pancake, 1983; Patterson, 1986b). Dan Olweus (1980) in his study of bullying and scapegoat behavior has described cases in which adequate parent–child relationships are as-

180

sociated with poor peer relationships. In contrast, there are numerous examples of antisocial conduct-disordered adolescents with adequate peer relationships but grossly inadequate relationships with authority figures. There is sufficient evidence to advance the notion that disordered peer relationships arise out of pathological experiences with peers, either through the absence of adequate experiences or through the presence of distorting experiences in the preschool and childhood period. They are not necessarily derived from internalized inadequate maternal or paternal relationship representations.

Despite the apparent autonomy of relationship representations, they likely undergo modification in the course of development. The infant's early mother–infant relationship representations are modified by new inputs from this relationship as the infant grows and develops and makes additional demands on the mother; similarly, as the mother develops in her parenting relationship in response to the child, her representations of the relationship change. Thus the relationship representation is not a static element within the repertoire of the child, or for that matter within the mother; it shifts over time. Further modification of these relationship representations likely occurs as other assimilated representations, such as fathers and siblings, are incorporated in the cognitive structure of the child. The modification of these multiple relationship representations over time as they influence one another is certainly an area demanding additional research. The nature of, and the basis for, these internalized transformations is not clear, but probably includes as a major determinant the continued physical growth and development of the child.

Relationship Pathology

DEFINITION

When does a relationship between two individuals become sufficiently deviant to be deemed pathological? Obviously a relationship is pathological when it does not provide for satisfaction and achievement of relationship functions. Such a relationship disturbance is characterized by rigidity, distress, and developmental inappropriateness. We have suggested (as does Sroufe in chapter 5) that relationship disturbance is present not merely when the goals and expectations of one or the other partner are not being met, but when there is disturbance in the regulatory components of the relationship. In this formulation, a relationship disturbance exists when the relationship is over- or underregulated, or when there is asynchrony of behavior in the fulfillment of the relationship functions. This formulation of disturbance is best seen in the mother–infant relationship but is probably a heuristically useful principle to apply to other relationships in the life cycle, especially when the context of the relationship is taken into account.

ASSESSMENT

At later stages in the life cycle the assessment of relationship pathology becomes a major problem. Assessment is relatively straightforward for the infancy period, since observational methods can be used to determine the variation of normal dyadic relationships and more extreme abnormal deviations. The attachment paradigm of Ainsworth provides an excellent example of the benefit of a behavioral approach to the assessment of pathological mother–infant relationships.

When we consider relationship representations beyond infancy, the focus cannot be solely on the manifest behavior expressed in the dyadic relationship, because this behavior might reflect an individual's relationship representations and not the pathological relationship expressed in the current interaction. This issue becomes a problem in older children when both partners have internalized relationship representations, a situation not likely to occur in early infancy when it is probable only the mother is expressing her representations.

In older individuals we detect relationship representations through fantasy, play, imagination, dreams, free associations in therapy, and the consistency of manifest behavior inferred from behavior in a variety of contexts. The presence of pathological relationship representations is especially apparent when evoked in situations of high stress, where the usual defenses or behavioral facades are broken down. (The problem of determining pathological relationship representations, of course, is no different from the problem of determining internalized individual pathology. In this instance, the concern is primarily with individual cognitive, perceptual, and affective dysfunction.)

Relationship pathology is most readily detected when both behavioral observations and verbal reports are combined. Behavioral observations can be made across many situations and with many different individuals, so that the pattern of the pathology reflected by the relationship representations becomes obvious. Presumably, if pathological relationship behavior is observed in a single situation and not in others, it might not reflect an ongoing pattern characteristic of the representation. Ideally a research approach that examines relationship representations by verbal report combined with direct observation of the individual in a variety of relationship situations would be the better approach to understanding relationship pathology (Dodge, Petit, McClasken, & Brown, 1986).

As an example of some of these issues, I will cite some observations obtained in a recent study of abused and neglected children (Wald, Carlsmith, & Leiderman, 1988). In this study of five- to ten-year-old white abused or neglected children and not abused or neglected children included for comparison, children were asked to describe their peer relationships at home and at school. Parents also described peer relationships of the child, as did teachers, who independently assessed peer relationships at school. (Teachers presumably were more objective than parents and children in observing the manifest behavior of the child. Independent observation of playground behavior of the children suggested that this was the case.) As anticipated, there was little agreement between parents and children about the children's peer relationships, a finding that cannot merely be attributed to the possibly distorted views of abusing and neglecting parents, since normal control group parents and children presented similar results. Within the limitations of this methodology, these findings raise serious questions about the congruence between internal representations as reflected in verbal reports, the observations of parents and teachers, and the manifest behavior of these children on the playground.

If the child's view of his or her social behavior is clearly at variance with the parents' and teachers', who also did not agree, how can we classify the relationship pathology of the abused and neglected children? Should we use the child's view of the relationship, the manifest behavior as observed by others, or a combination of the two? It turns out that there are relatively few extant studies that explore internal representations and manifest behavior simultaneously for children, a most remarkable circumstance considering the centrality of relationship representations in the theory of relationship disorders. A conclusion to be drawn is that more rigorous studies of verbal reports of relationships in conjunction with observed behaviors must be done if we are to develop a taxonomy of relationship pathology for older children, adolescents, and adults, individuals for whom internal representations play such a large role in shaping manifest behavior.

TAXONOMY

Is it possible to classify relationship disturbances given the current state of knowledge? The obvious answer, considering the paucity of empirical information for dyadic relationships on such aspects as internal representations and interactive behavior in a variety of contexts, is that it is probably premature to adopt specific classification schemas. However, an approach to the problem might be to describe any given relationship structure and context in terms of the relationship functions (protection/vigilance, responsivity/security, physiological need regulation, psychological need regulation, learning/teaching, play, empathic intimacy) salient for that structure and context. Such an approach would yield a multiaxial description of the normative relationship functions for that dyad. The evaluation could be iterated for other relationship situations and other partners. The pattern of nonnormative relationship functions would then provide the clues to permit delineation of the pathological relationship representations for that individual. A complete description of relationship disturbance would include these representations plus descriptions of contexts and specific pathological relationship functions. A complete taxonomy would be based upon the collection of pathological patterns over a number of individuals at various phases in the life cycle.

CLINICAL CASES

To illustrate some of the problems inherent in any classification schema of relationship pathology, two cases will be presented.

An Adolescent   Eighteen-year-old Franz was urged to seek help by his father, who had learned that Franz had written notes to a female friend at school threatening suicide. This friend did not have any special relationship to Franz other than participation in several classes with him at high school.

In the first interview Franz was cautious in tone and guarded in utterance. He spoke slowly and deliberately, clarifying and amending each statement with the comment, "I want to give you an accurate picture of my life." He reported that he first became aware of "blue" feelings at about age fourteen, when he first entered high school. At that time he recalled wanting to be involved with his classmates in clubs and to sit with them at lunch. When he attempted to participate in these activities, he did not know what to say or how to behave. He was aware of being attracted to the girls in his classes, but again had no self-confidence or skill in appropriate heterosexual behavior. The young woman who had received his notes had talked to him in the lunchroom on a few occasions because she wondered why he was "so quiet."

Franz was the older of two children. His sister, younger by two years, was socially precocious, now only a year behind Franz in high school, a member of the cheerleading team, a member of the honor society, and the center of attention of both male and female classmates. Franz felt that his sister was the favorite of his parents, though he acknowledged that both parents were considerate of him and concerned about his welfare. He did not experience overcontrol from them even though he was the focus of their efforts from early childhood because of poor school performance.

Franz's history of relationship disturbances goes back at least to primary school, where he was held back for a year for a speech problem. According to Franz, and confirmed by his parents, teachers reported that they could not understand him, though both he and his parents felt that he was perfectly understandable at home. Accordingly, he spent the first few years of primary school in special education classes, and in addition received special tutoring after school. There was virtually no contact with peers other than his sister until he entered the sixth grade. Sometime during the fifth year of primary school, his speech improved to normal and it was found that his IQ was slightly above average; everyone was surprised, since they had assumed that he was intellectually retarded.

Franz's relationships with his parents would be best described as passive-dependent. Though his parents appeared both involved with and concerned about Franz and his welfare, the parents and Franz did not communicate. Franz looked to them for information and guidance. Yet the parent–child relationship was satisfactory, compared with Franz's relationships with peers. Essentially he was a social isolate, without involvement with peers or near peers. His chief social contacts were with younger cousins, and even these relationships involved parallel play rather than direct interaction. Franz appeared capable of peer relationships, according to his parents' and sister's accounts. These relationships simply were absent from his social repertoire.

The disturbed relationship functions of Franz involved physiological need regulation (adolescent psychosexual activity), adolescent attachment relationships, play, and empathic intimacy involving peers and near peers in situations outside of his family home. Franz's relationship representations appeared to be those of a damaged, isolated, uncommunicative child, with vague or nonexistent peer partners. And when a partner did appear in his imagery, it was a figure who would help Franz in his dependent relationships.

In summary, this case represents mild parental–child relationship pathology, coexisting with massive peer relationship pathology in a socially deprived adolescent. The origin of this pathology appears to be early peer social deprivation beginning in primary school and continuing through age twelve. The familial relationships were adequate, attested to in part by Franz's current positive adult relationships. This case supports the view that peer and parental relationship representations derived from different sources in the course of development remain relatively autonomous, at least through the period of late adolescence and young adulthood.

A Married Couple   Martha and Amos, a couple in their late forties, had been married for almost twenty years and had raised three children, all of whom had established independent lives. Amos and Martha sought help when each recognized that with the departure of their children there was very little to communicate when they found themselves alone. Each had developed close relationships with colleagues at work, much more satisfying than their own relationship. Neither had developed outside emotional attachments, and their current sexual functioning was adequate and satisfying.

Martha had been a successful housewife, satisfied with domestic activities until the children entered high school. No longer happy at home, she decided to return to college to complete her degree. She followed this with two years of graduate school, receiving an advanced degree. She obtained employment locally and was extremely successful in her work, receiving two promotions in the first five years of employment.

Amos was a professional, much involved in his work, though always considerate of his children and concerned for their welfare. He approved of the domestic activities of his wife, though he remained distant from the home. He was pleased with her efforts to be a "good mother." Other than occasional domestic quarrels and some concern about the motivation and performance of one of his children, his life was reasonably serene. Though not at the top of his profession, he achieved reasonably high status with considerable recognition of his professional activities.

In the first interview, they described their current relationship as not feeling close to one another and not having fun together. They had at one time enjoyed such things as introducing the other to special skills: Martha had taught Amos gourmet cooking and Amos had taught Martha about backpacking, a sport he dearly loved. Neither felt lonely or depressed. Neither experienced the absence of laughter, joy, or appropriate intimacy with individuals in situations away from the family home. Both had siblings to whom they felt loyal and close. Each had a parent who had died sometime earlier, and both were dutiful in their obligations to the surviving parent. In sum, the relationship pathology reflected something in their current circumstances when together.

The relationship representations gleaned from descriptions of behavior in other contexts and at other points in their life cycle indicated that Amos had strong paternal needs expressed in the caretaking of his children and his view of his wife as a helpmate in the fulfillment of this need. A possible origin for this representation was his senior position in the family: he was the oldest child and assisted his mother in taking care of younger siblings, partly as a substitute for a father who was away on business much of the time during his childhood and adolescence. Amos expressed the view that fathers were at least as important as mothers in the family relationship. He experienced a feeling of loss with the departure of his last child from home. He never had developed a companionate attitude toward his wife and did not view her as a partner in their relationship. He described the relationship as one in which one person was superior and the other subordinate.

Martha, in contrast to Amos, is a second child. She saw herself as a cooperative member of the household, following the rules at the behest of her parents. She looked to her older brother to take the lead in family activities. Her image of male–female relationships was that the man makes major decisions in goals and direction and the woman helps carry them out. Her relationship with Amos early in the marriage seemed ideal, especially when this image of helpmate was enacted in their relationship. Only later in her marriage, after the children reached high school, did she develop a sense of incompleteness, derived in part from her own feelings about herself and in part from information gained from the women's movement. She no longer idealized the male in the superior position with the female subordinate to him.

This clinical vignette illustrates relationship pathology in a marriage arising out of pathological internalized representations that had remained virtually unchanged from childhood and that had been reinforced in the early phase of the couple's relationship. The pathological functions were those involved in teaching/learning, play, and empathic intimacy. The relationship pathology was confined to these functions and seemed to be specific to this relationship and not to others. However, it was not inconceivable that in other social situations, relationships similar to the marriage relationship would be recapitulated and would also be subject to relationship pathology.

Therapy was directed toward providing new experiences for the couple in a variety of contexts where behavior patterns could be modified. Experience with other couples in a couples group provided an opportunity for modeling; implicit in this experience was permission for the couple to test out a wider variety of relationships hitherto not considered by them. After several sessions in this combined approach, the couple had a greater sense of appreciation for one another. They embarked on a set of new activities, enjoyable to both, which alleviated some of the previously alienated feelings. They learned new relationship skills and were optimistic about their potential for solving relationship problems on their own.

THERAPY

The therapeutic approach to pathological relationships in the later phases of the life cycle in part involves the modification of pathological relationship representations, which can occur later in the life cycle under the press of major shifts in relationships or with highly salient experiences such as individual, family, or group psychotherapy. The therapeutic goal is to provide new experiences in relationships in order to modify old relationship representations and provide the template for new representations. The circumstances for producing change in relationship representations and in the conditions that maintain them are the object of much of current psychotherapeutic and sociotherapeutic research.

The possibility that parental and peer relationship disorders are relatively autonomous becomes an important issue when we consider therapeutic strategies. A frequently held assumption is that the results of therapy for relationship disturbances in the parent–child system also will have influence on relationship disorders in the child–peer system. This assumption has not been fully tested. If relative independence of these systems is assumed then the strategy of therapy will differ from strategies employed in circumstances where dependence is assumed. Under the assumption of relative autonomy, the efficacious therapeutic strategy for parent–child relationship disturbances is to use a parent–child therapeutic paradigm, that is, to have the therapist take a parent role in dyadic or family therapy.

Peer relationship disturbances arising in middle or later childhood or adolescence might best be treated by a peer-oriented therapeutic paradigm, either in small group therapy or, in the case of younger children, in a therapeutic nursery. More likely relationship pathology contains elements of dysfunction in both the parental and the peer systems. Therapy then includes both peer and parental relationship components, a mix frequently found in family therapy but also possible in a combination of dyadic therapy and group therapy.

There is, of course, a middle way in relationship therapies, especially for older children and adolescents. Affiliative therapy (Hilgard & Moore, 1969) uses elements of both peer and parental relationships and is especially appropriate for dysfunctional mentoring relationships. In this instance, therapists are peers immediately older than the client. These therapeutic mentors combine elements of both parental and peer figures, providing an experience consistent with the experience in childhood and adolescence of using older peers and siblings as models for normative behavior. In general, the mentoring relationship may well be one of the most powerful therapeutic tools for modifying behavior throughout the life cycle.

Conclusion

I have presented some of the problems that may be encountered in the use of the concept of relationship disturbance beyond infancy. Although the evidence indicates that the concept can be heuristically useful, it must be applied with caution because of the increased complexity of relationships in the preschool and school-age period, when relationships are no longer necessarily dyadic. Rather, relationships involve a variety of individuals, including peers, near peers, parents, and other adults. The interplay between dyadic and group phenomena during this stage does not permit easy classification of normative and pathological processes. Furthermore, even when we consider only dyadic relationships for the postinfancy period, other difficulties remain. Each dyadic relationship likely has a different meaning, salience, and emotional impact, in many instances dependent upon situational constraints. Thus there would be no easy way to assess the severity of relationship disturbances even if the dimensions of the dyadic interaction were known and the disturbance could be classified.

A second issue mitigating against use of the relationship disorder construct in the postinfancy period concerns the nongeneralizability of relationship representations beyond those individuals involved in the original representations. If relationship disturbances turn out to be person-specific then the concept of relationship disturbance will have limited utility. However, it is more likely that relationship disturbances with primary figures persist relatively autonomously, at least over the short term. In the longer term, relationship representations likely undergo some coalescence, which accounts for manifestations of relationship disturbance across individuals and across situations.

A major source of relationship disturbances is parent–infant relationship dysfunction. Disturbances—especially those involving peer and near peer relationships—also can arise in the postinfancy period regardless of earlier positive and secure attachment relationships with mother or father. Cross-cultural studies suggest that parental and peer relationship development is not necessarily congruent, especially in societies where nonparental figures have an important role in child rearing and where the age cohort rather than the family is the relevant reference group. The mentoring relationship provides a major mechanism for both modern and traditional societies in the socialization of the child and adolescent into an age-graded cultural system.

The family recently has become the focus of ecologically oriented child development researchers, and there has been relatively little study of other social institutions or situations. Despite the paucity of evidence, situation specificity in relationship disturbances is probably important for some relationships. Concurrent studies of relationships and relationship disturbances in such situations as the family, school, and community are long overdue.

The continuity of relationship disturbances can be explained both by internalized relationship representations and continuity of context. Internalized relationship representations are part of a child's self-concept, and they undoubtedly undergo modification during development. The child's manifest interactional behavior also changes, in part because of the increased complexity of the context and the number of interactional partners. Despite excellent theoretical models to point the way for the study of internal representations and manifest behavior, empirical evidence to capture the dynamic flux between the two domains in specific contexts remains elusive. Both internal representations and manifest behavior are influenced by cognitive and physical development as well as setting. The integration of these psychological domains remains a frontier for future research.

The attempt at a taxonomy of relationship disturbances for the infancy period may point the way to the task that should be attempted for relationship disturbances occurring later in the life cycle. The difficulties involved for this later age period are many. The benefits to be gained from such an attempt are considerable, especially if the goal is to alleviate relationship disturbances, whatever their genesis, throughout the life cycle.

Chapter 9

The Represented and Practicing Family: Contrasting Visions of Family Continuity

David Reiss

This book attempts to lay the groundwork for a rigorous, clinically useful and empirically based classification of relationship disorders; at several points an outline for a classification of this kind is presented. However, not the classification itself but the groundwork is the main objective. Specifically, this means to organize existing empirical data about the smooth and problematic aspects of the development of relationships and to clarify the nosological implications of such an organization.

This chapter is an attempt to clarify one of the central conceptual difficulties that has emerged in our efforts. The dilemma has become manifest as we have attempted to trace the evolution of relationships involving the infant from the earliest moments following birth through the years of early childhood. Our primary aim is to fashion a nosology from knowledge of disorders in these relationships. Do we focus primarily on the family relationships in which the growing child is embedded? This focus implies the disorder is external to individuals. Alternatively, can we, perhaps later in the development, talk of relationships that have become internal to the child, so that the disorder is a consequence, in some sense, of disturbed relationships? This question has led to a second one: Is there at any developmental phase or level a process by which family relationships are conserved or maintained within individuals? This, as it turns out, is not simply a question of the development of infants and children but an equally important question about families. It highlights two contrasting perspectives about the family and its relationship to individual development.

The first of these views emerges from a line of studies focusing on the determinants of social and emotional development in children. In general, according to this view, family relationships are an early *context* of development. To be sure, the child is no longer viewed by any contemporary developmentalist as a passive responder to this environment. Indeed, the child has been shown to have a considerable impact on his or her own family relationships. However, the thrust of inquiry guided by this perspective is to learn how these relationships become *absorbed or internalized* in the developing individuals (Ainsworth, Blehar, Waters, & Wall, 1978; Main & Goldwyn, 1984; Ricks, 1985; chapters 3 and 4). Indeed, from this perspective, the beginning of such relationships—usually those between parent and infant—are initiated and sustained by structures that are internal to the caregiver, such as the remembered relationships between the maternal caregiver and her own mother (Main & Goldwyn, 1984; Ricks, 1985). As the parent–infant relationship matures, the infant is thought to acquire an enlarging repertoire of internalized memories and abstractions of memories and models that forms an additional source of structured stability to the relationship itself (Bowlby, 1969, 1973, 1980). The pivotal concept in this perspective is that not only are the coherence, stability, and substance of the relationship represented by these internalized structures, but the stability and coherence of the relationship itself may be located and conserved through time by such structures. In sum, this perspective, although it considers a range of mechanisms, highlights internal representations as a source of stability in relationships. A child's or adult's working model or subjective construction of his or her relationship with others is a major source of stability and coherence of social behavior across time. Although it is rarely done in practice, it is possible to extend this perspective on dyadic relationships to frame a conception of the family as a mosaic of such internal representations. In this sense the family and this mosaic of representations are coterminous. We can highlight this mode of analysis by calling it the study of the represented family.

A fundamentally different perspective arises from clinical and observational studies of whole families theoretically guided by Kantor and Lehr (1975) and David Reiss (1981); clinically informed by Salvador Minuchin (1974) and others; and empirically investigated by Lewis, Beavers, Gossett, & Phillips (1976), Grotevant and Cooper (1985), Reiss (1981), and others. Although many of these studies are motivated by a concern for the social and cognitive competence of children, they are riveted on observations of the family itself: its boundaries, structures, regulatory principles, and development over time. A central inquiry within this perspective concerns the social interactional processes that maintain stability and coherence in family groups and the mechanisms by which such processes change in response to expectable developmental challenges, unforeseen crises, and therapeutic interventions.

According to this perspective, the stability and coherence of these processes reside not within individuals but in the *coordinated practices* of the entire family. Although individual memory in general and the individual's representations of relations in particular are accorded great importance in this perspective, the emphasis is on the interaction patterns themselves. Investigators in this tradition, implicitly or explicitly, assume that family interaction per se has a critical memorial function of its own. That is, the interaction of the group— above and beyond the memories of its individuals—conserves relationships and regulates and perpetuates many aspects of ongoing family life.

A prime example of a coordinated practice in family life is the family ritual. Rituals in simple societies, in religious practice, and in families are regularly enacted because it is in the coordinated practice of such behaviors that the group itself can be maintained. Although aspects of rituals may be stored (or represented) within individual memory, in this family perspective such storage is at best an accessory source of stability and coherence. Indeed, most major rituals have an initiation or corrective function. They realign individual representation with group practice. Most enduring groups rely on ritual objects, written regulations, hallowed grounds and sanctuaries, and other common property to provide the stability of the group's ritual life. Indeed, this common property endows interaction patterns with their substance and memorial function and allows for an image of the family very different from the represented family. Investigators in this tradition, because of their preoccupation with observable, external, and patterned coordinated practice in family life, may be said to be in search of a different species of family, which can be called the *practicing family*. These investigators are not much concerned with the reflections of past family experience in the current mental life of individuals; rather they seek to examine directly patterns in the whole family that account not only for differences among families but also for the continuity of the unique attributes of the family across time.

193

Although much has been written about the new epistemology arising out of family studies, the differences between the two perspectives are not, at the core, philosophical. Rather, each perspective can be understood as arising from different sets of observational data made in very different clinical and research contexts and thought about in different ways. The perspectives can and are being reconciled, and indeed each suggests to the other certain research agendas. It is a safe bet that a science of relationship disorders will draw on both perspectives because every relationship probably has represented and practiced aspects.

In this chapter I attempt to (1) clarify the different research strategies drawn from the two perspectives to suggest approaches by which the two perspectives may be brought to bear jointly on critical problems of relationships and their disorders and (2) outline some types of coordinated family practice that, according to current evidence, play a role in family perdurance.

The Represented and Practicing Family: Contrasting Research Strategies

THE MAIN AND GOLDWYN STUDY OF ATTACHMENT ACROSS GENERATIONS

Recently, Mary Main and Ruth Goldwyn (1984) have extended the fecund line of investigation into parent–child attachment. They have asked whether patterns of attachment between parents and children can be transmitted across generations, particularly whether the quality of relationship between a mother and her mother in childhood is reproduced, in some measure, by the mother's current relationship with her toddler. Main and Goldwyn developed a standardized interview. An initial review examined four components of the remembered relationship in childhood: how much rejection of the mother by her mother was recalled; how unrealistically idealized this relationship was; how much difficulty there was in remembering the childhood relationship; and what the mother's current feelings, understandings, and explanations were for the impact of this relationship on her. In sum, Main and Goldwyn attempted to sample a part of the represented family, specifically the mother's mother as internalized by the mother. They related this representation to transactions directly observed between the mother and her infant at twelve and eighteen months of age.

As expected, mothers who recalled their own mothers as rejecting had infants who rejected them in the reunion phase of the Strange Situation Test. However, there was evidence that the represented family could be modified with experience. Some mothers expressed anger and resentment or were particularly coherent in their accounts of their childhood relationships; this suggested that some perspective or internal containment of the represented family had been achieved. These mothers had more securely attached infants. In contrast, mothers whose memory of childhood was poor or who idealized their own rejecting parents had avoidant infants. These mothers, perhaps, had not worked through their troubled past; they were unable to understand or acknowledge emotionally the difficulties they had with their own mothers.

THE MINUCHIN STUDY OF ANORECTIC CHILDREN AND THEIR FAMILIES

In searching for a clear contrast drawn from studies of the practicing family, I could not locate programmatic research that specifically addresses the same questions as attracted Main and Goldwyn. Indeed, most observers of very early social and emotional development in children have studied the represented family. The Main and Goldwyn study is important not only in its own right but because it is drawn from a particularly productive line of investigation into infant attachments and shares many investigative strategies with a wider set of studies of the development of self-concept and social behavior in children. The work of Salvador Minuchin occupies an equally pivotal position in studies of the practicing family. The Minuchin group, like the attachment theorists, have produced an impressive body of programmatically linked theory and observation. Their questions are different, but their concerns overlap, in major ways, those of the attachment theorists. Their clinical interests focus on major psychiatric syndromes—in this case anorexia nervosa (Minuchin, Rosman, & Baker, 1978). This syndrome is particularly dramatic because it produces such bizarre behavior and dramatic weight loss, and because it is potentially fatal. Moreover, it has been quite resistant to most forms of treatment. However, a look behind the clinical exotica of this syndrome clearly reveals that the Minuchin group is concerned with issues of social emotional development, particularly of autonomy, in children and adolescents. Thus, the contrast between the two approaches—particularly the underlying intellectual strategies—offers a good opportunity to clarify the differences between the represented and practicing family.

The Minuchin group focuses on the whole family. The majority of their observations are drawn from laboratory, interview, and therapeutic sessions in which all members sharing the anorectic's household are observed in interaction. Minuchin's group defines several features that appear unique in these families: there is a high level of emotional connectedness or "enmeshment" among all members; the family as a group focuses intensely on the welfare and protection of the children, in part through detailed monitoring of their health and diet; and the family as a group avoids open conflict, often suppressing hostility by a commitment to ideals of harmony and serenity. Moreover, in families with anorectics, all these distinctive patterns are seen as particularly repetitive, rigid, and unchanging over time. The central theoretical concept of the study is that these patterns are self-maintaining because each individual contributes to and is shaped by them. Thus, for example, a father will insist that his daughter eat. Daughter agrees with father—to conceal that she is in fact not eating—but establishes restricted conditions (such as "when I'm hungry"). Mother, sensing the lingering possibility for conflict between father and daughter, explains how difficult it will be for her to eat. This restimulates father's anxiety about his child's welfare; thus he is encouraged to reimpose a halfhearted request for eating and the cycle repeats. In this way, an enmeshed, conflict-avoiding, and child-focused system can maintain rigid patterns unendingly across time.

THE STUDIES CONTRASTED

It is useful to contrast these studies to clarify differences in studies of the represented and the practicing family. Three separate dimensions highlight this contrast. First, as is clear from the examples, the *observational focus* is different; the two teams pick very different family phenomena for detailed scrutiny. Second, the two approaches differ in their *approach to the dyad;* it is a central focus in the work of Main and Goldwyn and a subsidiary focus of the Minuchin group. The contrasting focus and emphasis on dyads shape data-gathering strategies: which family members are included for study and which of their thoughts and behaviors are assessed. However, there are also contrasts in the way data are interpreted, in particular, in the *concepts of continuity across time.*

Observational Focus The Main and Goldwyn report, like many studies of the represented family, focuses on parent–child interaction. More specifically, from the complex fabric of family process the investigators of the represented family have cut away just the area of family process that immediately surrounds the infant or young child. In the initial Main and Goldwyn report the narrow focus is apparent in both the independent and the dependent variables. In the independent variable the central interest is in the remembered mother–child relationship (although this group has collected data on other relationships as well). Other remembered dyads within the family are not examined nor are transactions between the family—as individuals or as a group—and outsiders. For example, no inquiry is made concerning memories of the marital relationship or of the transactions among all members or between the family and strangers.

A correspondingly selective focus is apparent in the Minuchin study, as is typical of studies of the practicing family. As expected, a net is cast to capture a larger number of family members and a broader range of family processes, yet many relevant processes within the anorectic child (the "identified patient") are virtually ignored. Only a thin veneer of the child's external behavior is studied; only behavior most relevant to the ongoing flow of family interaction is brought into focus. Shorn from this study are the inner experiences of self, such as those finely delineated by Hilde Bruch (1973), a student of the represented anorectic family, and others. In Minuchin's short- and long-term follow-up of the anorectic children we know only bare facts about the children's behavior: they eat, they gain weight, they improve overall social and academic adjustment. We know little about changes in their body image, in their experience of initiative, self-efficacy, equality with peers. Indeed, investigators of the represented family—having already climbed under the skin to delineate subtle, subjective experiences of family life, have painted very sensitive and detailed portraits of these inner experiences of children (see chapters 3 and 4).

The Centrality of the Dyad   Once having selected a particular observational focus of family process, each approach parses the process in very different ways. Observers of the represented family usually focus on relationships constructed from dyads. The initial Main and Goldwyn report is concerned, primarily, with two dyads: grandmother–mother and mother–child. Current studies of the represented family often contain more than two people, but systems of relationships among these people are conceptualized as a system of dyads (chapter 5; Parke, Power, & Gottman, 1979). Investigators of the practicing family place dyads in subordinate positions. A more overriding concern is to delineate connections among people in larger groups. The concepts of enmeshment, conflict avoidance, and child-centeredness—used most often in studies of the practicing family—*could* apply to dyads but are equally applicable to groups of three or more.

This distinction goes to the heart of the contrast made here. Dyads lend themselves very well to two aspects of the represented family. First, forces that initiate and maintain dyads with relative conceptual ease can be located in the minds of one or both members. Further, the representational process itself seems well suited for encapsulating dyads. It is easier to grasp how such dyadic patterns as "bully–whipping boy" (Olweus, 1980) or "adult seducer–child seduced" (chapter 5) can be absorbed, remembered, and stored for long periods. On the other hand, even a simple multiperson concept like enmeshment cannot be so easily represented; further, it is not easy to understand how such a representation—left as an internalized residuum of childhood—could activate enmeshment in a current multiperson family group.

Concepts of Continuity across Time   Students of the represented family are, quite naturally, very interested in the unfolding of behavior and experience across time. The initial Main and Goldwyn report extends the usual time span of interest across two generations. At the core of the logic of this analysis is the representation itself: a hypothetical construct that is meant to account for how an event at time 1 can continue to exert an influence at time 2. Sophisticated concepts of the represented family allow for a variety of determining experiences across time, again as illustrated in the Main and Goldwyn report, to add or subtract to the influence of early experiences. Indeed, as the process goes forward a variety of forces and pressures combine in interaction to propel and shape current experience and behavior. Physiologists refer to this accumulated set of pressures in the cardiovascular system as *vis a tergo,* a force from the rear: the combination of stroke volume and force of cardiac contraction that propels blood forward in the vascular system.

I stress the concept of *accumulated* pressure because it is a mistake to see concepts of the represented family as implying simple, linear causality. Most sophisticated models in this genre allow for reciprocal effects, conditional relationships, and context-dependent outcomes. Nonetheless, the overall concept of continuity emphasizes a chain of sequentially dependent circumstances. That is why it seems so natural for attachment theorists to be going backward in time—once a typology of attachment patterns has been established—to ask: Where do these patterns come from?

A very different concept of continuity is emphasized in studies of the practicing family. The central focus is on *contemporaneous fit.* The social and emotional competence of the child is seen not as a product of accumulated circumstance but as part of an overall pattern of relationships: it is a solution to unbearable tensions, or a link between alienated components of the system, or a component of repeated sequence of interaction events, or part of a camouflage for an event that is even more painful. (For example, see Bermann [1973] for a study of a young boy's behavior disorder that was part of a family pattern to camouflage its anxiety about impending and dangerous heart surgery for father.)

Importantly, students of the represented family tend to take a more passive

198

stance toward their data. Their models of causality—although involving sequentially ordered events—are complex. There is a preference for learning the
natural history of this unfolding pattern. Students of the practicing family are
inclined to action. Because of their conviction of the centrality of the *current
fit* they have more optimism that a therapeutically induced change at almost
any point in the system will disrupt it and allow for a potential change in all
family members—including the identified patient. This is precisely the tack
taken by the Minuchin group. Their highly influential monograph is much less
concerned with the delineation of a natural history of the anorectic family
than with intervention—some of it very dramatic. The data of the book are
the interventions, many of which are reported extensively and verbatim. The
goal is changing the family system. For example, the therapist challenges the
family to feed the anorectic child, thus revealing the conflict-avoiding and
enmeshed patterns while inducing a change in those patterns to make the
eating disorder disappear.

This contrast in studies illumines gaps in the research agendas that use only
one perspective. Omissions in the Main and Goldwyn report can be identified.
The mother's role in shaping secure attachment in her child may not be
influenced directly by her representation of her childhood relationship with
her own mother, despite the positive correlations reported. The pattern of
current family ties—in which mother is embedded—needs to be carefully
examined to make a more secure decision. Some mothers who recall as adults
bad past relationships with their mothers may, at the same time, have tenuous
current ties with their peers and husband and remain alienated from husband's
kin and friends. Perhaps it is this current pattern of relationships that is
reflected in insecure attachment to her own child; the remembered grandmother–mother tie may be an epiphenomenon.

Likewise, there are gaps in the Minuchin agenda. Two areas emerge quite
clearly. First, little attention is given in the entire volume to the origins of the
destructive features of the anorectic family: enmeshment, child-centeredness,
and conflict avoidance. They may indeed arise in some way from representations of the family of orientation in one or both parents. Moreover, we have
no data on how the represented family (each member's experience of the
family) is changed by interventions and the role such changes play in the
long-term favorable outcomes for the family and the anorectic.

Coordinated Practice and Family Continuity

The theoretical forms for an individual and dyad-based concept of the represented family are well known to developmentalists. The concept that the development of the growing child reflects, in part, an absorption of the family environment was popular before the turn of the century. *Studies in Hysteria* (Breuer & Freud, 1895/1955) was a galvanizing clinical report of the return of this represented (but repressed) experience in adult neurotic behavior. A subsequent century of basic and clinical research in child development only reinforced this concept (see chapters 3 and 4 for an elaboration of this position).

The view that the coordinated family practice is a major source of family continuity is more elusive and slippery in developmental and developmentally oriented clinical studies. However, it is possible to sketch out a picture of this kind. The intellectual traditions here are drawn not from psychology or any of its philosophical progenitors but rather from history, sociology, and anthropology, specifically the studies of the rise and persistence of defined social groupings such as culture, castes, and organizations. It has been forcefully argued that family process as a primary mechanism of maintaining continuity of social forms (rather than a more passive vehicle of larger cultural and religious imperatives) is a relatively recent sociohistorical process (Aries, 1962). Sociology and anthropology, by analogy to other perduring social groups across the broad span of history, provide observations and concepts for characterizing two fundamental aspects of the continuity in the practicing family: the mechanisms by which in ordinary times it is regulated and stabilized and the mechanisms by which the family changes in predictable ways across the duration of its own group life. These mechanisms may not be fully independent of the representational processes of individual members, but neither are they wholly dependent on them.

Consider, for example, the maintenance of the continuity of religious practice. At certain phases in the development of religion, oral traditions lie at the core of maintaining consistency of religious practice across generations. For example, the native Navajo religion requires that a shaman have a verbatim memory of the details of religious practice because until very recently there were no written symbols to help preserve the detail of the practice of "sings" and other rites. Here, surely, is an instance in which a tribal expert does represent the practices of his group; these representations (the verbatim memory of religious protocol) are the guide or template of group process, much as a mother's working model of her relationship with her own mother may shape her initial ties with her own infant (see Main & Goldwyn, 1984).

200

But this example has another side. To be sure, verbatim memory is an asset to the would-be shaman and, through his meticulous religious practice, to the continuity of the group. But, according to the detailed studies of Clyde Kluckhohn and Dorothea Leighton (1958) and Gladys Reichard (1950), group process provides a continuing corrective to shamanistic practice. First, shamans learn the rudiments of their chants by long and active participation in group ritual life; few shamans begin their training until their mid-twenties, and most do not perfect their skills until middle or old age. Second, the quality of shamanistic practice is under constant regulation by the entire tribe through a simple device: better shamans receive more money for the rituals they guide. Finally, shamans themselves function as a closed subsociety: they regularly participate in informal "seminars" and "study groups" where they compare their approaches and, presumably, adjust the details of their practice. The evidence would suggest that the minutely detailed representations of religious practice by the shamans are precious vehicles of common group practice but are not its fundamental origin or its most critical error-correcting mechanism.

Oral traditions have been of central importance to the continuity of other religious groups even when a detailed and subtle written language is available and widely known among its practitioners. Judaism, before the fall of the Second Temple, is a particularly interesting example. Although the major laws of Jewish practice were inscribed in the first five books of the Bible—the Torah—the critical details of everyday Jewish life were guided by an intricate oral law that religious Jews believed had been given to Moses along with the written law. For centuries, preservation of the oral law was supported by the existence of the temple shrine in Jerusalem to which most Jews journeyed as often as possible and which was the only site permitted for certain major religious rituals. Thus, with a common, central, and revered shrine set in the central and hallowed city of Jerusalem, itself a mosaic of tradition and continuity, the oral law could be sustained through its retelling, its continuous oral interpretation, and its group practice. The oral law was a medium, not an origin, of the continuity of a religion that could worship at a common site. With the fall of the Second Temple the Jews were dispersed and lost the geographic and ceremonial center of their communal life. At that point the oral law was redacted and became, in time, the Talmud. Even the Talmud would have failed as a codex providing continuity of group life were it not the focus of continuing and searching interpretive commentary.

Families—like religions—can be viewed as but another perduring group. Each, in the course of its own development, goes through a process similar to redaction. Family experiences and traditions also become codified. The residue of major shared experiences of the family—such as illnesses, migrations, and financial disasters—may be conserved in a variety of their common practices. Some of these shared experiences are transformed into subtle or conspicuous coordinated *behavior.* Others are actually redacted, to use this term in its narrowest sense, into written *documents,* such as wills. Both behavior and documents go on to have major and continuing impact on the family, providing for both its uniqueness and its continuity. I will describe below five different kinds of coordinated practice that have received empirical attention. At present, research has been successful in delineating some basic modes of organization for each of these five kinds, from microchains of behavior occurring in just a few moments to molar patterns such as family rituals. However, there remain three important uncertainties in this scheme.

First, it is not clear from current data how experience may be conserved by each of these modes of coordinated practice. However, since the plausibility of the practicing family rests on this conservation process, I will try to indicate the memorial function of each kind of practice where existing data give some hint. In general, this becomes easier as one moves from the molecular chains of interaction to molar practices.

Second, it is not clear precisely who in the family ought to be regarded as critical participants in these coordinated practices. For example, most of the molecular studies of brief chains of behavior focus on marital or parent–child dyads. The observations of more molar behaviors, such as family rituals, include not only the immediate household but often embrace key members of the extended family and even close friends. Current research would suggest that some coordinated practices regularly involve the whole family and conserve critical properties of the whole group. Other practices may concern subsystems—the marriage or sibling relationships—and conserve experience unique to those systems.

Third, we are only beginning to obtain data about the capacity of the developing infant and young child to participate fully in the various levels of coordinated practice. I have assumed that there is a developmental sense to the way these levels of practice are ordered; that is, infants and very young children can fully participate in—and indeed shape—the molecular chains of behavior but require increasing developmental competence to participate in the more molar practices. (Daniel Stern has proposed an ordering from molecular to molar forms of representation; see chapter 3.)

MICROCHAINS

Recent advances in techniques for directly observing interaction as well as for analyzing statistical dependencies and sequences among units of interaction behaviors have revealed perhaps the most microcosmic coordinated practices in families. For the most part these sequences have involved dyads but there is no reason why existing techniques cannot be expanded to triadic and even tetradic interaction sequences. (The limits are mainly statistical ones. Large base rates of events are necessary for sequential analyses; on the whole, the minimum base rate per family, adequate for statistically secure analyses, must be multiplied by the number of interacting people if all individuals have roughly the same base rates of any particular behavior.)

Four domains have received particularly close attention: mother–infant sequences, various dyads in families of aggressive children, marital interaction, and family routines. Examples of these analyses include the studies of mutual regulation of excitation in mother–infant pairs (where a full range of verbal and nonverbal behavior is coded in mothers and gaze direction is the presumed control component in the infant (see Brazelton, Koslowski, & Main, 1974; Stern, 1985; Fogel, 1982). Also, on a somewhat more advanced level, Stern's (1985) studies of affective attunement qualify here. For older children another important example is Gerald Patterson's (1982) programmatic studies of coercive cycles—where parents reinforce coercive and even violent behavior in their children by selectively attending to it, or, by a process of negative reinforcement, stopping their own aversive behavior in response to coercion from their children.

A third area of programmatic research is the study of longer behavior chains in marital couples (Gottman, 1979). Here the focus has been on the management by couples of negative affect, because this accomplishment is among the most reliable discriminators of satisfied and unsatisfied (but not necessarily long-lived or short-lived) marriages. Unsatisfied marriages are characterized by a reverberating negative affect. If the husband complains about any aspect of his life to his wife, then she in turn complains about him or about some other topic. This is particularly true in early phases of a marital interaction sequence and has been called by John Gottman cross-complaining. Satisfied couples show a radically different sequence: a complaint will be followed by an affirmation or acknowledgment of the source of the difficulty; this is followed by the couple's rapidly moving into conclusive problem-solving interaction. The latter pattern, in satisfied marriages, may reflect a process similar to the negative excitation cycles between mothers and infants, studied by Tiffany Field (1979).

PROBLEM-SOLVING EPISODES

Microchains are molecular sequences of behavior. Usually they are set in motion by a relatively small perturbation or change in the behavior of one member: fussiness in an infant, aggressive behavior in a parent, irritability in a spouse. The level of organization of these sequences are two or, at most, three steps long. Similarly, three-step sequences are observed in mother–infant microchains. Gottman has carried his analyses to seven-step sequences.

Problem-solving episodes are more complex though they have been much less frequently studied. First the stimulus itself for these sequences is, in most instances, more complex than a perturbation in the behavior of one member. At times the stimulus may be interpersonal impasses among family members themselves. At other times the impasses may be externally imposed.

Peter Steinglass and his colleagues (Steinglass, Bennett, Wolin, & Reiss, 1987) called attention to these sequences in studying families of alcoholics. They noted that many of these families—some of whom were observed when the family unit was admitted to a research in-patient alcoholic ward—responded to brief, time-limited stressful events in ways that were highly typical for each family. The Steinglass group was interested in the extent to which alcohol was used as a routine part of the problem-solving sequence. They noted, for example, a family when faced with an unresponsive but critical person in their environment (a pediatrician who would not make a housecall for a sick child, in one instance) went through a regular sequence: frustrated rage of husband with no effective action by him, retreat by wife to isolation from husband, drinking by wife, disinhibition of wife's behavior, assertiveness with unresponsive outside person, effective response by outside person. The regularity of such sequences raised questions as to whether similarly precise ordering might be found in nonalcoholic families. Minuchin's work, among others, reports in detail conflict-avoiding sequences that occur repeatedly, for example, in response to defiance and limit testing in adolescent children. However, an empirically sound set of studies of problem-solving episodes is only just emerging.

ARTIFACTS AND HALLOWED GROUND

The aspects of organization that have been described thus far—microchains and problem-solving patterns—and those that will be described subsequently—rituals and stories—all refer to behavioral interactional regularities in family systems. Artifacts and hallowed ground constitute an aspect that focuses not on behaviors, as such, but on physical objects and spaces.

Artifacts, as intended here, are critical family possessions. Major systematic investigation has begun in at least two areas in this domain. Wills have been systematically explored from two different vantage points (Sussman, Cates, & Smith, 1970; Farber, 1981). Although a great deal of family interaction, considered as behavior, precedes and follows the writing of a will, the will itself may be considered a central artifact both reflecting and shaping the ongoing course of family interaction. Recent data suggest that wills and their impact can extend across a significant span of a family's development; their importance is rarely confined to the period just before or after the death of a family member. Other written artifacts—correspondence, suicide notes, diaries, albums—have been less thoroughly studied but may in many families play a critical role in the ongoing regulation of family interaction and development.

Recent, meticulous studies by Mihaly Csikszentmihalyi and Eugene Rochberg-Halton (1981) have brought another set of (mostly) nonwritten objects into view. These researchers focused on common household objects and their role in organizing family life. Their survey covered a full range from furniture to books, electrical equipment, and mementos. Their data strongly suggest that artifacts often play a role in integrating relationships. For example, in families characterized by high levels of expressed warmth among all members, the parents have carefully preserved mementos of their own parents and retain objects from their own childhood.

Families also come to possess spaces. The almost universal possession in our culture is the home. A growing literature documents the role of spatial layouts as contraints on interaction in and between families in residential areas (for example, Parke & Swain, 1979). Our research group has reported, for example, the effect on families of spatial changes required for the home care of the chronically ill. In one case a paraplegic father required his own special bed and exercise areas as a part of his long-term care. This necessitated the following spatial reassignments in the household: (1) father left the bed he shared with mother for his special bed in the bedroom of the twelve-year-old daughter; (2) the displaced daughter moved in with mother and took father's former place in the double bed; (3) however, there was no room to store daughter's belongings either in her old room (now filled with special equipment for father) or in her parents' room (still filled with parents' clothes), so her clothing was stored in the room of two older brothers; (4) exercise space for father's upper body rehabilitation occupied the solo bedroom of one of the older brothers who moved in with the other—to make very cramped quarters, indeed, compounded by the need to store sister's belongings in the same space. These changes had many long-term consequences on the form and flow of family organization; the most fundamental was to shape most of family interaction around father's illness. It is not simply metaphorical to speak of the spatial organization as a sanctification of the illness and its care with the necessary subordination and even defilement of other family functions. In this sense, the areas of the home devoted to the chronic care of father became hallowed grounds: special spaces for the conduct of the functions that most preoccupied the family group.

Although this example is particularly dramatic, most family homes constitute special settings that favor or support interaction patterns that are less frequent, different in character, or nonexistent outside the home. Equally important, the home may have critical internal differentiation: individuals may have their own inner sanctums for privacy, as Csikszentmihalyi and Rochberg-Halton have shown, and the family may have specially enshrined areas that sustain important functions.

A fundamental question about both artifacts and hallowed ground is whether they can be conceived of as *active sustaining forces* in family perdurance or whether they play a more passive role as *symbolic expressions* of other sources of perdurance in the family. Was the spatial layout in the family of the father with paraplegia a reflection of its mode of coping with illness rather than a "cause" of this coping? The answer here is necessarily complex. In many instances wills, heirlooms, and a family's home are handed down through the generations; in these instances they clearly play an active role in shaping and sustaining the family forms of the successor generations. At other times the family actively creates its own artifacts and hallowed ground. In this instance the family, in effect, is engaged in a process of redaction: the conversion of family experiences, coping strategies, ideals, and objectives into a physical and perceptible "record" that guides their subsequent behavior. This is certainly the case in the family with a paraplegic father. The changes in the household space occurred over several months with much trial and error and reflected the painful resolution of many competing demands for the family's time and resources. Once in place, however, the spatial arrangements functioned as a codex, a highly legitimized and canonical constraint on patterns of family interaction.

Wills, as family artifacts, are a more explicit manifestation of this process of redaction. The writing of a will reflects many features of family life in the period prior to the time the will is drawn: specific relationships between the testator and his surviving family as well as general, overall family values concerning intergenerational relationships. Farber (1981), for example, has distinguished families with collateral values—where members in the same generation, such as cousins and siblings, are beneficiaries—in contrast to those families with intergenerational values—where children or parents are the exclusive beneficiaries. However, once in effect the will—a redaction of these relationships and values—becomes a legally binding constraint, often with enormous impact on the surviving family for many years.

RITUALS

Rituals have been a central preoccupation in the study of continuities in culture. The sociologists Bossard and Boll (1950) recognized that families, as "minicultures," also develop their own rituals. More recently these concepts have been developed by David Reiss (1981) and studied systematically and empirically by Bennett, Wolin, Reiss, and Teitelbaum (1987). Rituals are more complex sequences than microchains or problem-solving episodes. In this schematic ascending series of behavioral forms in family life they are the first level of common practice that is rich with symbolic import; indeed, their primary function is symbolic.

Family rituals have several critical features that distinguish them from microchains and problem-solving episodes. First, they are generally practiced by the whole family. Second, they are fully self-aware. Families may not be aware of or able to report on microchains or problem-solving episodes but can recount key family rituals in great detail. Moreover, families are, for the most part, proud of their rituals. Third, rituals almost always have a preparatory phase: they are anticipated and prepared for. This serves to place them on an experiential pedestal and set them off from more mundane and routine aspects of family life. Fourth, a closely related feature: rituals are preemptory. Generally, they are carried out in invariant forms that require that families set aside their ordinary practices to give rituals first place. Fifth, they are self-sustaining and self-corrective. Families know their rituals well and members who deviate from one or another practice are usually reminded or persuaded to fall into place. Correspondingly, rituals usually assign clear roles or tasks to each member of the family. Sixth, as I have said, rituals are usually rich with symbolism; some families can interpret part of the symbolic components.

Rituals may originate at any point in family development and may be transmitted across generations. Indeed, this leads to their seventh feature—rituals are transmitting: because of their invariance across broad reaches of time, their rich symbolic and communicative nature, and the verve with which they are practiced, rituals are transmitting. They convey a rich and impressive image of family life to outsiders, to growing children, and in many instances to the next generation. Thus, Bennett, Wolin, Reiss, and Teitelbaum were able to demonstrate that rituals are likely mechanisms for the psychosocial transmission of alcoholism across generations: if alcoholism invades the rituals of the parental generation it is much more likely to emerge in the children's generation—either in the biological offspring *or in their spouses.*

207

STORIES

Most families tell stories about themselves; some are passed down from generation to generation. Many are told and retold across time. Aside from current work in our laboratory, by Molly Oliveri and myself, I am unaware of any systematic, quantative studies of such family stories. However, from the perspective of the individual teller or listener, stories have been a major center of interest for developmental and cognitive psychologists (Mandler, 1984; Nelson & Gruendel, 1981; Rumelhart, 1977; Cohler, 1982). In general, the direct elicitation and analysis of stories have been used as tools for understanding cognitive development in children or, in Bertram Cohler's work, for exploring an internal sense of consistency and coherence at midlife. Sociolinguists have been interested in stories as a special form of discourse; by recognizing that stories help organize a social group into a "teller" and "listeners," they have identified the story as a mechanism of social integration (see Sacks, 1978; Jefferson, 1978; Ryave, 1978).

Only recently have anthropologists, and folklorists in particular, approached the role of the story in the family. Steven Zeitlin, Amy Kotkin, and Holly Baker (1982) have collected large numbers of family stories through a special family folklore project at the Smithsonian Institution in Washington, D.C. In general, their collection suggests that family stories serve three broad functions. First, they highlight conspicuous heroes or rogues in the family's history. For example, a black family retells a story of a slave grandfather who violated the antireading laws of the slaveholding states by secretly learning to read from one of the slaveholder's children. Or an American family of German descent tells of an uncle who remained in Germany and stood up to the Nazis by defying their ban on building personal houses; his strategy was to construct one under a huge pile of junk.

A second function of family stories is to highlight, dramatize, and conserve the vividness of significant family transitions and stressful events. These include weddings, courtships, migrations, and lost family fortunes. Some families have elaborate stories about supernatural or religious experiences. Also, major family feuds, sometimes explaining current splits in the family, are told and retold. In our own work family stories are also readily elaborated around illnesses and recoveries.

A third function of stories is to enshrine and preserve certain family customs. Zeitlin, Kotkin, and Baker (1982) have recorded many stories, for example, that explain unique family expressions. For instance, when a grandmother in a family traveled to the city of Washington in the winter, as a very young girl, she looked out the hotel window and told her mother that it was "so icy, horses are falling left and right." But when her mother checked she could see only one horse slipping. Thus, the phrase "horses are falling left and right" became the family's expression for exaggeration, a phrase that endured for seventy years. Sometimes, family customs and even rituals are the focus of family stories. One family had a tradition of giving a can of Canadian seal meat as a wedding present. This ritual arose from the story of a cousin, in days of yore, who gave it as a jesting Christmas present after he returned to Kentucky from a long sojourn in Canada.

Stories have both a mythic and exalted component and a concealed and secret component. One story told to us by a family in our study concerned the presumably unintended shooting of their son by an enraged neighbor. The story, as it developed, emphasized the son as an innocent bystander who, but for the grace of God, might have been fatally wounded; it exalted the forbearance of the family, who "understood" the anguish of their neighbor, a tearful and anxious immigrant. His daughters, among the few children of their ethnic background in the neighborhood, had been mercilessly taunted by their peers. Concealed in the story was the family's fear that their son had been among the ethnically motivated taunters of the immigrant family. The hidden concern of the storytelling family emerged in a series of linked but subordinate stories—stories told as asides to the main story—about a grandfather who was killed in a tractor accident, perhaps through carelessness; about a childhood friend of mother's who was drowned because he refused to heed storm warnings; and stories about the son himself, which pictured him as a troublemaker.

Stories are easily remembered. Indeed, they are attractive to cognitive psychologists because they seem to delineate cognitive and memory structures that sustain them across time. Surely, of all the levels I have described, stories should exemplify more of the represented than the practicing family. I suggest otherwise. Like rituals and problem-solving episodes, and possibly even microchains, the longevity of stories depends on individual memory and hence on representational processes. However, in describing this level of structure in family life, I am focusing not on the remembered or represented story but on the *act* of storytelling itself. Thus, the focus shifts from the content of the story to its telling and retelling as a communal or shared act of historical reconstruction by the family as a group.

Although there are few empirical data to guide us here, there appear to be three circumstances in which families tell stories about themselves. First, stories are told to outsiders just as they were to the interviewers in our research project. For some families this was an opportunity to assemble a story for the first time, to begin a process of fitting and reconciling varying accounts and individual memories. The story was created as it was told. In these instances the interviewer—whose questions were guided by a brief manual—clearly was an active participant: her questions elicited some facets of the evolving group tale and helped suppress others. For other families it was clear that the main lines of the story were well rehearsed. For these families the retelling not only conveyed a standard line but permitted subordinated asides which expressed hidden or darker sides of the experienced family history or a partially concealed dissent or conflict among individuals about versions of the past. It was striking that in almost no instance did the story emerge fully formed: its retelling was always an event of re-creation, formulation, elaboration, active suppression, fresh dissent, reconciliation, or all of these.

These active, evolutionary processes probably typify the other circumstances of storytelling and retelling in family life where pure outsiders are not involved. One group of such instances may be termed initiations. Here a child or a potential or actual in-law (boyfriends, girlfriends, fiancés, and newlywed spouses are very frequently the audience of family stories) is regaled with a story that serves two functions simultaneously: it makes the recent arrival more of an insider and privy to the quasi-secrets that bind as well as fracture families. At the same time, like other initiation rites, storytelling serves to define family values and shared self-images. A second group of instances are the retelling of stories at family gatherings where everyone knows the basic plot and themes. Sometimes, as Zeitlin, Kotkin, and Baker have noted, storytelling is a regular feature of recurrent family rituals. At other times it is more spontaneous. The main outlines of the stories are clear and hence a special form of ellipsis or condensation may characterize the telling; the family may be left to fill in the blank spaces implicitly. The filling-in process is itself an affirmation of the special characteristics of the group. I have already described a particularly graphic instance of storytelling ellipsis: the phrase that substitutes for the entire family story, such as the "horses are falling left and right."

Thus, storytelling, as opposed to the stories themselves, remains a continuously and communally interpretive act. Stories in the practicing family are not individually represented images and experiences of family life. Rather, there are simultaneous redactions and interpretations that are communally performed. They serve as continuing error-correcting procedures in family life by acting as constant affirmations of family values and through pressure to reduce dissent.

We have also been impressed in our own research by how storymaking and storytelling are an active coping device for the family in the face of severe stress. In one study we asked all families to tell us about a recent stressful event and how they responded to it. We coded the entire story for a number of features. One dimension that emerged with clarity was the degree to which the story put the event in some perspective. The storytelling process was an effort to bind or heal the wounds of the event: to make sense out of the event, to reconcile conflicts in the family that it had produced, and, perhaps most important, to place the event within the context of a recognizable family history consistent with the family's image of itself. Clearly, some families had largely achieved this closure by the time we asked about the events, and their stories reflect a completion of this process. For others this process was just the beginning—perhaps stimulated by our requests for a story.

INTEGRATING LEVELS OF COORDINATED PRACTICE

Do these five kinds of practices operate separately from one another to maintain continuity of family process and family relationships across time? This seems unlikely. More likely they act in concert, although we have remarkably few data on the relationships among the kinds of common practices. One possibility is that levels are related to one another as foreground and background factors. For example, the maintenance of rituals across time—a foreground factor in this instance—depends on the family's executing particular kinds of interactional microchains—a background factor. The reverse may also be true. The perpetuation of microchains of a given character may also arise from a background of particular family rituals and stories. Indeed, we can sketch out a possible mechanism of this kind using the data on coercive microchains collected by Patterson and his group. Patterson's (1982) data on coercion in families of boys with conduct disorders provides a particularly rich set of detailed observations. These permit an initial analysis of how many of the kinds of common practices described above may be linked together in a coherent, ordered mechanism.

In studying these interaction patterns, Patterson's primary question was, what microsocial processes account for the greater frequency of aggressive behaviors in children in some families and less frequency in others? To answer this question Patterson and his group have observed hundreds of families over extended periods in their own homes. Their observations have been precise, objective, and quantitative, using an observational scheme called the Family Interaction Coding System. Approximately every six seconds a trained observer coded the nature of a social interaction in which the target member was engaged (every five minutes a new target member was randomly selected so that the interaction patterns of all members were sampled repeatedly over time).

In all families studied, both those with children who were highly aggressive and antisocial and those with children without behavior problems, Patterson discovered an interesting sequence of behavior. A parent, or a sibling in some cases, initiated the sequence with an aversive behavior, the two most frequent being either physical punishment by the parent or the parent's ignoring the child. The next behavior in the sequence was clearly a counterattack by the child, very frequently a form of destruction or yelling. The third step, and most crucial, was a *cessation* of aversiveness by the parent: the parental behavior immediately following the counterattack by the child was positive, not aversive. In normal families about 15 percent of all children's coercive behavior is embedded in such chains, whereas 21 percent of such behavior in families of aggressors is embedded in them. The number of initial, unprovoked attacks by the parent and counterattacks by the child are greater in the latter; as a consequence the overall frequency of such chains is much higher in families of aggressive children. Indeed, these three-step michrochains are a central part of their interactional style.

What maintains these sequences? Patterson focuses on reinforcement. When the parent stops his or her own aversive behavior after the child's counterattack, that parental *cessation* is a reinforcement of the counterattack. To extend Patterson's argument, it can also be seen that the child's cessation of attack following the parent's cessation reinforces the parent's cessation. Thus, each partner is reinforcing the other. However, as Patterson himself implies, reinforcement does not constitute a very powerful explanation. Rather, the temporal relationship between an antecedent event and a response is more probable if the antecedent and response are followed by the so-called reinforcing behavior rather than other alternatives. The interesting question is still unanswered: Why does the reinforcer have this effect?

There are several fragments of data that may yield a more satisfactory explanation, an explanation invoking several more complex or molar types of common practice. First, physiological data suggest that counterattacks, particularly successful ones (as in the negative reinforcement microchain), may reduce many indices of automatic arousal in the counterattacker (see Green, Stonner, & Shope, 1975). Second, Patterson's preliminary data suggest that these sequences may require a particular "agent" to both start and continue them. That is, in delineating a particular microchain, especially a coercive one, it is not possible to separate the person who initiates or reinforces the chain from the behavior itself. For example, in some families only the coercive behavior of the mother, not the father, may initiate such chains. Third, settings may play a significant role in maintaining these sequences. Preliminary data, for example, suggest that techniques that are effective in interrupting chains of this kind at home do not generalize to school settings, where the teacher replaces a parent in the chain (Patterson, 1982).

Drawing together these fragmentary data with the more solid data from the many lines of Patterson's work, I have constructed a possible scheme to account for the negative reinforcement microchains that have such importance in families of aggressive children.

Figure 9-1 shows three components of the basic scheme for illustrating the connection among kinds of common practices. The first component of this scheme, as shown at the top of figure 9-1, is the microchain of aversive behaviors which Patterson has described. These are the public social events illustrated on the top of the figure. These sequences or events, as I have noted, have been observed in the home, and approximate established fact. The second component of the scheme is a postulated series of internal events that are presumed to occur on a second-by-second basis within the parent and the child. These processes are linked by the same reciprocal relationships as the manifest, public interaction events. The third component of the scheme is what I am calling setting rules. This component references the apparent setting specificity of Patterson's findings. His contrasts between home and school have involved both a change of agents—from parent to teacher—and a change of setting. My own clinical experience indicates that the negative reinforcement sequences are less frequent, even when the same agents are involved, in public settings than at home. It is crucial to know whether the sequences are less frequent because the initiating event—the unprovoked attack—occurs less frequently or because the conditional probabilities of subsequent events, given an unprovoked attack, are also changed.

Let us examine the second component more carefully because it resides at the logical hub of our analysis. Patterson's data suggest that the negative reinforcement sequence may be propelled by sequential social cognitions of the parent and child. The child perceives the parent's initial unprovoked attack as a threat *unique to that parent;* a similar set of behaviors from the other parent or from siblings may or may not be perceived as a threat. Similarly, the parent perceives the child's response as a threat *unique to that child;* similar responses from the spouse or other children may not be perceived as threatening. A series of investigations (Mandler, 1967; Glass, 1977; Henry, 1980; Ekman, Leenson, & Friesen, 1983) suggests that perceived threat is a fundamental psychological experience activating autonomic arousal and that the combination of autonomic arousal and perceived threat constitutes in a broad range of species a powerful incentive for escape (Solomon & Wynne, 1954). If, in previous instances, a behavior has provided successful escape it will very likely be tried first in the current instance. The precise mechanism by which a repertoire of potential escape-avoidance responses is accessed is not known. Patterson has collected no biological data, but the

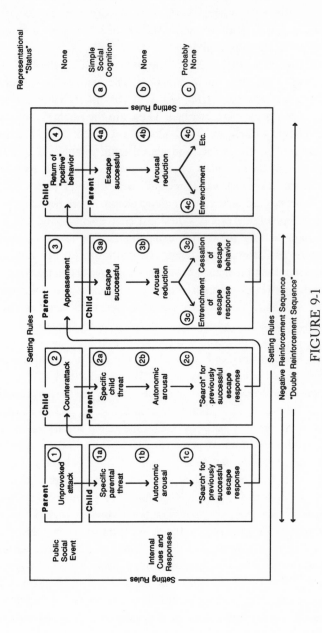

FIGURE 9-1

A hypothetical mechanism to explain the attack-counterattack sequence in families of aggressive boys observed by Patterson.

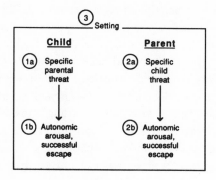

FIGURE 9-2

The minimum number of elements that must be "stored" over long periods of time in order to maintain the attack-counterattack sequence.

relationship between perceived threat and autonomic arousal in dyadic social interaction is clearly established in Gottman's recent (1979, 1986) work and the role of autonomic arousal in parent–infant interaction is also being explored. Moreover, we now have data on escape-avoidance learning and the role of autonomic arousal in this process (Green, Stonner, & Shope, 1975). A major value of exploring escape-avoidance processes in this sequence rests on the relative permanence of behavior that is "learned" as successful in escape situations. Escape avoidance is an attractive paradigm in seeking to explain behavior perdurance even though it raises as many questions as it answers. It is relevant that Gottman has proposed an escape-avoidance mechanism to account for perdurance of marital interaction patterns.

The scheme in figure 9-1 is unnecessarily elaborate. It clarifies a sequence of observable and internal events that characterize and partially explain a typical coercive cycle. However, something less than that scheme needs to be stored over the long haul to account for perdurance of the coercive micro-chain. Figure 9-2 is my effort to delineate the minimum requirements. I suggest that the following three components may suffice.

First, we need the readiness in a particular parent–child pair—say, a father and his oldest son—to perceive threat uniquely in the activities of the other. This readiness probably includes specific behavior in the other that somehow activates the perceived threat.

Second, we need an established connection between autonomic arousal and escape behavior. I assume that the linkage between perceived threat and autonomic arousal is built into many species and is certainly not specific to particular families.

215

Finally, we need the operation of setting constraints. The setting rule, as I have said, may operate to moderate the frequency of the initial behaviors in the microchain or the conditional probabilities of subsequent behaviors.

The three may be the necessary and sufficient elements. Once father emits a threatening behavior the whole microchain is set in motion. The son may begin an incomplete chain by emitting a threatening behavior. (The child's threatening behavior would be sufficient, according to my scheme, to elicit an appeasement from father since it is sufficient to produce autonomic arousal in him.) It would be important to know whether these incomplete chains are also more frequent in families of aggressive children; Patterson does not report data that I can interpret in this way.

In this scheme, four elements constitute a mechanism for perdurance of family patterns. The first element is the observable microchain itself, the four-step coercive sequence. The second element is the set of shared perceptions—similar or complementary—that family members hold of each other. In the current scheme these are illustrated by father's and son's perceptions of each other as dangerous. As I will outline below, I posit that these perceptions are sustained more through common practices such as rituals and storytelling in the whole family than by their perdurance as individual representations. The third element is the group of relevant setting rules, which may be simpler versions of processes I described earlier in relationship to artifacts and hallowed ground. Finally, there is a fourth element, socially oriented biological mechanisms—in this case the linkage between autonomic arousal and escape-avoidance learning.

Let us return to our example of a family in which the coercive cycle is maintained by the father and oldest son, although it involves other family members as well. The cycle is perpetuated through a multilevel mechanism that includes a mutual perception of dangerousness. Are not these mutual perceptions just a reincarnation of internalized relationships similar to those studied by Main and Goldwyn (1984), as reviewed at the outset? Might we not argue that both father and son have internalized a generalized perception of a relationship with one another, including mutual suspicions, victimization, and violence? Perhaps the son may retain such a generalized perception to be reactivated when he has a son of his own. In the long run, data may support this hypothesis.

However, data are of relatively little use unless other lines of analysis are considered, and where data permit, ruled out (or in). I am suggesting that there has been a bias to view perceptions of this kind as phenomena within individuals. The sociologists Phillip Berger and Thomas Luckmann (1966) provided an alternative analysis. Perceptions of this kind, they argued, are not subjectively experienced as "viewpoints" or interpersonal "attitudes." The perceiver regards them as *reality*. The father, in our own example, perceives his son as, *in fact*, dangerous, and vice versa. As perceptions of reality, according to Berger and Luckmann, these social cognitions cannot be sustained without active social support. Berger and Luckmann argue that virtually no one can sustain a vision of reality unless, sooner or later, he or she is joined by others—in politics, religion, and everyday life.

Our research group was among the first to examine empirically the plausibility of this perspective for families (Reiss, 1981). Indeed, a line of investigation strongly suggests that all families develop subtle and persistent shared experiences of themselves—cognitions about the reality of their own strengths and weaknesses *as a group*—as well as shared convictions about the immediate social world in which they live. These convictions—we have called them *family paradigms*—concern the relative safety and stability of the social world, the degree to which it is experienced as novel or related to past experiences, and its inclusion of the family either as an integrated unit or as a group of unrelated individuals.

Although we have no data that directly bear on our example of coercive cycles, extensive clinical experience suggests to me that it is impossible for father and son to sustain the reality of their convictions of mutual dangerousness unless these convictions are supported by the whole family. This does not mean that everyone else in the family must have the identical perceptions. For example, mother may view the son as fragile and vulnerable. This enhances her image of father as dangerous and may sustain the son's image of father's danger as well. In response to mother's image of son, father may view his son as even more dangerous because he is capable of "fooling" his mother and "seducing" her to protect him. Likewise, an older sister may view the father as vulnerable to a brother she sees as a clever manipulator. To retaliate for his occupying so much of father's attention she may bait her brother into violent behavior, enhancing father's perception of his son as dangerous, and subsequent to his retaliation, confirming the reality of his own dangerousness in his son's eyes. Family rituals and stories may maintain these interlocking and self-sustaining perceptions. Eric Bermann (1973) reported a particularly illuminating in-home study of the support of perceptions like these by family stories and rituals that sustained and supported the reality conviction.

The Represented and Practicing Family Reconciled

Are the contrasting visions of the represented and practicing family reconcilable? In my view, yes, but only by research that pays equal heed to both. The differences are more modest when we recognize that they are based on distinctions not in epistemology but in analogy. In the sciences, particularly when we try to think beyond the data at hand, we often reason by analogy. The represented and practicing families are generous, even extravagant, elaborations of simple analogies.

A central analogy of the represented family is the concept of the working model, which has two components. The first is that the social world as beheld through the neutral eyes of the observer does not directly shape the social behavior of the individual or the enduring relationships that he or she forms. Rather, the individual's active and ongoing construction of a model or image of that world is the critical governor of social behavior. The images may be simple and relatively undifferentiated, as in infants and very young children, or they may be more complex and subtle. The second component of the working model is its proactive or anticipatory features. The person can set a model into motion; thus a "working" model. The person can think, if I do this, then X will do that and Y will then do something else. Thus a person's social behavior is shaped by a model that actively anticipates specific social responses as consequences of the person's own social acts.

Deborah Egeland, Byron Jacobvitz, and Alan Sroufe (1988) provide a dramatic example of this form of working model. They describe daughters who as children were sexually exploited by their fathers and emotionally estranged from their mothers (see chapter 4). These daughters, it may be said, develop a model that anticipates a sequence of reactions whenever parent and child interact: "Parent sexually stimulates the child of the opposite sex and distances or derides child of same sex." Thus, this daughter as a parent sexually stimulates her son but scorns her daughter.

In contrast, the central analogy of the practicing family is embedded in the word *practicing* itself, as in to practice a religion—or to practice an art (perhaps even an occult art). Another sense of the word is as in rehearsal of a play or of a musical instrument; here repeated problem-solving efforts, once mastered, become routine. But the core image, at least as I have articulated this perspective, describes not a kind of an *individual*—such as an intuitive, model-building scientist—but a kind of a *group*. The parallels to religious groups or ideologically driven political parties are perhaps the closest.

Berger and Luckmann argue that models in the minds of individuals cannot long endure without being sustained by common group practice. In my own work, guided by the vision of the practicing family, I have been attracted to Thomas Kuhn's (1962) notion of the paradigm and have reported, as alluded to earlier, a considerable range of data supporting the notion of a family paradigm. Kuhn's ideas caught my attention as a set of analogies because they specifically addressed the social context of a scientist's working model. For most scientists, the perdurance of scientific models does not depend on the retentive powers of individual scientific minds; it rests instead on the routinized common practice of the scientific community.

Recognizing that these two visions are separated by a chasm no wider than an analogy, the sad fact is that we have little data to permit us to integrate the perspectives. Arguing by example, I have already indicated in my comparisons of the initial Main and Goldwyn report with that of the Minuchin group some research pathways that lie before us. It is beyond the scope of this chapter to outline a research agenda to make critical choices here. In general, we need a clearer picture of the relative power of internal models and common practices to predict sustained patterns of both competent and maladaptive social relationships. More precisely, we need to know what specific predictions are possible from each perspective. Two areas of active, current research are ideal arenas for comparing the relative power of these two contrasting visions or analogies.

The first area is studies of long-term continuity of social behavior. Sroufe, for example, in chapters 4 and 5 has provided dramatic examples of continuity in social behavior from early childhood to school age and from early childhood experience in the family of origin to adult social experience in the family of procreation. What are the mechanisms that maintain this continuity? Visions of the represented family prompt hypotheses that working models are internalized early in childhood and persist across great spans of time. I would argue that this hypothesis cannot be critically tested without attention to alternate hypotheses drawn from the vision of the practicing family. Continuities in social behavior from early to later childhood may be plausibly attributed to constancy in the social groups of which the child is a member: the family first and foremost, but also other intimate groups. Likewise, the even broader continuities from childhood to adulthood may be sustained through equally enduring common practices in long-term social groups. Research is now only beginning to uncover, for example, the extraordinary impact of surviving members of early family life (aging parents, for example) on the current marriage and parenting practices of their adult children. And the powerful effects of sibling relationships across the lifespan are only beginning to be recognized. Sibling relationships may be an excellent vehicle for maintaining continuity in social roles and relationships from early childhood through adulthood.

A second and related body of research is on the effect of interventions, both preventative and therapeutic. In this connection, it is important not to be misled by the official label of the intervention. We know, for example, that "individual psychotherapy" may have as much effect on family patterns as do "family therapy" interventions (see, for example, Pilkonis, Imber, Lewis, & Rubinsky, 1984). Likewise, family therapy can have profound effects on individual experiences, perspectives, mood, and outlook (see, for example, Friedman, 1975). What is needed most is a careful assessment of the mechanisms of change: How much does the therapeutic induction of new perduring relationship patterns depend on alterations of individually based working models and how much on alterations of common practice?

Relationship Disturbances in Context

Arnold J. Sameroff and Robert N. Emde

Human existence is social existence. Although a few hardy souls may at points in their lives survive as isolates, infants never can. Their physical survival is tied to the care provided by other human beings. If society's physical care ceased to exist, the infant would cease to exist. The question we have been addressing in this book is, to what extent can the same be said for the infant's psychological existence? What are the psychological consequences of human relationships for the infant?

The special consequences of most concern to us are disorders of infant behavior. We are very troubled by the diagnostic principle that is the foundation of all existing psychiatric classification systems, that disorder is a characteristic of the individual. Our experience with early development has made it very difficult for us to see infants apart from their caregivers in normal growth, and by extension, in deviant growth. We were struck that in the first volume with "infant psychiatry" as part of the title, the editors (Rexford, Sander, & Shapiro, 1976) argued that infants were part of a complex set of relationships:

> This viewpoint places the infant always in a context and in an ongoing continuity of exchange within that context. From this standpoint, organization of behavior at any one place in time, and the changes in organization of behavior during a child's development, are not considered to be issues belonging at the level of the

individual but rather are viewed as issues properly belonging at the level of the system, that is, the baby in interaction with the caretaking environment. The infant and the caretaking milieu are the constituents of an open, interactive, regulative system, each component member participating in exchanges which mutually influence and regulate the behavior of the other. (pp. xvi–xvii)

If the individual is not a suitable level of analysis for understanding infant development, neither is the individual a suitable level of analysis for understanding infant behavioral disorders. This is not to say that infants are not individuals or that infants do not make contributions to the systems in which they participate. But individuality must be considered in context, and therefore diagnosis must include context as a major parameter. Easier said than done. One of the major hindrances to the growth of infant psychiatry has been the poor quality of assessments of individual behavior. To try for quality assessments of relationships as well has been a further critical stumbling block. On the other hand, if the treatment of infant symptoms requires the treatment of relationships, then defining the quality of those relationships is a paramount issue.

Infant Adaptation and Early Relationships

DEVELOPMENTAL REGULATION

The theme of regulation that permeates our understanding of psychological growth is first presented by Arnold Sameroff (chapter 1) in a general description of developmental processes. From the perspective of general systems theory (Sameroff, 1983, 1989), the definition of an individual depends on the ability to engage in autonomous functioning in the face of environmental variation. Human beings have psychological processes that represent the highest level of self-regulation, the ability not only to be self-aware but to self-reflect and to construct more comprehensive modes of adaptation. The excitement to be found in the study of infants is that we can watch the creation of this psychological world out of their experience with the biological and social history of their culture. What we have to avoid is the illusion that infants are self-created. Without their biological heritage there would be no capacity to exist and without their social heritage there would be no opportunity to exist.

Despite the infant's burgeoning abilities, an initial limited repertoire of thought and action do not provide for a capacity to adapt alone. The regulating system of the child must include another: a caregiver. Thus when we refer to the self-regulation of the child's development, we refer to a dyadic system. Infants need caregivers, of whatever kind, to monitor their state and produce changes in the environment to compensate whenever their condition requires. For these reasons regulation by self and others must be considered the core function of human existence.

The domain of human developmental regulation is described by Sameroff as comprising transactions between the genotype, the phenotype, and the environtype. The social environtype is hypothesized to be a coded regulatory system, analogous to the biological genotype, that has evolved in each culture to assure the growth of children to be productive adults. It operates through a developmental agenda that is comprised of influences from cultural, family, and individual parent codes. Differences in developmental agendas produce differences in the adult products that characterize different cultures. Developmental psychopathology results from disorganization or lack of coherence in developmental agendas, reflecting states of disorganization in the culture, the family, or the parent. Because the environtype is conceptualized as always in a transactional relationship to the child, the quality of the relationship becomes a prime ingredient in each child's adaptation.

DEVELOPMENT AND AFFECT IN THE RELATIONSHIP EXPERIENCE

The infant's physiological needs are useful as obvious examples of the infant's inability to be considered as independent. When we move to the consideration of psychological development, the picture has been less clear. In recent years a heavy focus has been placed on the attachment relationship between infant and parent as a major indicator of the social and emotional adaptive capacities of the child. Robert Emde (chapter 2) considers a much larger range of functional aspects of the parent–child relationship. He defines a set of complementary roles for parent and child that are embedded in the biological history of the human species. He describes the asymmetry of the parent's and child's roles in each of these domains, which assures the developmental needs of the child. The infant's attachment to the parent is the counterpart to the parent's bonding to the infant. The parent's protective behavior is complemented by the child's vigilance for danger. The physiological regulation of the infant is balanced by the need satisfaction provided by the parent. Infant learning is complemented by parent teaching. Self-control by the child is intertwined with discipline and structure provided by the parent. And, of most consequence to Emde, affect regulation and sharing by the infant is enabled by empathic responsiveness of the parent.

Affect is seen by Emde as a core of human psychological experience. A strong biological preparedness for the infant's activity, self-regulation, and social fit in human interactions is made possible by a strong biological preparedness for affective monitoring. The infant's ability to experience different emotions and to recognize different emotions in others provides a sense of coherence and connection, linking the infant's own past and current experiences and linking the infant with other humans. The experience of affect is described as undergoing developmental transformations in the form of biobehavioral shifts during the first two years of life. These shifts are biologically potentiated but consolidated in a relationship context. As an organizer of experience, affect provides incentives for integration as well as maintaining an individual's sense of coherence. Affect is universally human, fundamentally social, and a major ingredient of the child's emerging sense of self.

The quality of the affective core, and thus of the infant's sense of self, is conditioned by the relationship with the parent. Security arises out of caregiving relationships, as does a positive emotional balance. Conversely, insecurity and a negative emotional balance are also a consequence of relationship experiences. The developing personality of the child is founded in these early relationship experiences. The next question to be addressed is how these experiences are carried forward.

REPRESENTING RELATIONSHIPS

The development of the infant's ability to represent relationship experience is described by Daniel Stern (chapter 3) in answer to three questions: (1) Where does a relationship pattern reside? (2) What gives relationship patterns continuity? and (3) What is a representation of interactive history?

The answer to the first question addresses psychodynamic theories that treat relationship representations as individual creations that are fantasy-based. Stern argues that relationship patterns or object relations are rooted in the reality of social interactions. They reside outside the individual and initially are constituted only during social interactions. What gives relationship patterns continuity is the child's memory of past interaction history. The mental representation of interactive events is the repository of continuity, but of what does this representation consist?

In accord with a developmental model, Stern outlines a hierarchy of representational units that increase in complexity as the child's cognitive abilities grow. In the beginning specific interactions are encoded as episodic memories of specific lived events. These memories become integrated into functional categories comprised of representations of generalized experience. The functional categories of experience are prototypes encompassing elements from multiple domains: motor, perceptual, affective, cognitive, and motivational. None of these features has priority, in general, but a prototype may be dominated by affect or one of the other features as the most salient domain. The representations of generalized interactive events become organized into interaction scenarios with increasing invariance; different ones are available for different activities. Scenarios become incorporated into working models, but not only in regard to attachment. Working models are formed in every domain of a child's activity, including those described by Emde as the functional aspects of development. The working model is conceived of as a motivational system that regulates behavior. It permits the child to form expectations and evaluate consequences. However, it operates not consciously but rather as a "presymbolic" guide to action, interpretation, and feeling. Consciousness becomes evident with the development of narrative models of interaction regulation during the third year of life. Narratives are different from working models in that they can be told to oneself or another.

This developmentally and organizationally hierarchic view of relationship representations offers a model for the internalization of relationship experiences. The quality of these experiences will affect the quality of the representations and thus the quality of new relationships where these representations are called forth. The organized self will carry forward and enact these representations into later periods of life.

THE EMERGING SELF

The role of social relationships in the emergence and formation of the self is elaborated by Alan Sroufe (chapter 4). He argues that the dyadic caregiving relationship not only precedes but gives rise to the sense of self. In line with the general systems view of development presented by Sameroff, the affective core of self emerging in the context of the caregiving relationship presented by Emde, and the hierarchical organization of representation discussed by Stern, Sroufe sees behavior as not simply what people do but how it is organized. Development is not simply the capacity to do new things but, more fundamentally, changes in the organization of behavior. Individual differences in the organization of behavior produce differences among normal individuals and between normal and disordered individuals.

The self is seen as emerging developmentally from the negotiation of a series

225

of issues within the parent–child relationship. The issues arise as changes in the infant's behavior that are driven by a combination of biological and burgeoning psychological abilities perturb the parent's interactive behavior. In Sameroff's terms, the changing phenotype triggers the developmental agenda of the environtype. A view of the specifics of this process is to be found in Louis Sander's (1975) description of an epigenetic sequence of adaptive issues. He describes how the rapidly growing and changing infant introduces new qualities and quantities of behavior into the interaction. Although we have referred to Sander's work several times throughout the book, we are committed more to his conceptualization than to the specific issues and phases he describes. There is not yet a sufficient empirical base for describing any universal sequence of parenting issues.

In Sroufe's organizational theory, smoothly organized attachment behavior and affect regulation in the infant are seen to emerge from a history of responsive care. Prompt and effective parental response has been associated with secure infant attachment behavior. The experience of the child becomes one of self as potent and worthy. These aspects of the self are carried forward into the expanding world of social interactions beyond the parent. For securely attached infants the sense of others as available and valuable is carried forward into adaptive relationships with peers and teachers in the preschool setting. In contrast, for insecurely attached infants preschool interactions are characterized by frequent hostility, unprovoked aggression, and generally negative and exploitative peer relationships.

Sroufe's description of the emergence of self and Stern's description of the development of relationship representation converge on the importance of working models for mediating the early relationships experienced by the child and the later ones created by the child. Children are seen as behaving in ways to confirm existing models. Working models of secure attachments promote positive interactions that further confirm the models. Working models of insecure attachments also are confirmed by the social rejection elicited by the child's negativity and aggressiveness. Developmental competence is carried forward in the organization of self that has emerged from the parent–child negotiation of interactional issues.

Relationship Experience and Disturbance

DESCRIBING AND ASSESSING RELATIONSHIPS

A basis for the description of variation in relationships is needed in order to provide a foundation for relationship classification. Relationships are defined by Sroufe (chapter 5) as regularities in patterns of social interaction over time; they are the product of both partners. There has been a traditional focus on the content of interactions as the most salient influence on child behavior. We would argue that for social and emotional outcomes the quality of the interaction may be more important. The "how" of the relationship includes a description of the patterning, functions, and goals of the partners over a wide variety of circumstances.

A major problem in the assessment of relationships is that, unlike the individuals who participate in them, they are intangible. Yet Sroufe argues that their reality is evident in the predictable consequences for individual behavior that result from patterns of interactional behavior.

The structure of relationships is in the patterns of interaction. The rules, roles, and coalitions in relationships, well-articulated in family therapy descriptions, are an important aspect of structural assessment. In early development the assessment of structural elements must be quite dynamic because of the rapidly changing characteristics of the infant. The parent is faced with a continuous need for adaptation to the changing contribution of the child. The assessment of this adaptation is an important element in the evaluation of relationship disturbance.

The criteria for assessing relationship disorders, although similar to the criteria for assessing individual disorders, are in many important ways quite distinct. Criteria for disturbance in relationships—as in individuals—include pain, inflexibility, and compromised adaptation in various areas of functioning. Uniquely relational criteria are the balance between individual and relationship needs, the appropriateness of boundaries between individuals, and how relationship serves the developmental needs of its members.

Often relationships are assessed as disturbed without accompanying evidence of overt child disturbance. In such cases there are strong possibilities that these conditions place the child at risk for later negative consequences. Here probablistic predictions have more support than deterministic ones. Deviance in parental communication during adolescence meets the criteria for such a risk condition because of the limitations it places on the child's individuation or emancipation (Goldstein, 1988). Similarly, during infancy the

227

parent–infant attachment relationship may limit the child's exploration of the environment.

The formal assessment of relationships and relationship disturbances has been approached at many levels. Although the clinical literature is replete with descriptive categorizations, few of these have been examined empirically, especially with attention to developmental issues. Traditional schemes for describing parenting behavior have paid little attention to the dyadic dimension of parenting; studies have focused on the style of parenting behavior with little attention to either the developmental level or the interactive contribution of the child.

CLASSIFICATION OF PSYCHOPATHOLOGY

The formidable task of reconciling descriptive models of developing relationships and the psychopathology expressed by infants and young children is tackled by Thomas Anders (chapter 6). His primary objective is to stimulate the development of a nosology of early relationship psychopathology that can supplement existing diagnostic systems.

Anders aims for agreement on descriptions of limited syndromes, offering possible links to etiology, indications for treatment, and prognosis. The need for a classification system for relationship psychopathology is emphasized by the inadequacy of current diagnostic systems in this area. In neither DSMIII-R (American Psychiatric Association, 1987) nor ICD-9 (World Health Organization, 1977, 1979) is there a recognition of the importance of developmental stages or the regulatory functions of parents for the individual behavior of infants. Of the three mental disorders of infancy listed in DSMIII-R, there is good evidence that for at least two of them—reactive attachment disorder and rumination disorder—the disorder may reside more in the parent than in the child.

The diagnosis of relationship disorder requires a comprehensive assessment of individuals within their relationships to family and social context. Areas of assessment must include the current status and history of the child's relationship with parenting figures, the individual characteristics and past histories of the participants, and social support and stresses for the family.

Anders proposes that for diagnostic purposes the relationship must be evaluated in terms of its regulatory pattern, affective tone, and developmental phase. The developmental phase of the relationship requires a focus on both partners as individuals and as partners. The child's range of initiatives for independent regulation must be juxtaposed with the parent's ability to accept and respond to these initiatives. In Sander's (1975) system, for example, as children develop they move from an initial achievement of physiological regulation to an ability to participate in interactions, to an ability to direct interactions, to an ability to intentionally thwart interactions. These changes perturb relationships with caregivers, who must readjust at each phase to the increasing autonomy of the child, modifying specific behaviors while maintaining an adaptively organized, appropriately regulated, affectively attuned relationship with the child.

Unfortunately for evaluation purposes, relationship problems may not be manifest in all domains of interaction. The office assessment of interactions may not find evidence for existing disturbances in feeding or bedtime settings, and even feeding and bedtime interactions might be quite divergent. The development of testing procedures will follow quickly, once clear hypotheses for relationship classification are articulated. We have not given detailed analysis of such procedures because few validated measures have been described. The Ainsworth Strange Situation is a procedure for evaluating the child's working model of the relationship and perhaps for assessing how well the relationship works for the child but not for judging the relationship itself. The underlying rationale of the Strange Situation procedure is to gradually increase the stress level of parental separations until most children will evidence their characteristic responses based on their individual working models. A similar assessment strategy may be successful in which interactive tasks are given that gradually increase the amount of initiative and mutual regulation required of the partners.

Anders argues that not only the personalities and temperaments of the partners but also the past relationship histories of the parents must be taken into account. Once the relationship and the partners have been assessed, there is still a need to see the convergence of the relationship with social norms, stresses, and supports. It is well recognized that impoverished economic circumstances can subvert the opportunity for otherwise competent parents to regulate their child's development adequately. It is less well recognized that cultural differences give different meaning to the contributions of different family members to relationships with the child and have different implications for future consequences of early relationship characteristics.

RELATIONSHIP DISORDERS

The classification of a relationship as disordered is based for Anders on a number of consequences: (1) that an individual is symptomatic because of the relationship experience, (2) that symptoms are disruptive to daily life, (3) that the interactions of the partners are inflexible or insensitive, and (4) that the relationship inhibits the normal developmental progress of the partners (parent as well as child). Disorder itself is the most severe category of relationship dysfunction. Less severe categories, perturbation and disturbance, are far more common and far less prognostic of individual problems.

Perturbation   Perturbations are normative variations in relationships caused on the child's side by either developmental or illness factors. In the case of a perturbation, changes in the child's behavior require changes in the parent's interaction patterns. The progression of developmental perturbations is in line with that described by Sander (1975) and with the biobehavioral shifts in affective development described by Emde (chapter 2). The ubiquity of illnesses during the first years of life is another major source of perturbation more fully described by Arthur Parmelee (chapter 7). To the extent that parents are prepared for these changes in child behavior, either through education or the rearing of their other children or siblings, an adaptation can be made in the relationship as soon as the parent can identify the change in the child's behavior. These aspects of the developmental agenda (see chapter 1) are what assure the parent of a general sense of efficacy in child rearing, based on the history of the culture, the family, and the individual parent.

Disturbance   On the other hand, when the parent's developmental agenda does not contain responses to expectable changes in child behavior, the perturbation may produce a relationship disturbance. Whereas a perturbation may resolve itself relatively quickly, a disturbance results when a problem in regulation persists over time. Such a disturbance need not be considered pathological, but it does represent a risk condition. There is a higher probability that a disturbed relationship will be carried forward into later developmental phases or spill over into other developmental domains than that a well-functioning relationship will.

Disorder   When the relationship disturbance begins to restrict developmental processes, a disorder is indicated. Disorders have been discussed by Anders within a number of commonly observed syndromic categories, including regulation of feeding, sleep, affective exchange, security-exploration, control, boundary, and gender. These syndromes are defined as disorders when they are characterized by dysfunctional relationship regulation patterns and one or both partners are deviating from their developmental trajectories.

Anders's presentation underscores the importance of the diagnosis of relationship qualities when a child is presented as having a behavioral problem. The belief shared by the authors of this volume is that there is no necessary implication that developmental problems are tied to fixed individual characteristics. There is always a dynamic balance between the individual's behavior,

230

developmental processes, and social forces. Changes in the balance can produce disorder or health.

ILLNESS AS A DEVELOPMENTAL PERTURBATION

The idea that developmental changes can produce perturbations in established relationships is familiar to most infancy specialists. On the other hand, to recognize a similar role for illnesses is a foreign idea. Parmelee (chapter 7) contends that it is unusual for illnesses not to perturb family relationships and conversely that there are few disturbed family relationships that will not affect the child's health. He takes an even stronger position by asserting that infant illnesses are important contributors to normative development.

One of the main themes of the development section of this book is that infants learn to define themselves through relationship experiences. In one of the primary caregiving domains, the role of the parent is to provide protection and nourishment. It is during periods of illness that the child may be most sensitive to variations in parental nurturant behavior. The parent's own sense of security with the child's physical fragility will influence many aspects of the child's social and emotional adjustment.

The parent is able to identify the children's illnesses by empathy with their behavioral states. Feelings of illness in both child and parent are not always associated with disease but can be the outcome of behavioral experiences, such as separation or loss. Through the relationship the child learns the emotional concomitants of illness and develops an understanding of the sick role. The child learns to understand empathy and being empathic with others.

In Parmelee's view most parents see wellness and illness as the most salient markers of earlier developmental progress. Caregiving is focused on eating and weight gain rather than social and emotional development. The problem areas are breastfeeding failures, spitting-up problems, and excessive crying. The modal consequence of these perturbations is that caregiving shifts toward overregulation as parents try to bring these difficulties under control.

The parent who remains sensitized to the early spate of childhood illnesses may be further stressed by the continuing number of illnesses experienced by the average child. The care of very sick children may delay and even prevent the parents from reinforcing their own relationship, further reducing their flexibility in the face of the child's illness. Once the illness abates, the child regains the ability for self-regulation and the parents can reduce the level of their involvement. The sensitized parent may not be able to permit the child to take over again, retaining an overprotective attitude well after the child has recovered.

The major transactions between childhood illness and family relationships make the role of pediatricians especially important for supporting appropriate patterns of relationship regulation. Because most early relationship problems manifest themselves as physical conditions in the infant, such as feeding or sleeping problems, the pediatric setting is where most parents will bring their infants for treatment. Despite their increasing prominence, infant mental health professionals are infrequently the point of contact with the service community, and they may be unnecessary except for the most severely disordered relationships if the pediatric contacts are sensitive to relationship issues.

Pediatric sensitivity should take two forms. The first is to be aware of influences of relationships on common behavioral problems in infancy. The second is to be aware of the influences of illness on relationships. Unfortunately, the focus for most medical training is on the symptomatic patient and not on the social context that is affecting and being affected by the symptoms. For Parmelee a key role for pediatricians is behavioral intervention into family functioning. Among these interventions is to assure parents that illnesses are a common and unavoidable part of rearing children, to help parents to understand that a child's illness requires them to take a greater role in caregiving and that the child's improvement requires them to relinquish this overregulation, and to help parents to see themselves as competent caregivers and their children as durable beings. Physical problems and illness have important functions in helping parents and children appreciate the limits of their abilities to take care of themselves and others.

Relationship Continuity through the Life Cycle

The description and classification of early relationships has two purposes. The first is to provide a basis for understanding disorders during early childhood and to discover ways of resolving these disorders. The second is to provide a basis for exploring the continuity between early relationships and later ones. Continuity is influenced by the resemblance in partners and functions from one age to another as well as by the means through which the qualities of relationships are carried forward in time.

PARTNERSHIPS THROUGH LIFE

One goal of this book is to raise professional consciousness about the ubiquity of relationship influences during infancy and early childhood. But as with most consciousness raising, many adherents may be sensitive only to the first steps in the process. We have argued for a shift in focus from the individual child to the caregiving dyad, typically the mother–child relationship. Now we must confront the fact that the mother–child dyad is of declining prominence among the many relationships in which children take part, especially as they grow older. Indeed, as Herbert Leiderman (chapter 8) points out, in many other cultures the mother–infant relationship may be of secondary importance in many domains of a child's life.

Leiderman argues that the normal variation in relationships and their development must be comprehended before one can make judgments about disorder. Pathological deviancy must be separated from cultural deviancy based on norms of Western society. In many cultures the toddler is expected to enter into a variety of relationships with siblings and other members of the culture. In some cultures the process begins earlier and siblings take on virtually all caregiving and socializing functions when the infant begins walking.

Another source of variation in relationships is the child's own development. As children grow they enter into a number of relationship types, according to the scheme presented by Emde and elaborated by Leiderman. Children move from the early asymmetrical caregiving/care receiving partnership with the mother; to more symmetrical affiliation with same-age peers; to new mentoring relationships with older near peers, which combine features of the asymmetric parent relationship and the symmetric peer relationship; to the most complex romantic relationships. Each of these types involves different social roles and relationship processes, although the functions associated with each type continue through the life cycle.

The genesis and continuity of relationship problems has not been studied well enough to make developmental links between early and later problems. Research on early development has attended to continuities in relationship problems during early childhood, especially investigations of attachment. Research on later development has not attended to continuities in relationship behavior, but only to aspects of personality, especially antisocial behavior. Conversely, there have not yet been demonstrations in the continuity of early personality, and there has been little research on the continuity of relationships in older children.

One of the major problems in understanding the continuity of relationship problems is to identify their mode of transmission. A strong case has been made by Stern (chapter 3) and Sroufe (chapter 5) for the role of representation, especially of working models of relationships, as the primary conserver of relationship deviancy. In a similar vein, Emde has argued that continuity is carried by an affective core of self that has become conditioned and tuned by early relationship experiences and whose representations become reactivated in later affectively similar relationship experiences. Leiderman, in contrast, believes that a case can be made for continuity of context as the conserver of relationship patterns. Past relationship deviations are related to present relationship problems because those early relationships have been enacted continuously and concurrently. It may not be so much that the relationship experience with the parent in the first few years of life influences later competency as that the same parent is still interacting with the child and still in a disturbed relationship. The contrast between the influence of relationship representations and that of the ongoing relationship between child and parents is the central focus of David Reiss's (chapter 9) contribution to understanding family influences.

REPRESENTED VERSUS PRACTICED RELATIONSHIPS

Research on early relationships has maintained a dyadic focus excluding much of family life. To the extent that the role of the father is taken into consideration, it has been as part of a contrasting or competing parent–child dyad with that of the mother (Parke & Tinsley, 1987). Small beginnings have been made at revealing the more complicated relationships in the family, where not only do mother–child and father–child relationships have complementary roles, but the mother–father marital relationship is an important modifier of each parent's relationship with the child (Belsky, Rovine, & Fish, 1989).

But still there has been little work on the family as a total system in early childhood. One of the major stumbling blocks in such efforts has been the lack of models on which to base research efforts. Reiss has brought together a wide range of conceptions in family research into a model that may serve as such a basis. He describes two aspects of family functioning that must be included in any adequate theory—the represented family and the practicing family. The represented family is defined through reports of internal representations of social relationships. The practicing family is defined through observations of patterned, coordinated family behavior. For the represented family stability of relationship behavior through development and across generations is maintained by the stability of working models of relationships. For the practicing family stability is maintained by interaction patterns among the members.

These two perspectives have important implications for the treatment of relationship disorders. If the disorder is in representations, a different approach must be taken than if the disorder is in practice. In the former case the individual is the repository of the disorder, whereas in the latter the disorder is in the individual's lived relationships with others. Where representations are seen as the source of relationship problems, a psychodynamic intervention would seem most fruitful. Where practice is seen as the source, modifications in the behavioral interactions of family members would seem most fruitful. Although the distinction is important, Reiss maintains that the two perspectives are alternative descriptions of relationships and that both are essential to an integrated view of family disorder and therapy.

Reiss's own work (1981) has been devoted to the study of family paradigms, subtle and persistent shared experiences of family members and convictions about the world in which they live. Although he sees paradigms as examples of family practice, it is not unreasonable to consider them as being based in part on working models, a represented, generally unaware, aspect of individual functioning. His use of paradigm derives from the work of Thomas Kuhn (1962) on scientific revolutions. Reiss interprets Kuhn as believing that scientific models do not depend on the minds of individual scientists but on the common practice of the scientific community. Thus the family paradigm depends not only on the working models of individual members but on the common practice of the family as a unit. Which of these perspectives is the richer will be determined through empirical research in which intervention strategies based on individual and family models can be studied. In truth, it is most likely that all current relationships are a product of developmental history and contemporary circumstances and that these circumstances include both represented and practiced elements. To produce an adequate understanding of relationship disorders requires attention to each of these factors. The clinical and empirical reality we are confronting is that such analyses are the exception rather than the rule.

Where Do We Go from Here?

We have told what we believe is an exciting story of what we see in early relationships. Unfortunately, it must remain a story until the database we have reviewed is greatly expanded. There are major lacks in every empirical domain connected to our concerns. Yet we may have advanced the possibility of empirical confirmations by providing a theoretical framework for organizing the study of early relationships and their representation. We have moved into a territory where there is much to be explored and little integrating theory. The history of science has provided ample evidence that blind empiricism rarely advances our knowledge. At the most fundamental levels of physics, it has been theory that has guided the search for new particles that would never have been found without a focused spotlight. What is further remarkable about the search for the ultimate individual units of existence is that the current answer is a relationship. The elementary units known as quarks can exist only in pairs; the existence of our universe is based on relationships. In regard to the study of early social relationships, there must be a theory that organizes what we know and points to the gaps.

Research on basic developmental processes has always sought to discover what leads to what under what circumstances. With the conceptual advances we have made in our understanding of dyadic regulation, affective communication, and early schematic memory processes, can we now discern more about developmental change? Can we predict factors that influence change and continuity within the context of the early caregiving relationship experience? Can we delimit the conditions that foster adaptive relationships? Some of the research reviewed here offers a promising start to answering these questions. But there is still a world of knowledge to be discovered.

Our book describes much of what is known about variations in the child and the child's experience of the quality of early relationships. Moreover, we have attempted to structure a system of clinical classification for early relationships, one that might prove useful for identifying and assessing relationships that are currently disturbed or are at risk for future disturbance.

We need to know the conditions under which maladaptive early caregiving relationships exist, persist, and are subject to ameliorative change. Our suggested classification system of relationship deviance needs validation (and probable modification) through the process of clinical trial and through correlations with other domains of meaningful clinical data. What conditions affect regulatory problems in relationships that are characterized by rigidity of response, by distress, by inappropriate boundaries, and by interference with the development of the participants? A conceptual focus on relationship disorders seems to challenge the very basis of one of the medical model's features of diagnosis, one that dates back to Hippocratic times, namely, an emphasis on individual prognosis. Individuals may or may not be disordered outside of the context of the relationship. This point raises another important set of research questions. What are the conditions under which relationships affect other relationships? When do individuals continue to suffer maladaptation beyond the bounds and context of the original problematic relationship?

Is a classification of relationship disorders, such as the one we have proposed, valid for some kinds of social relationships and not valid for others? We have argued that the parent–infant relationship is special. We have also implied that our classification approach may be generalizable to other problematic relationships. But we do not know the extent of such a conclusion, and research is needed. As Leiderman has discussed, our scheme seems likely to be most apt for the caregiving relationship of infancy, in which intimacy and commitment predominate. Still, it would seem that other relationships characterized by a degree of intimacy and commitment would profit from a similar classification approach in the midst of perturbation, disturbance, and disorder. Intimacy and commitment are requisites for the mutual respect and autonomy that go along with the connectedness of any well-functioning relationship. Perhaps a classification of relationship disorders would be applicable to a limited set, such as parent–child, spousal, lover, and some peer relationships only. More research is needed to clarify these matters.

We described some connections between the quality of early relationships and the quality of later relationships. But there is little doubt that this question faces us with still more uncharted territory. Our ideas that relationships in infancy have to do with other concurrent relationships and that early relationship experiences become internalized to influence later relationships is part of a more general idea that is in dire need of research. That is, in many ways relationships seem to have powerful effects on other relationships. As we have discussed in this book, there is research evidence of intergenerational effects of relationships on other relationships and there is additional research evidence of the effects of concurrent relationships on other relationships. Yet there is little knowledge of the conditions under which such effects may occur.

MAJOR ISSUES FOR FUTURE RESEARCH

Two major issues cut across our orienting questions of adaptation, variation, and continuity through the lifespan; they are sure to become the subject of increased theory building and research. The first of these issues concerns mutual influences among different levels of functioning, and the second concerns the conscious accessibility of meaning or working models.

The issue of boundaries and mutual influences arose at virtually every point of our group's discussions. Not only must we decide when it is more appropriate to think in terms of relationship adaptiveness and relationship problems versus individual adaptation and individual problems, but we must also think about mutual influences between the two levels. For example, when the relationship has a boundary problem, what happens to the child's affective representations? Or when the child has a motor disorder, what happens to the synchrony of the relationship? Under what conditions do dyadic relationships affect larger holistic units—the family or the community at work or school or play—or, reciprocally, how do larger contexts affect the parent–child dyad? Such reciprocal influences are not usually thought of in our theories or in our clinical work, which is all too often concerned with the assessment of influences at a single level, usually that of the individual.

When one relationship influences another across generations, there must be a means of transmitting the quality of the first to the second. Reiss (chapter 9) has framed the issue of whether the maintenance of relationships is through representation or practice. A further issue is to identify the represented or practiced elements and then to determine the reciprocal influences between them.

This discussion now leads us quite naturally to our last issue. In the practicing world and in the represented world many influences are unconscious rather than conscious and not accessible in a way that they can be told to another. Where in consciousness can we place the working model? Where in consciousness can we place practicing experiences within the family? We are aware of only a small part of what counts for us in terms of both individual meaning and meaning as found in relationship enactments. The study of conscious and unconscious processes is regaining respectability in empirical circles. We hope this volume has brought to consciousness a number of important relationship themes for dealing with problems of infants and their parents. Whether these themes were repressed by our past overemphasis on the individual or were beyond our past levels of conceptualization is not totally clear. What is clear, paradoxically, is that the study of individuals, and especially individual infants, has made a compelling case for the significance of relationships. Only through the study of early relationships can we fully comprehend early individual development.

REFERENCES

Adams, J. A., & Weaver, S. J. (1986). Self-esteem and perceived stress of young adolescents with chronic disease: Unexpected findings. *Journal of Adolescent Health and Care, 7,* 173–177.

Ainsworth, M. D. S. (1973). The development of infant-mother attachment. In B. Caldwell & H. Ricciuti (Eds.), *Review of child development research* (Vol. 3). Chicago: University of Chicago Press.

Ainsworth, M. D. S., & Bell, S. (1974). Mother-infant interaction and the development of competence. In K. Connelly & J. Bruner (Eds.), *The growth of competence.* New York: Academic Press.

Ainsworth, M. D. S., Bell, S., & Stayton, D. J. (1974). Infant-mother attachment and social development "socialization" as a product of reciprocal responsiveness to signals. In M. P. M. Richard (Ed.), *The integration of a child into a social world* (pp. 99–135). Cambridge: Cambridge University Press.

Ainsworth, M. D. S., Blehar, M. C., Waters, E., & Wall, S. (1978). *Patterns of attachment: A psychological study of the strange situation.* Hillsdale, NJ: Lawrence Erlbaum Associates.

Ainsworth, M. D. S., & Wittig, B. (1969). Attachment and exploratory behavior of one-year-olds in a strange situation. In B. M. Foss (Ed.), *Determinants of infant behavior* (Vol. 4, pp. 111–136). New York: Wiley.

Als, J., Tronick, E., & Brazelton, T. B. (1979). Analysis of face-to-face interaction in infant-adult dyads. In M. Lamb, S. Suomi, & G. R. Stephenson (Eds.), *The study of social interaction* (pp. 33–76). Madison: University of Wisconsin Press.

American Psychiatric Association. (1980). *Diagnostic and statistical manual of mental disorders* (3rd ed.). Washington, DC: Author.

American Psychiatric Association. (1987). *Diagnostic and statistical manual of mental disorders* (3rd ed., rev.). Washington, DC: Author.

Amsterdam, B. (1972). Mirror self-image reactions before age two. *Developmental Psychobiology, 5,* 297–305.

Anders, T. F. (1979). Night-waking in infants during the first year of life. *Pediatrics, 63,* 860–864.

Anders, T. F., & Zeanah, C. H. (1986, August). *Subjectivity in parent-infant relationships: A discussion of internal working models.* Paper presented at the Third World Congress of Infant Psychiatry and Allied Disciplines, Stockholm, Sweden.

Andolphi, M., Angelo, C., Menghi, P., & Nicolo-Corigliano, A. (1983). *Behind the family mask: Therapeutic change in rigid family systems.* New York: Brunner/Mazel.

Apple, D. (1960). How laymen define illness. *Journal of Health and Human Behavior, 1,* 219–225.

Arend, R. (1984). *Preschoolers' competence in a barrier situation: Patterns of adaptation and their precursors in infancy.* Unpublished doctoral dissertation, University of Minnesota.

Arend, R. A., Gove, F. L., & Sroufe, L. A. (1979). Continuity of individual adaptation from infancy to kindergarten: A predictive study of ego-resiliency and curiosity in preschoolers. *Child Development, 50,* 950–959.

Aries, P. (1962). *Centuries of childhood.* New York: Vintage.

Azarnoff, P., & Flegal, S. (1975). *A pediatric play program.* Springfield, IL: Charles C. Thomas.

Baldwin, J. M. (1897). *Social and ethical interpretations in mental development.* New York: Macmillan.

Bass, L. W., & Cohen, R. L. (1982). Ostensible versus actual reasons for seeking pediatric attention: Another look at the parental ticket of admission. *Pediatrics, 70,* 870–874.

Bates, J., Maslin, C., & Frankel, K. (1985). Attachment security, mother-child interaction, and temperament as predictors of behavior problem ratings at age three years. In I. Bretherton & E. Waters (Eds.), Growing points of attachment theory and research. *Monographs of the Society for Research in Child Development, 50*(1–2, Serial No. 209).

Baumrind, D. (1967). Child care practices anteceding three patterns of preschool behavior. *Genetic Psychology Monographs, 75,* 43–88.

Belsky, J. (1980). Child maltreatment: An ecological integration. *American Psychologist, 35,* 430–435.

Belsky, J., & Isabella, R. (1987). Maternal, infant, and social-contextual determinants of attachment security: A process analysis. In J. Belsky & T. Nezworski (Eds.), *Clinical implications of attachment.* Hillsdale, NJ: Lawrence Erlbaum Associates.

Belsky, J., Rovine, M., & Fish, M. (1989). The developing family system. In M. Gunnar & E. Thelen (Eds.), *Systems and development.* Hillsdale, NJ: Lawrence Erlbaum.

Belsky, J., & Russell, A. I. (1985). Marital and parent-child relationships in family of origin and marital change following the birth of a baby: A retrospective analysis. *Child Development, 56,* 342–349.

Bennett, L. A., Wolin, S., Reiss, D., & Teitelbaum, M. A. (1987). Couples at risk for the transmission of alcoholism: Protective influences. *Family Process, 26,* 111–129.

Berger, P. L., & Luckmann, T. (1966). *The social construction of reality.* New York: Doubleday.

Bermann, E. (1973). *Scapegoat.* Ann Arbor: University of Michigan Press.

Bertalanffy, L. von. (1968). *General system theory: Foundations, development, applications.* New York: Braziller.

Block, J. H., & Block, J. (1980). The role of ego-control and ego-resiliency in the organization of behavior. In W. A. Collins (Ed.), *Development of cognition, affect, and social relations.* Hillsdale, NJ: Lawrence Erlbaum.

Block, J. H., Block, J., & Morrison, A. (1981). Parental agreement-disagreement on child rearing orientations and gender-related personality correlates in children. *Child Development, 52,* 965–974.

Bloom, B. S. (1964). *Stability and change in human characteristics.* New York: Wiley.

Bornstein, M. (1981). Psychological studies of color perception in human infants. In L. P. Lipsitt (Ed.), *Advances in infancy research* (Vol. 1, pp. 1–4). Norwood, NJ: Ablex.

Bossard, J. H. S., & Boll, E. S. (1950). *Ritual in family living.* Philadelphia: University of Pennsylvania Press.

Boszormenyi-Nagy, I., & Spark, G. (1973). *Invisible loyalties: Reciprocity in intergenerational family therapy.* New York: Harper & Row.

Bowen, M. (1978). *Family therapy in clinical practice.* New York: Aronson.

Bowen, M. (1980). Family systems theory. In S. Harrison & J. McDermott, Jr. (Eds.), *New directions in childhood psychopathology* (Vol. 1). New York: International Universities Press.

Bowlby, J. (1958). The nature of the child's tie to his mother. *International Journal of Psycho-Analysis, 39,* 350–373.

Bowlby, J. (1969). *Attachment and loss: Vol. 1. Attachment.* New York: Basic Books.

Bowlby, J. (1973). *Attachment and loss: Vol 2. Separation, anxiety and anger.* New York: Basic Books.

Bowlby, J. (1980). *Attachment and loss: Vol 3. Loss, sadness and depression.* New York: Basic Books.

Bowlby, J. (1988). Developmental psychiatry comes of age. *American Journal of Psychiatry, 145,* 1–10.

Brazelton, T. B. (1962). Crying in infancy. *Pediatrics, 4,* 579–588.

Brazelton, T. B. (1969). *Infants and mothers: Differences in development.* New York: Dell.

Brazelton, T. B. (1973). *Neonatal behavioral assessment scale.* Philadelphia: J. B. Lippincott.

Brazelton, T. B. (1974). *Toddlers and parents.* New York: Delacourt Press.

Brazelton, T. B. (1975). Anticipatory guidance. *Pediatric Clinics of North America, 22,* 533–544.

Brazelton, T. B., Als, H., Tronick, E., & Lester, B. (1979). Specific neonatal measures: The Brazelton neonatal behavioral assessment scale. In J. Osofsky (Ed.), *Handbook of infant development.* New York: Wiley.

Brazelton, T. B., Koslowski, B., & Main, M. (1974). The origins of reciprocity: The early mother-infant interaction. In M. Lewis & L. A. Rosenblum (Eds.), *The effects of the infant on its caregiver.* New York: Wiley.

Breger, L. (1974). *From instinct to identity.* Englewood Cliffs, NJ: Prentice Hall.

240

REFERENCES

Brenner, J., & Mueller, E. (1982). Shared meaning in boy toddlers' peer relations. *Child Development, 53,* 380–391.

Bretherton, I. (1985). Attachment theory: Retrospect and prospect. In I. Bretherton & E. Waters (Eds.), Growing points of attachment theory and research. *Monographs of the Society for Research in Child Development, 50*(1–2, Serial No. 209).

Bretherton, I., & Waters, E. (Eds.). (1985). Growing points of attachment theory and research. *Monographs of the Society for Research in Child Development, 50*(1–2, Serial No. 209).

Breuer, J., & Freud, S. (1895/1955). Studies on hysteria. In J. Strachey (Ed.), *The standard edition of the complete psychological works of Sigmund Freud.* London: Hogarth.

Brill, M. S., Fauvre, M., Klein, N., Clark, S., & Garcia, L. (1987). Caring for chronically ill children: An innovative approach to children's health care. *Chronic Illness, 16,* 105–113.

Bronfenbrenner, U. (1977). Toward an experimental ecology of human development. *American Psychologist, 32,* 513–531.

Bronfenbrenner, U. (1986). Ecology of the family as a context for human development: Research perspective. *Developmental Psychology, 22,* 723–742.

Bruch, H. (1973). *Eating disorders: Obesity, anorexia, and the person within.* New York: Basic Books.

Bruner, J. (1982). *Child's talk: Learning to use language.* New York: Norton.

Bruner, J. S., Jolly, A., & Sylva, K. (Eds.). (1976). *Play: Its role in development and evolution.* New York: Basic Books.

Burkett, L. (1985). *Parenting behavior of women who were sexually abused as children in their families of origin.* Unpublished doctoral dissertation, University of Minnesota.

Cadman, D., Boyle, M. M., Szatmari, P., & Offord, D. R. (1987). Chronic illness, disability and mental and social wellbeing: Findings of the Ontario Child Health Study. *Pediatrics, 79,* 805–813.

Call, J. (1983). Toward a nosology of psychiatric disorder in infancy. In J. Call, E. Galenson, & R. Tyson (Eds.), *Frontiers of infant psychiatry* (Vol. 1). New York: Basic Books.

Call, J. D., Galenson, E., & Tyson, R. L. (Eds.). (1983). *Frontiers of infant psychiatry* (Vol. 1). New York: Basic Books.

Call, J. D., Galenson, E., Tyson, R. L. (1984). *Frontiers of infant psychiatry* (Vol. 2). New York: Basic Books.

Campbell, J. D. (1975). Illness is a point of view: The development of children's concepts of illness. *Child Development, 46,* 92–100.

Campbell, J. D. (1978). The child in the sick role: Contributions of age, sex, parental status, and parental values. *Journal of Health and Social Behavior, 19,* 35–51.

Campos, J. J., Barrett, K. D., Lamb, M. E., Goldsmith, H. H., & Stenberg, C (1983). Socioemotional development. In M. Haith & J. J. Campos (Eds.), *Handbook of child psychology* (Vol. 2, pp. 783–915). New York: Wiley.

Campos, J., Hiatt, S., Ramsay, D., Henderson, C., & Svejda, M. (1978). The emergence of fear on the visual cliff. In M. Lewis & L. Rosenblum (Eds.), *The development of affect.* New York: Plenum.

Campos, J. J., & Stenberg, C. (1981). Perception, appraisal, and emotion: The onset of social referencing. In M. Lamb & L. R. Sherrod (Eds.), *Infant social cognition* (pp. 273–314). Hillsdale, NJ: Lawrence Erlbaum Associates.

Carey, W. B., & Sibinga, M. S. (1972). Avoiding pediatric pathogenesis in the management of acute minor illness. *Pediatrics, 49,* 553–555.

Carr, S., Dabbs, J., & Carr, T. (1975). Mother-infant attachment: the importance of the mother's visual field. *Child Development, 46,* 331–338.

Casey, P., Sharp, M., & Loda, F. (1979). Child-health supervision for children under 2 years of age: A review of its content and effectiveness. *Journal of Pediatrics, 95,* 1–9.

Casey, P. H., & Whitt, J. K. (1980). Effect of the pediatrician on the mother-infant relationship. *Pediatrics, 65,* 815–820.

Cicchetti, D. (1984). The emergence of developmental psychopathology. *Child Development, 55,* 1–7.

Cicirelli, V. G. (1973). Effects of sibling structure and interaction in children's categorization style. *Developmental Psychology, 9,* 132–139.

Clarke, A. M., & Clarke, A. D. B. (1977). *Early experience: Myth and evidence.* London: Open Books (1976); New York: Free Press.

Cohen, S. E., Brill, N., Fauvre, M., Clark, S., Garcia, L., & Kline, N. (1987). *A guide for planning for the psychological needs of the young hospitalized child.* Los Angeles: Department of Pediatrics, University of California, Los Angeles.

Cohler, B. J. (1982). Personal narrative and life course. In P. B. Baltes & O. G. Brim, Jr. (Eds.), *Life-span development and behavior* (Vol. 4). New York: Academic Press.

Condon, W. S., & Sander, L. W. (1974). Synchrony demonstrated between movements of the neonate and adult speech. *Child Development, 45,* 456–462.

Connell, D. B. (1976). *Individual differences in attachment: An investigation into stability, implications and relationships to structure of early language development.* Unpublished doctoral dissertation, Syracuse University.

Cottrell, L. (1969). Interpersonal interaction and the development of the self. In D. Goslin (Ed.), *Handbook of socialization theory and research* (pp. 543–570). Chicago: Rand-McNally.

Crockenberg, S. (1981). Infant irritability, other responsiveness and social support influences on the security of infant-mother attachment. *Child Development, 52,* 857–865.

Csikszentmihalyi, M., & Rochberg-Halton, E. (1981). *The meaning of things: Domestic symbols and the self.* Cambridge: Cambridge University Press.

Darwin, C. (1872). *The expression of emotions in man and animals.* London: John Murray; Chicago: University of Chicago Press (1965).

Decarie, T. G. (1969). A study of the mental and emotional development of the Thalidomide child. In B. M. Foss (Ed.), *Determinants of infant behavior: Vol. 4* (pp. 167–187). London: Methuen.

Denny, F. W., & Clyde, W. A., Jr. (1983). Acute respiratory tract infections: An overview. In W. A. Clyde, Jr., & F. W. Denny (Eds.), Workshop in acute respiratory disease among children of the world. *Pediatric Research, 17,* 1026–1029.

deVries, M. W., & Sameroff, A. J. (1984). Culture and temperament: Influences on temperament in three East African societies. *American Journal of Orthopsychiatry, 54,* 83–96.

Dingle, J. H., Badger, B. F., & Jordan, W. S., Jr. (1964). *Illnesses in the home: A study of 25,000 children in a group of Cleveland families.* Cleveland: Western Reserve University Press.

Dittrichova, J., & Lapackova, V. (1964). Development of the waking state in young infants. *Child Development, 35,* 365–370.

Dixon, S. (1987). Three to four months: Having fun with the picture-book baby. In S. D. Dixon & M. T. Stein (Eds.), *Encounters with children* (pp. 131–142). Chicago: Year Book.

Dodge, K. A., Petit, G. S., McClasken, C. C., & Brown, M. M. (1986). Social competence in children. *Monographs of the Society for Research in Child Development, 51* (2, Serial No. 213).

Drotar, D., & Bush, M. (1985). Mental health issues and services. In N. Hobbs & J. M. Perrin (Eds.), *Issues in the care of children with chronic illness: A source book on problems, services and policies.* San Francisco: Jossey-Bass.

Drotar, D., Crawford, T., & Bush, M. (1984). The family context of childhood chronic illness: Implications for psychosocial intervention. In M. G. Eisenberg, L. C. Suttin, & M. A. Jansen (Eds.), *Chronic illness and disability through the lifespan: Effects on self and family* (pp. 103–129). New York: Springer.

Dunn, J. (1980). Individual differences in temperament. In M. Rutter (Ed.), *Scientific foundations of developmental psychology* (pp. 101–109). London: William Heinemann.

Dunn, J., & Kendrick, C. (1982). *Siblings: Love, envy and understanding.* Cambridge: Harvard University Press.

Dunn, J., & Munn, P. (1986). Siblings and the development of prosocial behavior. *International Journal of Behavioral Development, 9,* 265–284.

Egeland, B., & Farber, E. (1984). Infant-mother attachment: Factors related to its development and changes over time. *Child Development, 55,* 753–771.

Egeland, B., Jacobvitz, D., & Papatola, K. (1986). Intergenerational continuity of parental abuse. In J. Lancaser & R. Gelles (Eds.), *Biosocial aspects of child abuse.* San Francisco: Jossey-Bass.

Egeland, B., Jacobvitz, D., & Sroufe, L. A. (1988). Breaking the cycle of abuse: Relationship predictors. *Child Development, 59,* 1080–1088.

Egeland, B., & Sroufe, L. A. (1981). Developmental sequelae of maltreatment in infancy. In R. Rizley & D. Cicchetti (Eds.), *Developmental perspectives in child maltreatment.* San Francisco: Jossey-Bass.

Eisenberg, L. (1977). Disease and illness. *Culture, Medicine and Psychiatry, 1,* 9–23.

REFERENCES

Ekman, P., Friesen, W., & Ellsworth, P. (1972). *Emotion in the human face.* New York: Pergamon Press.

Ekman, P., Leenson, R. W., & Friesen, W. V. (1983). Autonomic nervous system activity distinguishes among emotions. *Science, 221,* 1208–1210.

Elder, G. H. (1974). *Children of the great depression.* Chicago: University of Chicago Press.

Elkind, D. (1981). *The hurried child: Growing up too fast too soon.* Reading, MA: Addison-Wesley.

Emde, R. N. (1980a). Emotional availability: A reciprocal reward system for infants and parents with implications for prevention of psychosocial disorders. In E. Goldson (Ed.), *Parent-infant relationships* (pp. 87–115). Orlando, FL: Grune & Stratton.

Emde, R. N. (1980b). Levels of meaning for infant emotions: A biosocial view. In W. A. Collins (Ed.), *Development of cognition, affect, and social relations* (pp. 1–37). Hillsdale, NJ: Lawrence Erlbaum.

Emde, R. N. (1983). The prerepresentational self and its affective core. *Psychoanalytic Study of the Child, 38,* 165–192.

Emde, R. N., & Buchsbaum, H. K. (in press). Toward a psychoanalytic theory of affect: Emotional development and signaling in infancy. In S. I. Greenspan & G. H. Pollock (Eds.), *The course of life: Psychoanalytic contributions toward understanding personality development* (2nd ed.). Washington, DC: U.S. Government Printing Office.

Emde, R. N., & Easterbrooks, M. A. (1985). Assessing emotional availability in early development. In W. K. Frankenburg, R. N. Emde, & J. W. Sullivan (Eds.), *Early identification of children at risk: An international perspective* (pp. 79–101). New York: Plenum.

Emde, R. N., Gaensbauer, T. J., & Harmon, R. J. (1976). Emotional expression in infancy: A biobehavioral study. *Psychological Issues: A Monograph Series, 10*(37).

Emde, R. N., Gaensbauer, T., & Harmon, R. J. (1982). Using our emotions: Principles for appraising emotional development and intervention. In M. Lewis & L. Taft (Eds.), *Developmental disabilities: Theory, assessment and intervention* (pp. 409–424). New York: S. P. Medical and Scientific Books.

Emde, R. N., & Harmon, R. J. (1972). Endogenous and exogenous smiling systems in early infancy. *Journal of the American Academy of Child Psychiatry, 11,* 177–200.

Emde, R., & Harmon, R. (Eds.). (1984). *Continuities and discontinuities in development.* New York: Plenum.

Emde, R. N., Johnson, W. F., & Easterbrooks, M. A. (1988). The do's and don'ts of early moral development: Psychoanalytic tradition and current research. In J. Kagan & S. Lamb (Eds.), *The emergence of morality.* Chicago: University of Chicago Press.

Emde, R. N., & Robinson, J. (1979). The first two months: Recent research in developmental psychobiology and the changing view of the newborn. In J. Call, J. Noshpitz, R. Cohen, & I. Berlin (Eds.), *Basic handbook of child psychiatry* (Vol. 1). New York: Basic Books.

Engel, G. L. (1977). The need for a new medical model: A challenge for biomedicine. *Science, 196,* 129–136.

Engelhardt, H. T., Jr. (1981). The concepts of health and disease. In A. L. Caplan, H. T. Engelhardt, Jr., & J. J. McCartney (Eds.), *Concepts of health and disease: Interdisciplinary perspectives* (pp. 30–45). London: Addison-Wesley.

Erickson, M. F., Sroufe, L. A., & Egeland, B. (1985). The relationship of quality of attachment and behavior problems in preschool in a high risk sample. In I. Bretherton & E. Waters (Eds.), Growing points of attachment theory and research. *Monographs of the Society for Research in Child Development, 50*(1–2, Serial No. 209), 147–186.

Erikson, E. (1963). *Childhood and society* (rev. ed.). New York: Norton.

Farber, B. (1981). *Conceptions of kinship.* New York: Elsevier.

Farrington, D. P. (1978). The family background of aggressive youths. In L. A. Herzov, M. Gerger, & D. Shaffer (Eds.), *Aggression and emotional behavior in childhood and adolescence* (pp. 73–94). Oxford: Pergamon Press.

Feinman, S., & Lewis, M. (1983). Social referencing at ten months: A second-order effect on infants' responses to strangers. *Child Development, 54,* 878–887.

Field, T. M. (1978). The 3 Rs of infant-adult social interaction: Rhythms, repertoires and responsivity. *Pediatric Psychology, 3,* 131–136.

Field, T. M. (1979). Interaction patterns of preterm and term infants. In T. M. Field, A. M.

Sostek, & H. H. Schuman (Eds.), *Infants born at risk: Behavior and development.* New York: S. P. Medical and Scientific Books.

Fisher, L. (1977). On the classification of families. *Archives of General Psychiatry, 34,* 424–433.

Flavell, J. H. (1977). *Cognitive development.* Englewood Cliffs, NJ: Prentice Hall.

Fleeson, J. (1988). *Assessment of parent-adolescent relationships: Implications for adolescent development.* Unpublished dissertation, University of Minnesota.

Fogel, A. (1982). Affective dynamics in early infancy: Affective tolerance. In T. Field & A. Fogel (Eds.), *Emotions and interactions: Normal and high-risk infants.* Hillsdale, NJ: Lawrence Erlbaum Associates.

Forsyth, B. W. C., Leventhal, J. M., & McCarthy, P. L. (1985). Mothers' perceptions of problems of feeding and crying behaviors. *American Journal of Diseases of Children, 139,* 269–272.

Fouts, G., & Atlas, P. (1979). Stranger distress: Mother and stranger as reinforcers. *Infant Behavior and Development, 2,* 309–317.

Fraiberg, S. (1977). *Insights from the blind.* New York: Basic Books.

Fraiberg, S. (1980). *Clinical studies in infant mental health.* New York: Basic Books.

Fraiberg, S. (1982). Pathological defenses in infancy. *Psychoanalytic Quarterly, 51,* 612–635.

Fraiberg, S., Adelson, E., & Shapiro, V. (1975). Ghosts in the nursery: A psychoanalytic approach to the problems of impaired mother-infant relationships. *Journal of the American Academy of Child Psychiatry, 14,* 378–421.

Freedman, D. A., Cannady, C., & Robinson, J. S. (1971). Speech and psychic structure. *Journal of the American Psychoanalytic Association, 19,* 765–779.

Freud, A. (1952). The role of bodily illness in the mental life of children. *Psychoanalytic Study of the Child, 7,* 69–81.

Freud, S. (1920). *Beyond the pleasure principle.* London: Hogarth Press.

Friedman, A. S. (1975). Interaction of drug therapy with marital therapy in depressive patients. *Archives of General Psychiatry, 32,* 614–637.

Frommer, E., & O'Shea, G. (1973). Antenatal identification of women liable to have problems in managing their infants. *British Journal of Psychiatry, 123,* 145–156.

Fuchs, E. (Ed.). (1976). *Youth in a changing world: Cross cultural perspective on adolescence.* The Hague: Mouton.

Fury, G. (1984). *Qualitative differences in relationships formed by preschool children with different attachment histories.* Unpublished summa cum laude thesis, University of Minnesota.

Gaensbauer, T. J., & Harmon, R. J. (1982). Attachment behavior in abused/neglected and premature infants: Implications for the concept of attachment. In R. N. Emde & R. J. Harmon (Eds.), *The development of attachment and affiliative systems* (pp. 263–279). New York: Plenum.

Garber, J., Cohen, E., Bacon, P., Egeland, E., & Sroufe, L. A. (1985, April). *Depression in preschoolers: Reliability and validity of a behavioral observation measure.* Paper presented at the meeting of the Society for Research in Child Development, Toronto.

Gesell, A., & Ilg, F. L. (1943). *Infant and child in the culture of today.* New York: Harper & Brothers.

Glass, D. D. (1977). *Behavior patterns, stress and coronary artery disease.* Hillsdale, NJ: Lawrence Erlbaum Associates.

Goldberg, S., Brachfeld, S., & DiVitto, R. (1980). Feeding, fussing and play: Parent-infant interaction in the first year as a function of prematurity and perinatal medical problems. In T. M. Field, S. Goldberg, D. Stern, & A. M. Sostek (Eds.), *High-risk infants and children: Adult and peer interactions* (pp. 133–153). New York: Academic Press.

Goldsmith, H., & Campos, J. (1982). Toward a theory of infant temperament. In R. N. Emde & R. J. Harmon (Eds.), *Advances in infant behavior and development.* Hillsdale, NJ: Lawrence Erlbaum Associates.

Goldstein, M. (1988). The family and psychopathology. *Annual Review of Psychology, 39,* 283–299.

Goodnow, J. J. (1988). Parents' ideas, actions, and feelings: Models and methods from developmental and social psychology. *Child Development, 59,* 286–320.

Gortmaker, L. S., & Sappenfield, W. (1984). Chronic childhood disorders: Prevalence and impact. In R. J. Haggerty (Ed.), Chronic disease in children. *Pediatric Clinics of North America, 31*(1), 3–18.

Gottman, J. M. (1975). *The interpersonal world of the infant.* New York: Basic Books.

REFERENCES

Gottman, J. M. (1979). *Marital interaction: Experimental investigations.* New York: Academic Press.

Gottman, J. M. (1983). How children become friends. *Monographs of the Society for Research in Child Development, 48*(3, Serial No. 201).

Gottman, J. M. (1986). *How marriages change.* Unpublished manuscript.

Graham, P., & Rutter, M. (1973). Psychiatric disorders in the young adolescent: A follow-up study. *Proceedings of the Royal Society of Medicine, 66,* 1226–1229.

Green, M., & Solnit, A. (1964). Reactions to the threatened loss of a child: A vulnerable child syndrome: Part III. *Pediatrics, 34,* 58–66.

Green, R. G., Stonner, D., & Shope, G. L. (1975). The facilitation of aggression by aggression: Evidence against the catharsis hypothesis. *Journal of Personality and Social Psychology, 31,* 721–726.

Greenspan, S. I. (1981). *Psychopathology and adaptation in infancy and early childhood.* New York: International Universities Press.

Greenspan, S. I., & Lourie, R. S. (1981). Developmental and structural approaches to the classification of adaptive and personality organization: Infancy and early childhood. *American Journal of Psychiatry, 138,* 725–735.

Greenspan, S. I., Nover, R. A., & Scheuer, A. Q. (1987). A developmental diagnostic approach for infants, young children, and their families. In S. I. Greenspan, S. Wieder, A. Lieberman, R. A. Nover, R. S. Lourie, & M. Robinson (Eds.), *Infants in multirisk families: Case studies in preventive intervention* (pp. 431–498). New York: International Universities Press.

Grossman, K. E., Grossman, K., Huber, F., & Wartner, U. (1981). German children's behavior toward their mothers at 12 months and their fathers at 18 months in Ainsworth's strange situation. *International Journal of Behavioral Development, 4,* 157–181.

Grossman, K., Grossman, K. E., Spangler, G., Suess, G., & Unzer, L. (1985). Maternal sensitivity and newborns' orientation responses as related to quality of attachment in Northern Germany. In I. Bretherton & E. Waters (Eds.), Growing points of attachment theory and research (pp. 223–257). *Monographs of the Society for Research in Child Development, 50*(1–2, Serial No. 209).

Grotevant, H., & Cooper, C. R. (1985). Patterns of interaction in family relationships and the development of identity exploration. *Child Development, 29,* 82–100.

Gunnar, M. R. (1980). Control, warning signals and distress in infancy. *Developmental Psychology, 16,* 281–289.

Haggerty, R. J., Roghmann, K. J., & Pless, I. B. (1975). *Child health in the community.* New York: Wiley.

Haith, M. M. (1977). Eye contact and face scanning in early infancy. *Science, 198,* 853–855.

Haith, M. M., & Campos, J. J. (Eds.). (1983). *Handbook of child psychology: Vol. 2. Infancy and developmental psychobiology.* New York: Wiley.

Haith, M. M., Hazan, C., & Goodman, G. S. (1988). Expectation and anticipation of dynamic visual events by 3.5-month-old babies. *Child Development, 59,* 467–479.

Hamburg, D. A. (1963). Emotions in the perspective of human evolution. In Ph. D. Knapp (Ed.), *Expression of the emotions in man* (pp. 300–315). New York: International Universities Press.

Hartup, W. (1983). Peer relationships. In E. M. Hetherington & P. H. Mussen (Eds.), *Handbook of child psychology: Vol. 4. Socialization, personality and social development.* New York: Wiley.

Hartup, W. (1986). On relationships and development. In W. Hartup & Z. Rubin (Eds.), *Relationships and development* (pp. 1–26). Hillsdale, NJ: Lawrence Erlbaum Associates.

Hayes, A. (1984). Interaction, engagement, and the origins of communication: Some constructive concerns. In L. Feagans, C. Garvey, & R. Golinkoff (Eds.), *The origins and growth of communications.* Norwood, NJ: Ablex.

Hayne, H., Rovee-Collier, C., & Perris, E. E. (1987). Categorization and memory retrieval by 3 month olds. *Child Development, 58,* 750–767.

Heinicke, C., & Westheimer, I. (1966). *Brief separations.* New York: International Universities Press.

Heisenberg, W. (1952). *Philosophic problems of nuclear science.* New York: Pantheon.

Henry, J. P. (1980). Present concepts of stress theory. In E. Usdin, R. Kventnansky, & I. J. Kopin (Eds.), *Catecholamines and stress: Recent advances.* New York: Elsevier.

Hetherington, E. M., Cox, M., & Cox, R. (1978). The aftermath of divorce. In J. Stevens & M.

Mathews (Eds.), *Mother-child, father-child relations.* Washington, DC: National Association for the Education of Young Children.

Hilgard, J., & Moore, U. (1969). Affiliative therapy with young adolescents. *Journal of the Academy of Child Psychiatry, 8,* 577–603.

Hinde, R. A. (1979). *Towards understanding relationships.* London: Academic Press.

Hinde, R. A., & Stevenson-Hinde, J. (1986). Relating childhood relationships to individual characteristics. In W. W. Hartup & Z. Rubin (Eds.), *Relationships and development* (pp. 27–50). Hillsdale, NJ: Lawrence Erlbaum Associates.

Hobbs, N., Perrin, J. M., & Ireys, H. T. (1985). *Chronically ill children and their families.* San Francisco: Jossey-Bass.

Hoffman, M. (1979). Development of moral thought, feeling, and behavior. *American Psychologist, 34,* 958–966.

Horner, T. M. (1980). Two methods of studying stranger fearfulness in infants: A review. *Journal of Child Psychology, 21,* 203–219.

Hornik, R., & Gunnar, M. R. (1988). A descriptive analysis of infant social referencing. *Child Development, 59,* 626–634.

Humphrey, L., & Benjamin, L. (1986). Using structural analysis of social behavior to assess critical but elusive family processes: A new solution to an old problem. *American Psychologist, 41,* 979–989.

Hyatt, S., Emde, R., & Campos, J. (1979). Facial patterning and infant emotional expression: Happiness, surprise and fear. *Child Development, 50,* 1020–1035.

Izard, C. (1971). *The face of emotion.* New York: Meredith & Appleton-Century-Crofts.

Izard, C., Huebner, R., Risser, D., McGinnes, G. C., & Dougherty, L. (1980). The young infant's ability to produce discrete emotional expressions. *Developmental Psychology, 16,* 132–140.

Jackson, D. (1977). The study of the family. In P. Watzlawick & J. Weakland (Eds.), *The interactional view.* New York: Norton.

Jacobvitz, D., & Sroufe, L. A. (1987). The early caregiver-child relationship and attention deficit disorder with hyperactivity in kindergarten: A prospective study. *Child Development, 58,* 1488–1495.

Jefferson, G. (1978). Sequential aspects of storytelling in conversation. In J. Schenkein (Ed.), *Studies of the organization of conversational interaction.* New York: Academic Press.

Kagan, J. (1981). *The second year: The emergence of self-awareness.* Cambridge: Harvard University Press.

Kagan, J. (1984). *The nature of the child.* New York: Basic Books.

Kagan, J., Kearsley, R., & Zelazo, P. (1978). *Infancy: Its place in human development.* Cambridge: Harvard University Press.

Kantor, D., & Lehr, W. (1975). *Inside the family.* San Francisco: Jossey-Bass.

Kaye, K. (1982). *The mental and social life of babies: How parents create persons.* Chicago: University of Chicago Press.

Kelley, H. H., Berscheid, E., Christensen, A., Harvey, J. H., Huston, T. L., Levinger, G., McClintock, E., Peplau, L. A., & Peterson, D. R. (1983). *Close relationships.* San Francisco: Freeman.

Kermoian, R., & Leiderman, P. H. (1986). Infant attachment to mother and child caregiver in an East African community. *International Journal of Behavioral Development, 9,* 1–26.

Kessen, W. (1979). The American child and other cultural inventions. *American Psychologist, 34,* 815–820.

Kessler, J. (1966). *Psychopathology of childhood.* Englewood Cliffs, NJ: Prentice Hall.

Kierkegaard, S. (1938). *Purity of heart is to will one thing.* New York: Harper & Row.

Klaus, M. H., & Kennell, J. H. (1982). *Parent infant bonding* (2nd ed.). St. Louis: Mosby.

Klein, G. L. (1967). Peremptory ideation: Structure and force in motivated ideas. In R. R. Holt (Ed.), Motives and thoughts: Psychoanalytic essays in honor of David Rapaport. *Psychological Issues, 5*(2–3, Monograph 18/19).

Klein, M. (1952) *Developments in psychoanalysis* (J. Rivere, Ed.). London: Hogarth Press.

Klinnert, M. D., Campos, J. J., Sorce, F. J., Emde, R. N., & Svejda, M. J. (1983). Social referencing: Emotional expressions as behavior regulators. In R. Plutchik & H. Kellerman (Eds.), *Emotion: Theory, research and experience* (Vol. 2, pp. 57–86). New York: Academic Press.

Kluckhohn, C., & Leighton, D. (1958). *The Navaho.* Cambridge: Harvard University Press.

246

Kohut, H. (1977). *The restoration of the self*. New York: International Universities Press.

Korsch, B. M. (1966). Practical techniques of observing, interviewing and advising parents in pediatric practice as demonstrated in an attitude study project. *Pediatrics, 18,* 467–490.

Kotelchuck, M., Zelazo, P., Kagan, J., & Spelke, E. (1975). Infant reaction to parental separation when left with familiar and unfamiliar adults. *Journal of Genetic Psychology, 126,* 255–262.

Krappman, L., & Oswald, H. (1983, April). Types of children's integration into peer society. Paper presented at the biennial meeting of the Society for Research in Child Development, Detroit.

Kreisler, L., & Cramer, B. (1983). Infant psychopathology: Guidelines for examination, clinical groupings, and nosological propositions. In J. D. Call, E. Galenson, & R. L. Tyson (Eds.), *Frontiers of infant psychiatry* (pp. 129–135). New York: Basic Books.

Kreppner, K., Paulse, S., & Schuetze, Y. (1982). Infant and family development: From triads to tetrads. *Human Development, 25,* 373–391.

Kuhn, T. S. (1962). *The structure of scientific revolutions*. Chicago: University of Chicago Press.

Kurdek, L. A. (1981). An integrative perspective on children's divorce adjustment. *American Psychologist, 36,* 856–866.

LaFontaine, A. (1970). Two types of youth groups in Kinshasa (Leopoldville). In P. Mayer (Ed.), *Socialization: The approach from social anthropology* (pp. 191–214). London: Tavistock.

LaFreniere, P., & Sroufe, L. A. (1985). Profiles of peer competence in the preschool: Interrelations between measures, influence of social ecology, and relation to attachment history. *Developmental Psychology, 21,* 58–68.

Leiderman, P. H., & Leiderman G. F. (1974). Affective and cognitive consequences of polymatric infant care in the East African highlands. In A. D. Pick (Ed.), *Minnesota symposium on child psychology*, Vol. 8 (pp. 81–110). Minneapolis: University of Minnesota Press.

Levinson, D. J., Darrow, C. N., Klein, E. B., Levinson, M. H., & McKee, B. (1978). *The seasons of a man's life*. New York: Knopf.

Lewis, J. M., Beavers, R. W., Gossett, J. T., & Phillips, V. A. (1976). *No single thread: Psychological health in family systems*. New York: Brunner/Mazel.

Lewis, M., & Brooks, J. (1978). Self-knowledge and emotional development. In M. Lewis & L. Rosenblum (Eds.), *The development of affect*. New York: Plenum.

Lewis, M., Feiring, C., McGuffog, C., & Jaskir, J. (1984). Predicting psychopathology in six-year-olds from early social relations. *Child Development, 55,* 123–136.

Lewis, M., & Rosenblum, L. A. (Eds.). (1975). *Friendship and peer relations*. New York: Wiley.

Loda, F. A., Glezen, W. T., & Clyde, W. A., Jr. (1972). Respiratory disease in group day care. *Pediatrics, 49,* 428–437.

Loevinger, J. (1976). *Ego development*. San Francisco: Jossey-Bass.

Londerville, S., & Main, M. (1981). Security of attachment, compliance and maternal training methods in the second year of life. *Developmental Psychology, 17,* 289–299.

Luborsky, L. (1985). Psychotherapy integration is on its way. *Counseling Psychologist, 13,* 245–249.

Maccoby, E., & Martin, J. A. (1983). Socialization in the context of the family. In E. M. Hetherington (Ed.), *Handbook of Child Psychology: Vol. 4. Socialization personality and social development*. New York: Wiley.

Mahler, M. S., Pine, F., & Bergman, A. (1975). *The psychological birth of the human infant: Symbiosis and individuation*. New York: Basic Books.

Main, M., & Cassidy, J. (1988). Categories of response to reunion with the parent at age 6: Predictable from infant attachment classifications and stable over a 1-month period. *Developmental Psychology, 24,* 415–426.

Main, M., & Goldwyn, R. (1984). Predicting rejection of her infant from mother's representation of her own experience: Implications for the abused-abusing intergenerational cycle. *Child Abuse and Neglect, 8,* 203–217.

Main, M., Kaplan, N., & Cassidy, J. (1985). Security in infancy, childhood and adulthood: A move to the level of representation. In I. Bretherton & E. Waters (Eds.), Growing points of attachment theory and research. *Monographs of the Society for Research in Child Development, 50*(1–2, Serial No. 209).

Main, M., & Stadtman, J. (1981). Infant response to rejection of physical contact by the mother: Aggression, avoidance and conflict. *Journal of the American Academy of Child Psychiatry, 20,* 292–307.

Main, M., & Weston, D. (1981). The quality of the toddler's relationship to mother and to father:

Related to conflict behavior and readiness to establish new relationships. *Child Development,* 52, 932–940.

Mandler, G. (1967). The conditions for emotional behavior. In D. C. Glass (Ed.), *Neurophysiology and emotion.* New York: Rockefeller University Press.

Mandler, J. M. (1984). *Stories, scripts and scenes: Aspects of schema theory.* Hillsdale, NJ: Lawrence Erlbaum Associates.

Mans, L., Cicchetti, D., & Sroufe, L. A. (1978). Mirror reactions of Down's syndrome infants and toddlers: Cognitive underpinnings of self-recognition. *Child Development, 49,* 547–556.

Maslow, A. H. (1971). *The farther reaches of human nature.* New York: Viking.

Matas, L., Arend, R., & Sroufe, L. A. (1978). Continuity of adaptation in the second year. The relationship between quality of attachment and later competent functioning. *Child Development, 49,* 547–555.

Mattsson, A., & Weisberg, I. (1970). Behavioral reactions to minor illness in preschool children. *Pediatrics, 46,* 604–610.

Mayer, P. (Ed.). (1970). *Socialization: The approach from social anthropology.* London: Tavistock.

Mayer, P., & Mayer, I. (1970). Socialization by peers: The youth organization of the Red Xhosa. In P. Mayer (Ed.), *Socialization: The approach from social anthropology* (pp. 159–190). London: Tavistock.

McCall, R. B. (1979). The development of intellectual functioning in infancy and the prediction of later I.Q. In J. Osofsky (Ed.), *Handbook of infant development.* New York: Wiley.

McClelland, J. L., & Rumelhart, D. E. (1985). Distributed memory and the representation of general and specific information. *Journal of Experimental Psychology, 114,* 159–188.

McClintock, M. K. (1987). A functional approach to the behavioral endocrinology of rodents. In D. Crews (Ed.), *Psychobiology of reproduction* (pp. 176–203). Englewood Cliffs, NJ: Prentice Hall.

McInerny, T. (1984). The role of the general pediatrician in coordinating the care of children with chronic illness. In R. J. Haggerty (Ed.), Chronic Disease in Children. *Pediatric Clinics of North America, 31.*

Mead, G. H. (1934). *Mind, self and society.* Chicago: University of Chicago Press.

Minde, K., & Minde, R. (1986). *Infant psychiatry: An introductory textbook.* Beverly Hills, CA: Sage.

Minkowski, A. (1967). *Regional development of the brain in early life.* Oxford: Blackwell.

Minuchin, S. (1974). *Families and family therapy.* Cambridge: Harvard University Press.

Minuchin, S., Rosman, B., & Baker, L. (1978). *Psychosomatic families: Anorexia nervosa in context.* Cambridge: Harvard University Press.

Miyake, K., Chen, S. J., & Campos, J. J. (1985). Infant temperament, mother's mode of interaction, and attachment in Japan: An interim report. In I. Bretherton & E. Waters (Eds.), Growing points of attachment theory and research. *Monographs of the Society for Research in Child Development, 50*(1–2, Serial No. 209).

Morris, D. (1980). *Infant attachment and problem solving in the toddler: Relations to mother's family history.* Unpublished doctoral dissertation, University of Minnesota.

Myers, R. E. (1967). *Cortical localization of emotion control.* Invited lecture presented at the meeting of the American Psychological Association, Washington, DC.

Natapoff, J. N. (1978). Children's views of health: A developmental study. *American Journal of Public Health, 68,* 995–1000.

Nelson, K. (in press). *Narratives from the crib.* Cambridge: Harvard University Press.

Nelson, K., & Gruendel, J. M. (1981). Generalized event representations: Basic building blocks to cognitive development. In M. E. Lamb & A. L. Brown (Eds.), *Advances in developmental psychology* (Vol. 1). Hillsdale, NJ: Lawrence Erlbaum.

Olson, D. H., Sprenkle, D. H., & Russell, C. S. (1979). Circumplex model of marital and family systems: 1. Cohesion and adaptability dimensions, family types, and clinical applications. *Family Process, 18,* 3–28.

Olweus, D. (1980). Bullying among school boys. In R. Barnan (Ed.), *Child and violence.* Stockholm: Academic Literature.

Olweus, D., Block, J., & Radke-Yarrow, M. (1986). *Development of antisocial and prosocial behavior.* New York: Academic Press.

248

REFERENCES

Oremland, E. K., & Oremland, J. D. (Eds.). (1973). *The effects of hospitalization on children*. Springfield, IL: Charles C. Thomas.

Osofsky, J. D. (Ed.). (1987). *Handbook of infant development* (2nd Ed.). New York: Wiley.

Palfrey, J. S., Levy, J. C., & Gilbert, K. L. (1980). Use of primary care facilities by patients attending special clinics. *Pediatrics, 65,* 567–572.

Palmer, S. E. (1987). PDP: A new paradigm for cognitive theory. *Contemporary Psychology, 32,* 925–928.

Pancake, V. R. (1985, April). *Continuity between mother-infant attachment and ongoing dyadic peer relationships in preschool.* Paper presented at the biennial meeting of the Society for Research in Child Development, Toronto.

Papousek, H., & Papousek, M. (1979). Early ontogeny of human social interaction: Its biological roots and social dimensions. In M. von Cranach, K. Foppa, W. Lepenies, & D. Ploog (Eds.), *Human ethology: Claims and limits of a new discipline.* New York: Cambridge University Press.

Papousek, H., & Papousek, M. (1981). How human is the human newborn, and what else is to be done? In K. Bloom (Ed.), *Prospective issues in infancy research* (pp. 137–155). Hillsdale, NJ: Lawrence Erlbaum Associates.

Parke, R. D., Power, T. G., & Gottman, J. M. (1979). Conceptualizing and quantifying influence patterns in the family triad. In M. E. Lamb, J. S. Suomi, & G. R. Stephenson (Eds.), *Social interaction analysis: Methodological issues.* Madison: University of Wisconsin Press.

Parke, R. D., & Sawin, D. B. (1979). Children's privacy in the home: Developmental, ecological and child-rearing determinants. *Environment and Behavior, 11,* 87–104.

Parke, R. D., & Tinsley, B. J. (1987). Family interaction in infancy. In J. Osofsky (Ed.), *Handbook of infant development* (2nd ed.). New York: Wiley.

Parkes, R. M., & Stevenson-Hinde, J. (1982). *The place of attachment in human behavior.* New York: Basic Books.

Parmelee, A. H., Jr. (1977). Remarks on receiving the C. Anderson Aldrich award. *Pediatrics, 59,* 389–395.

Parmelee, A. H., Jr. (1986). Children's illnesses: Their beneficial effects on their behavioral development. *Child Development, 57,* 1–10.

Parmelee, A. H., Jr., & Schimmel, B. F. (1958). Absence from school: Its relationship to illness in the community. *California Medicine, 88,* 144–148.

Parsons, T. (1951). *The social system.* Glencoe, IL: Free Press.

Patterson, G. (1982). *Coercive family process.* Eugene, OR: Castalia.

Patterson, G. R. (1986a). Maternal rejection: Determinant of product for deviant child behavior. In W. Hartup & Z. Rubin (Eds.), *Relationship and development* (pp. 73–94). Hillsdale, NJ: Lawrence Erlbaum Associates.

Patterson, G. R. (1986b). Performance models for antisocial boys. *American Psychologist, 41,* 432–444.

Patterson, G. R., & Dishion, T. J. (1988). A mechanism for transmitting the antisocial trait across generations. In R. A. Hinde & J. Stevenson-Hinde (Eds.), *Relations between relationships within families.* Oxford: Oxford University Press.

Patterson, G. R., & Strodthamer-Loeber, M. (1984). The correlation of family management practices and delinquency. *Child Development, 55,* 1299–1307.

Pedersen, F., Anderson, B., & Cain, R. (1977, April). *An approach to understanding linkages between the parent, infant, and spouse relationships.* Paper presented at the meeting of the Society for Research in Child Development, New Orleans.

Perrin, E. D., & Garrity, T. S. (1984). Development of children with chronic illness. *Pediatric Clinics of North America, 31,* 19–31.

Peterson, C., & McCabe, A. (1983). *Developmental psycholinguistics: Three ways of looking at a child's narrative.* New York: Plenum Press.

Piaget, J. (1952). *The origins of intelligence in children* (2nd ed.). New York: International Universities Press.

Pianta, R., Egeland, B., & Sroufe, L. A. (1989). Maternal stress in children's development: Predictions of school outcomes and identification of protective factors. In J. Rolf, A. Masten, D. Cicchetti, K. Neuchterlen, & S. Weintraub (Eds.), *Risk and protective factors in the development of psychopathology.* Cambridge: Cambridge University Press.

249

Pilkonis, P. A., Imber, S. D., Lewis, P., & Rubinsky, P. (1984). A comparative outcome study of individual, group and conjoint psychotherapy. *Archives of General Psychiatry, 41,* 431–439.

Pine, F. (1981). In the beginning: Contributions to a psychoanalytic developmental psychology. *International Review of Psychoanalysis, 8,* 15–33.

Plank, E. (1971). *Working with children in hospitals* (2nd ed.). Cleveland: Case Western Reserve University Press.

Plomin, R. (1986). *Development, genetics and psychology.* Hillsdale, NJ: Lawrence Erlbaum Associates.

Popler, D. J., Abromovitch, R., & Croter, C. (1981). Sibling interaction in the home: A longitudinal study. *Child Development, 52,* 1344–1347.

Posner, M. I., & Keele, S. W. (1968). On the genesis of abstract ideas. *Journal of Experimental Psychology, 77,* 353–363.

Posner, M. I., & Keele, S. W. (1970). Retention of abstract ideas. *Journal of Experimental Psychology, 83,* 304–308.

Powers, S., Hauser, S., Schwartz, J., Noam, G., & Jacobson, A. (1983). Adolescent ego development and family interaction. In H. Grotevant & C. Cooper (Eds.), *Adolescent development in the family.* San Francisco: Jossey-Bass.

Radke-Yarrow, M., Zahn-Waxler, C., & Chapman, M. (1983). Children's prosocial dispositions and behavior. In P. Mussen (Ed.), *Charmichael's manual of child psychology* (Vol. 4) (4th ed.). New York: Wiley.

Rashkis, S. R. (1965). Child's understanding of health. *Archives of General Psychiatry, 12,* 10–17.

Reichard, G. (1950). *Navaho religion: A study of symbolism.* New York: Pantheon.

Reiss, D. (1981). *The family's construction of reality.* Cambridge: Harvard University Press.

Reiss, D. (1982). The working family: A researcher's view of health in the household. *American Journal of Psychiatry, 139,* 1412–1420.

Resnick, J. S., & Kagan, J. (1983). Category detection in infancy. In L. P. Lipsitt (Ed.), *Advances in infancy research* (Vol. 2, pp. 79–111). Norwood, NJ: Ablex.

Rexford, E. N., Sander, N., & Shapiro, L. W. (1976). *Infant psychiatry: A new synthesis.* New Haven: Yale University Press.

Rheingold, H., & Eckerman, C. (1973). Fear of the stranger: A critical examination. In H. Reese (Ed.), *Advances in child development and behavior* (Vol. 8). New York: Academic Press.

Richie, J., & Richie, J. (1979). *Growing up in Polynesia.* Sydney, Australia: Allen and Unwin.

Ricks, M. H. (1985). The social transmission of parental behavior: Attachment across generations. In I. Bretherton & E. Waters (Eds.), Growing points of attachment theory and research (pp. 211–227). *Monographs of the Society for Research in Child Development, 50*(1–2, Serial No. 209).

Robins, L. N. (1966). *Deviant children grow up: A sociological and psychological study of sociopathic personality.* Philadelphia: William & Wilkins.

Robins, L. N. (1978). Sturdy childhood predictors of adult antisocial behavior. *Psychological Medicine, 8,* 611–622.

Robson, K. S. (1967). The role of eye-to-eye contact in maternal-infant attachment. *Journal of Child Psychology and Psychiatry, 8,* 13–25.

Roff, M., Sells, S. B., & Golden, M. M. (1972). *Social adjustment and personality development in children.* Minneapolis: University of Minnesota Press.

Rogoff, B. (1981). Schooling and the development of cognitive skills. In H. C. Triandis & A. Heron (Eds.), *Handbook of cross-cultural psychology: Vol. 4. Developmental psychology.* Boston: Allyn & Bacon.

Rommetveit, R. (1976). On the architecture of intersubjectivity. In L. H. Strickland, K. J. Gergen, & F. J. About (Eds.), *Social psychology in transition.* New York: Plenum.

Rosch, E. (1978). Principles of categorizations. In E. Rosch & B. B. Lloyd (Eds.), *Cognition and categorization.* Hillsdale, NJ: Lawrence Erlbaum Associates.

Rosenberg, D. (1984). *The quality and content of preschool fantasy play: Correlates in concurrent social/personality function and early mother-child attachment relationships.* Unpublished doctoral dissertation, University of Minnesota.

Rumelhart, D. E. (1977). Understanding and summarizing brief stories. In D. Leberge & S. J. Samuels (Eds.), *Reading: Perception and comprehension.* Hillsdale, NJ: Lawrence Erlbaum Associates.

REFERENCES

Rutter, M. (1970). Psychosocial development: Predictions from infancy. *Journal of Child Psychology and Psychiatry, 11,* 49–62.
Rutter, M. (1978). Diagnostic validity in child psychiatry. *Advances in Biological Psychiatry, 2,* 2–22.
Rutter, M. (1980). *Changing youth in a changing society.* Cambridge: Harvard University Press.
Rutter, M., & Garmezy, N. (1983). Developmental psychopathology. In E. M. Hetherington (Ed.), *Carmichael's Manual of Child Psychology: Vol. 4. Social and personality development.* New York: Wiley.
Rutter, M., & Gould, M. (1985). Classification. In M. Rutter & L. Hersov (Eds.), *Child and adolescent psychiatry: Modern approaches* (pp. 304–321). London: Blackwell Scientific Publications.
Rutter, M., & Shaffer, D. (1980). DSM-III: A step forward or back in terms of the classification of child psychiatric disorders? *Journal of the American Academy of Child Psychiatry, 19,* 371–394.
Rutter, M., Shaffer, D., & Shepherd, M. (1975). *A multiaxial classification of child psychiatric disorders.* Geneva: World Health Organization.
Rutter, M., Tizard, J., & Whitmore, K. (Eds.). (1981). *Education, health, and behaviour.* Huntington, NY: Krieger.
Ryave, A. L. (1978). On the achievement of a series of stories. In J. Schenkein (Ed.), *Studies in the organization of conversational interaction.* New York: Academic Press.
Sacks, H. (1978). Some technical considerations in a dirty joke. In J. Schenkein (Ed.), *Studies in the organization of conversational interaction.* New York: Academic Press.
Sagi, A., Lamb, M. E., Lewkowicz, K. S., Shoham, R., Dvir, R., & Estes, D. (1985). Security of infant-mother, -father, and -metapelet attachments among Kibbutz-reared Israeli children. In I. Bretherton & E. Waters (Eds.), Growing points of attachment theory and research. *Monographs of the Society for Research in Child Development, 50*(1–2, Serial No. 209).
Sameroff, A. J. (1981). Psychological needs of the mother in early mother-infant interaction. In G. Avery (Ed.), *Neonatology* (2nd ed.) (pp. 303–321). New York: Lippincott.
Sameroff, A. (1983). Developmental systems: Context and evolution. In P. Mussen (Ed.), *Handbook of child psychology: Vol 1. History, theory and methods.* New York: Wiley.
Sameroff, A. J. (1985, August). *Can development be continuous?* Paper presented at the annual meeting of the American Psychological Association, Los Angeles.
Sameroff, A. J. (1989). General systems and the regulation of development. In M. Gunnar & E. Thelen (Eds.), *Systems and development.* Hillsdale, NJ: Lawrence Erlbaum Associates.
Sameroff, A. J., & Chandler, M. J. (1975). Reproductive risk and the continuum of caretaking casualty. In F. D. Horowitz, M. Hetherington, S. Scarr-Salapatek, & G. Siegel (Eds.), *Review of child development research* (Vol. 4, pp. 187–244). Chicago: University of Chicago Press.
Sameroff, A. J., & Feil, L. (1985). Parental concepts of development. In I. E. Sigel (Ed.), *Parental belief systems: The psychological consequences for children* (pp. 84–104). Hillsdale, NJ: Lawrence Erlbaum Associates.
Sameroff, A. J., & Fiese, B. H. (1989). Transactional regulation and early intervention. In S. J. Meisels & J. P. Shonkoff (Eds.), *Early intervention: A handbook of theory, practice, and analysis.* New York: Cambridge University Press.
Sander, L. (1962). Issues in early mother-child interaction. *Journal of the American Academy of Child Psychiatry, 1,* 141–166.
Sander, L. (1975). Infant and caretaking environment: Investigation and conceptualization of adaptive behavior in a system of increasing complexity. In E. J. Anthony (Ed.), *Explorations in child psychiatry* (pp. 129–166). New York: Plenum.
Sander, L. (1980). Investigation of the infant and its caretaking environment as a biological system. In S. Greenspan & G. Pollock (Eds.), *The course of life: Psychoanalytic contributions toward understanding personality development: Vol. 1. Infancy and Childhood.* Washington, DC: National Institute of Mental Health.
Sander, L. (1985). Toward a logic of organization in psychobiological development. In K. Klar & L. Siever (Eds.), *Biologic response styles: Clinical implications.* Washington, D.C.: American Psychiatric Press.
Sandler, J., & Joffe, W. G. (1969). Towards a basic psychoanalytic model. *International Journal of Psycho-Analysis, 50,* 79–90.

251

Santostefano, S. (1978). *A biodevelopmental approach to clinical child psychology.* New York: Wiley.

Satir, V. (1967). *Conjoint family therapy.* Palo Alto, CA: Science and Behavior Books.

Schachar, R., Rutter, M., & Smith, A. (1981). The characteristics of situationally and pervasively hyperactive children: Implications of syndrome definition. *Journal of Child Psychology and Child Psychiatry, 22,* 375–392.

Schade, J., Meeter, K., & van Goeningen, W. (1962). Maturational aspects of the dendrites of the human cortex. *Acta Morphologische Scandinavica, 5,* 37–48.

Schaefer, E. (1959). A circumflex model for maternal behavior. *Journal of Abnormal and Social Psychology, 59,* 226–235.

Schaffer, H., & Callender, M. (1959). Psychologic effects of hospitalization in infancy. *Pediatrics, 21,* 528–539.

Scherer, K. (1986). Vocal affect expression: A review and model for future research. *Psychological Bulletin, 99,* 143–165.

Scruton, R. (1982). *From Descarte to Wittgenstein.* New York: Harper & Row.

Selvini-Palazzoli, M., Boscolo, L., Cecchin, G., & Prata, G. (1978). *Paradox and Counterparadox.* New York: Aronson.

Shank, R. C., & Abelson, R. (1977). *Scripts, plans, goals and understanding.* Hillsdale, NJ: Lawrence Erlbaum Associates.

Shore, M. F., Geiser, R. L., & Wolman, H. M. (1965). Constructive uses of a hospital experience. *Children, 12,* 3–8.

Shrand, H. (1965). Behavior changes in sick children nursed at home. *Pediatrics, 36,* 604–607.

Sigal, J., Chagoya, E. L., Villeneuve, C., & Mayerovitch, J. (1973). Later psychosocial sequelae of early childhood illness (severe croup). *American Journal of Psychiatry, 130,* 786–789.

Sigal, J., & Gagnon, D. (1975). Effects of parents' and pediatrician's worry concerning severe gastroenteritis in early childhood and later disturbances in the child's behavior. *Journal of Pediatrics, 87,* 809–814.

Sigel, I. E. (Ed.). (1985). *Parental belief systems: The psychological consequences for children.* Hillsdale, NJ: Lawrence Erlbaum Associates.

Skolnick, A. (1986). Early attachment and personal relationships across the life course. In P. Baltes, D. Featherman, & R. Lerner (Eds.), *Life span development and behavior* (pp. 124–206). Hillsdale, NJ: Lawrence Erlbaum Associates.

Snow, C. E. (1972). Mothers' speech to children learning language. *Child Development, 43,* 549–565.

Solnit, A. J. (1960). Hospitalization: An aid to physical health in childhood. *American Journal of Diseases of Children, 99,* 45–53.

Solomon, R. L., & Wynne, L. C. (1954). Traumatic avoidance learning: The principles of anxiety conservation and partial irreversibility. *Psychological Review, 61,* 353–384.

Sorce, J. F., & Emde, R. N. (1982). The meaning of infant emotional expressions: Regularities in caregiving responses in normal and Down's syndrome infants. *Journal of Child Psychology and Psychiatry, 23,* 145–158.

Sorce, J. F., Emde, R. N., Campos, J. J., & Klinnert, M. D. (1985). Maternal emotional signaling: Its effect on the visual cliff behavior of one-year-olds. *Developmental Psychology, 21,* 195–200.

Spencer, P. (1970). The function of ritual in the socialization of the Samburu Moran. In P. Mayer (Ed.), *Socialization: The approach from social anthropology* (pp. 127–150). London: Tavistock.

Spitz, R. A. (1957). *No and yes: On the genesis of human communication.* New York: International Universities Press.

Spitz, R. A. (1959). *A genetic field theory of ego formation.* New York: International Universities Press.

Spitz, R. A. (1961). Some early prototypes of ego defense. *Journal of the American Psychoanalytic Association, 9,* 626–651.

Spitz, R. A. (1965). *The first year of life.* New York: International Universities Press.

Sroufe, L. A. (1977). *Knowing and enjoying your baby.* New York: Spectrum.

Sroufe, L. A. (1979a). The coherence of individual development. *American Psychologist, 34,* 834–841.

Sroufe, L. A. (1979b). Socioemotional development. In J. Osofsky (Ed.), *Handbook of infant development* (pp. 462–516). New York: Wiley.

252

References

Sroufe, L. A. (1983). Infant-caregiver attachment and adaptation in the preschool: The roots of competence and maladaptation. In M. Perlmutter (Ed.), *Development of cognition, affect, and social relations* (pp. 41–81). Hillsdale, NJ: Lawrence Erlbaum Associates.

Sroufe, L. A. (1985). Attachment classification from the perspective of infant-caregiver relationships and infant temperament. *Child Development, 56,* 1–14.

Sroufe, L. A., & Fleeson, J. (1986). Attachment and the construction of relationships. In W. Hartup & Z. Rubin (Eds.), *Relationships and development.* Hillsdale, NJ: Lawrence Erlbaum Associates.

Sroufe, L. A., & Fleeson, J. (1988). Relationships within families: Mutual influences. In R. A. Hinde & J. Stevenson-Hinde (Eds.), *The coherence of family relationships* (pp. 27–47). Oxford: Oxford University Press.

Sroufe, L. A., Fox, N., & Pancake, V. (1983). Attachment and dependency in developmental perspective. *Child Development, 54,* 1615–1627.

Sroufe, L. A., Jacobvitz, J., Mangelsdorf, S., DeAngelo, E., & Ward, M. J. (1985). Generational boundary dissolution between mothers and their preschool children: A relationships systems approach. *Child Development, 56,* 17–29.

Sroufe, L. A., & Rosenberg, D. (1980, March). *Coherence of individual adaptation in lower SES infants and toddlers.* Paper presented at the International Conference on Infant Studies, Providence, RI.

Sroufe, L. A., & Rutter, M. (1984). The domain of developmental psychopathology. *Child Development, 55,* 17–29.

Sroufe, L. A., Schork, E., Motti, F., Lawroski, N., & LaFreniere, P. (1984). The role of affect in social competence. In C. Izard, J. Kagan, & R. Zajonc (Eds.), *Emotions, cognition and behavior.* New York: Cambridge University Press.

Sroufe, L. A., & Ward, M. J. (1980). Seductive behavior of mothers and toddlers: Occurrence, correlates, and family origins. *Child Development, 51,* 1222–1229.

Sroufe, L. A., & Waters, E. (1976). The ontogenesis of smiling and laughter: A perspective on the organization of development in infancy. *Psychological Review, 83,* 173–189.

Sroufe, L. A., & Waters, E. (1977). Attachment as an organizational construct. *Child Development, 48,* 1184–1199.

Sroufe, L. A., Waters, E., & Matas, L. (1974). Contextual determinants of infant affective responses. In M. Lewis & L. Rosenblum (Eds.), *The origins of fear.* New York: Wiley.

Stechler, G., & Halton, A. (1987). The emergence of assertion and aggression during infancy: A psychoanalytic systems approach. *Journal of the American Psychoanalytic Association, 35,* 821–838.

Stein, R. E. K., Jessop, D. J., & Riessman, C. K. (1982). Health care services received by chronically ill children. *American Journal of Disabled Children, 137,* 225–230.

Steinglass, P., Bennett, L., Wolin, S., & Reiss, D. (1987). *The alcoholic family.* New York: Basic Books.

Stenberg, C., Campos, J., & Emde, R. (1983). The facial expression of anger in seven-month-old infants. *Child Development, 54,* 178–184.

Stern, D. (1974). The goal structure of mother-infant play. *Journal of the American Academy of Child Psychology, 13,* 402–421.

Stern, D. (1977). *The first relationship: Infant and mother.* Cambridge: Harvard University Press.

Stern, D. N. (1985). *The interpersonal world of the infant: A view from psychoanalysis and developmental psychology.* New York: Basic Books.

Stern, D., & Stern-Bruschweiler, N. (1987). The mother's representation of her infant: Considerations of its nature. Unpublished manuscript.

Stone, L., Smith, H., & Murphy, L. (Eds.). (1973). *The competent infant: Research and commentary.* New York: Basic Books.

Strauss, M. S. (1979). Abstraction of prototypical information by adults and 10 month old infants. *Journal of Experimental Psychology: Human Learning and Memory, 5,* 618–632.

Stuart, H. C., & Sobel, E. H. (1954). The thickness of the skin and subcutaneous tissue by age and sex in childhood. *Journal of Pediatrics, 28,* 637–647.

Sullivan, H. S. (1953). *The interpersonal theory of psychiatry.* New York: Norton.

Sussman, M. B., Cates, J. N., & Smith, D. (1970). *The family and inheritance.* New York: Academic Press.

Tarjan, G., & Eisenberg, L. (1972). Some thoughts on the classification of mental retardation in the United States of America. *Journal of the American Psychiatric Association, 128,* 14–18.

Thompson, R. S., & Lamb, M. E. (1986). Infant-mother attachment: New directions for theory and research. In P. Baltes, D. Featherman, & R. Lerner (Eds.), *Life span developmental behavior* (pp. 1–42). Hillsdale, NJ: Lawrence Erlbaum Associates.

Thorne, B. (1986). Boys and girls together—but mostly apart: Gender arrangements in elementary school. In W. Hartup & Z. Rubin (Eds.), *Relationships and development* (pp. 167–184). Hillsdale, NJ: Lawrence Erlbaum Associates.

Tompkins, S. S. (1962–1963). *Affect, imagery, consciousness* (Vols. 1–2). New York: Springer.

Tronick, E., Als, H., Adamson, L., Wise, S., & Brazelton, T. B. (1978). The infant's response to entrapment between contradictory messages in face-to-face interaction. *Journal of Child Psychiatry, 17,* 1–13.

Troy, M., & Sroufe, L. A. (1987). Victimization among preschoolers: The role of attachment relationship history. *Journal of the American Academy of Child and Adolescent Psychiatry, 26,* 166–172.

Tulving, E. (1972). Episodic and semantic memory. In E. Tulving & W. Donaldson (Eds.), *Organization of memory.* New York: Academic Press.

Uddenberg, N. (1974). Reproductive adaptation in mother and daughter [Supplement]. *Acta Pschiatrica Scandinavica, 254.*

U.S. Department of Health and Human Services (1980). *The international classification of diseases* (9th rev., 2nd ed.). Washington, DC: Health Care Financing Administration.

Uzgiris, I. (1976). *Organization and sensorimotor intelligence.* New York: Plenum.

Valadian, I., Stuart, H. C., & Reed, R. B. (1961). Studies of illnesses of children followed from birth to 18 years. *Monographs of the Society for Research in Child Development, 26*(3, Serial No. 81).

Vaughn, B. (1978). *An ethological study of greeting behaviors in infants from six to nine months of age.* Unpublished doctoral dissertation, University of Minnesota.

Vaughn, B. E., Deane, K. E., & Waters, E. (1985). The impact of out-of-home care on child-mother attachment quality: Another look at some enduring questions. In I. Bretherton & E. Waters (Eds.), Growing points of attachment theory and research. *Monographs of the Society for Research in Child Development, 50*(1–2, Serial No. 209).

Vaughn, B., & Sroufe, L. A. (1979). The temporal relationship between infant heart rate acceleration and crying in an aversive situation. *Child Development, 50,* 565–567.

Vital Health Statistics (1980). Current estimates from the national health interview survey. *Public Health Service Series 10* (No. 139). Washington, DC: Government Printing Office.

Vygotsky, L. S. (1978). *Mind in society: The development of higher psychological processes.* Cambridge: Harvard University Press.

Waddington, C. H. (1962). *New patterns in genetics and development.* New York: Columbia University Press.

Wald, M. S., Carlsmith, J. M., & Leiderman, P. H. (1988). *Protecting abused and neglected children.* Stanford, CA: Stanford University Press.

Walk, R., & Gibson, E. (1961). A comparative and analytical study of visual depth perception. *Psychological Monographs, 75*(15, Serial No. 519).

Waters, E. (1978). The stability of individual differences in infant-mother attachments. *Child Development, 49,* 483–494.

Waters, E., & Deane, K. E. (1985). Defining and assessing individual differences in attachment relationships: Q-methodology and the organization of behavior in infancy and early childhood. In I. Bretherton & E. Waters (Eds.), Growing points of attachment theory and research. *Monographs of the Society for Research in Child Development, 50*(1–2, Serial No. 209).

Waters, E., Noyes, E., Vaughn, B., & Ricks, M. (1985). Q-sort definitions of social competence and self-esteem: Discriminant validity of related constructs in theory and data. *Developmental Psychology, 21,* 508–522.

Waters, E., Vaughn, B., & Egeland, B. (1980). Individual differences in infant-mother attachment relationship at age one: Antecedents in neonatal behavior in an urban economically disadvantaged sample. *Child Development, 51,* 203–216.

Waters, B., Vaughn, B., Egeland, B., & Sroufe, L. A. (1979). Individual differences in infant-mother attachment at 12 and 18 months: Stability and change in families under stress. *Child Development, 50,* 971–975.

Waters, E., Wippman, J., & Sroufe, L. A. (1979). Attachment, positive affect, and competence in the peer group: Two studies in construct validation. *Child Development, 50,* 821–829.

Watt, N. F., Anthony, E. J., Wynne, L. C., & Rolf, J. E. (Eds.). (1984). *Child at risk for schizophrenia: A longitudinal perspective.* Cambridge: Cambridge University Press.

Weisner, T. S. (1977). My brother's keeper: Child and sibling caretaker. *Contemporary Anthropology, 18,* 169–191.

Weiss, R. (1982). Attachment in adult life. In C. Parke & J. Stevenson-Hinde (Eds.), *The place of attachment in human behavior.* New York: Basic Books.

Weiss, R. S. (1986). Social relationships from childhood to adulthood: Continuities and transformations. In W. W. Hartup & Z. Rubin (Eds.), *Relationships and development* (pp. 95–110). Hillsdale, NJ: Lawrence Erlbaum Associates.

Werner, H. (1957). The concept of development from a comparative and organismic point of view. In D. Harris (Ed.), *The concept of development.* Minneapolis: University of Minnesota Press.

Wertheim, E. (1975). The science and typology of family systems: 2. Further theoretical and practical considerations. *Family Process, 14,* 285–309.

Wessel, M. A., Cobb, J. C., Jackson, E. B., Harris, G. S., Jr., & Detwiler, A. C. (1954). Paroxysmal fussing in infancy, sometimes called "colic." *Pediatrics, 14,* 421–434.

West, D. J., & Farrington, D. P. (1973). *Who becomes delinquent?* London: William Heinemann.

Wiggins, J. (1974). *In defense of traits.* Unpublished manuscript, University of British Columbia, Vancouver.

Wilkinson, S. R. (1988). *The child's world of illnesses: The development of health and illness behaviors.* New York: Cambridge University Press.

Wilson, E. O. (1975). *Sociobiology.* Cambridge: Belknap Press.

Wing, J. K. (1973). International variations in psychiatric diagnosis. *Triangle, 12,* 31–36.

Wing, J. K. (1980). Methodological issues in psychiatric case identification. *Psychological Medicine, 10,* 5–10.

Winnicott, D. (1965). *The maturational processes and the facilitating environment.* New York: International Universities Press.

World Health Organization (1977). *Manual of the international statistical classification of diseases, injuries, and causes of death* (Vol. 1). Geneva: World Health Organization.

World Health Organization (1979). *Manual of the international statistical classification of diseases, injuries, and causes of death* (Vol. 2). Geneva: World Health Organization.

Wynne, L. (1984). The epigenesis of relational systems: A model for understanding family development. *Family Process, 23,* 297–318.

Youniss, J. (1980). *Parents and peers in social development: A Sullivan-Piaget perspective.* Chicago: University of Chicago Press.

Zeanah, C. H., & Anders, T. F. (1986, August). *Subjectivity in parent-infant relationships: A discussion of internal working models.* Paper presented at the Third World Congress of Infant Psychiatry and Allied Professions, Stockholm.

Zeanah, C., Benoit, D., & Barton, M. (1987). *Working model of the child interview.* Unpublished manuscript, Brown University.

Zeitlin, S. J., Kotkin, A. J., & Baker, H. C. (1982). *A celebration of American family folklore.* New York: Pantheon Books.

Zigler, E., & Trickett, P. K. (1978). IQ, social competence, and evaluation of early childhood intervention programs. *American Psychologist, 33,* 789–799.

Zubin, J., & Spring, B. (1977). Vulnerability: A new view of schizophrenia. *Journal of Abnormal Psychology, 86,* 103–126.

INDEX

Abnormal psychology, 113
Abuse syndromes, *see* Child abuse
Adaptability, 110–11
Adolescence, 5, 22, 85, 227; and anorexia nervosa, 195–96; causes and effects of relationship pathology in, 176–78; and changes in working models of self, 94; and cultural code, 25; and family communication behaviors, 113–14; and family interaction patterns, 106, 114; psychiatric disorders in, 177; psychosocial development in, 168; relationships characteristic of, 173, 174; and relationships through the life cycle, 165, 180, 184–85, 188
Affect: biological preparedness, 39, 44, 46; as core of psychological experience, 223–24; and developmental transformation, 40–44; and emergence of self, 76–77, 81–85; and emotional availability, 45–47, 48–50; functions and goals of relationships revealed in, 100; and organization of experience, 44–47; regulation of, 22, 35, 37, 107, 109; and relationships through the life cycle, 180
Affective exchange syndromes, 136, 137
Affective sharing, 35, 37, 105, 129; and emergence of self, 72, 76, 77; individual differences in quality of, 72–73
Affective tone, 105–6, 129
Age groups, *see* Adolescence; Infants; Older children; Preschool-age children; School-age children; Toddlers
Aggression, 93, 117, 226; and control syndromes, 137; and coordinated practice, 211–17; and patterning of interactions,

99; and persistence of relationship pathology, 176, 177; *see also* Bullying behavior
Ainsworth, Mary, 74, 84, 85, 86, 92, 114–18, 124, 131, 174, 176, 182, 229
Alcohol abuse, 108, 204; and rituals, 207
American Psychiatric Association's DSMIII-R, 4, 8, 9, 120, 127, 128, 136, 137, 228
Anders, Thomas, 228, 229, 230
Anorexia nervosa, 195–96, 199
Antisocial behavior, 181, 233; and avoidant attachment, 93, 117; and coordinated practice, 211–17; and environtype, 32; predictors of, 176–77
Anxiety, in caregiver, 111–12
Anxious attachment: and classification of relationships, 115–18; and emergence of self, 84–85; and environtype, 31; genesis and consequences of, 174–78; as risk factor for later problem behavior, 171, 172; and school-setting behavior, 98
Apathy, 3, 137
Arousal, regulation of, 107; and environtype, 31–32; and physical health problems, 154–55, 156–57
Artifacts, 204–6
Asynchronous relationships, 97, 99, 109, 172
Attachment, 9, 118, 119, 165, 233; and adaptation throughout lifespan, 5, 165–67, 171–72, 174–81; functional aspects of, 35–36; and function of emotions, 45; across generations, 194–95; genesis and consequences of, 174–78;